FOOD SAFETY AND INFORMAL MARKETS

Animal products are vital components of the diets and livelihoods of people across sub-Saharan Africa. They are frequently traded in local, informal markets and this can pose significant health risks. This book presents an accessible overview of these issues in the context of food safety, zoonoses and public health, while at the same time maintaining fair and equitable livelihoods for poorer people across the continent.

The book includes a review of the key issues and twenty-five case studies of the meat, milk, egg and fish food sectors drawn from a wide range of countries in East, West and southern Africa, as part of the 'Safe Food, Fair Food' project. It gives a realistic analysis of food safety risk by developing a methodology of 'participatory food safety risk assessment', involving small-scale producers and consumers in the process of data collection in the data-poor environment often found in developing countries. This approach aims to ensure market access for poor producers, while adopting a realistic and pragmatic strategy for reducing the risk of food-borne diseases for consumers.

Kristina Roesel is co-ordinator of the 'Safe Food, Fair Food' project, based at the International Livestock Research Institute, Nairobi, Kenya, and also a doctorate candidate at the Free University, Berlin, Germany.

Delia Grace is Program Leader, Food Safety and Zoonoses, Integrated Sciences, at the International Livestock Research Institute, Nairobi, Kenya.

FOOD SAFETY AND INFORMAL MARKETS

Animal products in sub-Saharan Africa

Edited by Kristina Roesel and Delia Grace

LONDON AND NEW YORK

First published 2015 by Routledge

2 Park Square, Milton Park, Abingdon, Oxon, OX14 4RN
605 Third Avenue, New York, NY 10017

Routledge is an imprint of the Taylor & Francis Group, an informa business

First issued in paperback 2020

British Library Cataloguing-in-Publication Data
A catalogue record for this book is available from the British Library

Library of Congress Cataloging-in-Publication Data
Food safety and informal markets : animal products in Sub-Saharan Africa / edited by Kristina Roesel and Delia Grace.
pages cm
Includes bibliographical references and index.
1. Food adulteration and inspection—Africa, Sub-Saharan. 2. Food—Africa, Sub-Saharan.—Safety measures. 3. Wildlife as food—Africa, Sub-Saharan. 4. Informal sector (Economics)—Africa, Sub-Saharan. I. Roesel, Kristina. II. Grace, Delia.
TX360.A357F66 2014
363.19'2640967—dc23 2014019289

ISBN: 978-1-138-81873-6 (hbk)
ISBN: 978-0-367-73958-4 (pbk)

Typeset in Bembo
by Keystroke, Station Road, Codsall

CONTENTS

About CTA

The Technical Centre for Agricultural and Rural Cooperation (CTA) is a joint international institution of the African, Caribbean and Pacific (ACP) Group of States and the European Union (EU). Its mission is to advance food and nutritional security, increase prosperity and encourage sound natural resource management in ACP countries. It provides access to information and knowledge, facilitates policy dialogue and strengthens the capacity of agricultural and rural development institutions and communities.

CTA operates under the framework of the Cotonou Agreement and is funded by the EU.

For more information on CTA, visit www.cta.int

LIST OF ILLUSTRATIONS

Figures

Tables

Boxes

LIST OF CONTRIBUTORS

Kebede Amenu, Joy Appiah, Kennedy Bomfeh, Bassirou Bonfoh, Solenne Costard, Yolande Aké Assi Datté, Fanta Desissa, Gilbert Fokou, Alexander Heeb, Saskia Hendrickx, Kevin Kabui, John Kago, Erastus Kang'ethe, Kaiza Kilango, Valentin Bognan Koné, Sylvie Mireille Kouamé-Sina, Lusato Kurwijila, Cheryl McCrindle, Edgar Mahundi, Kohei Makita, André Markemann, Helena Matusse, Margaret Molefe, Ana Bela Cambaza dos Muchangos, Cameline Mwai, Flavien Ndongo, James Oguttu, Amos Omore, Nenene Qekwana, Shashi Ramrajh, Ibrahim Sow, Marisa Spengler, Kwaku Tano-Debrah, Haruya Toyomaki, Sylvain Gnamien Traoré, Antoine Bassa Yobouet, Girma Zewde, Erika van Zyl

Language editing and proofreading: Tezira Lore

PREFACE

Food-borne diseases have enormous impacts on the health of people around the globe and are of great and increasing concern to consumers, producers and policy-makers. In most developing countries, gastro-intestinal disease remains in the top five causes of sickness and death and unsafe food is an important contributor to this avoidable burden.

The most risky foods are livestock and fish products and fresh fruits and vegetables contaminated with animal or human waste. Yet these are also the foods of highest potential in providing the proteins and micro-nutrients which poor consumers desperately need. They are also high-value foods, well suited to production by small farmers, hence important sources of income for smallholder farmers.

A central premise of this book is that food systems should deliver not only safe food, but also enough food and food that supports the livelihoods of poor farmers and nutrition of poor consumers: safe food should be fair food.

This book brings together twenty-five case studies on food safety in East, West and southern Africa. As such, it provides a broad snapshot of issues around a wide selection of livestock and fish value chains. It also synthesises the evidence from the case studies to answer some questions about the relation between food safety and gender, poverty, participation and culture. This is important, as much food safety thinking in Africa is translated from elsewhere and not grounded in contemporary reality.

The case studies and syntheses challenge conventional thinking around food safety in Africa: they show how informal wet markets continue to be the major sources of perishable foods and probably will into the near future; they suggest that hazards are not always important if risks can be managed and that traditional food preparation can be surprisingly effective at reducing risk; they find that food sold by the formal sector often has no better compliance with food standards than food sold in the informal sector; they show how important culture is as a determinant of food safety, and why information may not be enough to change food safety behaviour; they argue that food safety problems are usually manageable, most often best solved through stakeholder engagement and incentives, rather than regulation and enforcement.

The book introduces an important concept for managing food safety: 'Participatory Risk Analysis'. Over the last decade, risk analysis has been accepted as the gold standard for assuring food safety. It has been adopted by the international community and underpins trade in foods and livestock. However, risk analysis has not had much success in tackling food safety problems in the informal sectors where most of the poor sell and buy their food. Conventional risk analysis is often expensive and time consuming, requires considerable amounts of data and quantitative analysis, and is often led by technocrats. By taking the core concepts of risk analysis, and combining them with development methods such as participatory appraisal and gender analysis, an approach has emerged that can be successfully applied to food safety problems in developing countries. The concept and practice of participatory risk analysis fits well with current ecohealth and one health thinking, which employs multi-disciplinary and multi-stakeholder approaches to solve complex health problems.

We are in an era of unprecedented change in Africa, with growth in population, rapid urbanization and changing technical, business and social change. Safe Food, Fair Food provides us with a unique picture of contemporary food safety in diverse systems in Africa. Its lessons on applying risk analysis and engaging stakeholders also provide a very useful participatory approach for understanding and managing food safety in a more dynamic future. Given the rapid socio-economic changes that will occur in Africa in the coming years, such approaches will be critical in challenging conventional thinking and developing and evaluating a variety of needed innovations.

John McDermott
Director, CGIAR Research Program on
Agriculture for Nutrition and Health
International Food Policy Research Institute
Washington, DC

ACKNOWLEDGEMENTS

We acknowledge the financial support of the German Federal Ministry for Economic Cooperation and Development, the CGIAR Research Program on Agriculture for Nutrition and Health, led by the International Food Policy Research Institute and the CGIAR Research Program on Livestock and Fish led by the International Livestock Research Institute.

ABBREVIATIONS

AIDS	acquired immunodeficiency syndrome
BaP	benzo(a)pyrene
BfR	German Federal Institute for Risk Assessment
BMZ	German Federal Ministry for Economic Cooperation and Development
CCP	critical control point
DAFF	Department of Agriculture, Forestry and Fisheries
DALY	disability-adjusted life year
DOH	Department of Health
DTI	Department of Trade and Industry
EU	European Union
FAO	Food and Agriculture Organization of the United Nations
FUB	Freie Universität Berlin
GDP	gross domestic product
HACCP	hazard analysis and critical control point
HIV	human immunodeficiency virus
ILRI	International Livestock Research Institute
ISO	International Organization for Standardization
KEBS	Kenya Bureau of Standards
MRA	microbial risk assessment
NRCS	National Regulator for Compulsory Specifications
OIE	World Organization for Animal Health
PAH	polycyclic aromatic hydrocarbon
SABS	South African Bureau of Standards
SWOT	strengths, weaknesses, opportunities and threats
WHO	World Health Organization
YLD	years lost due to disability
YLL	years of life lost
YOPIs	young, old, pregnant and immunocompromised

EXECUTIVE SUMMARY

In sub-Saharan Africa, the great majority of livestock and fish products are sold in informal or wet markets, that is, markets which escape effective health and safety regulation, are often untaxed and unlicensed, and where traditional processing, products and prices predominate.

Informal markets usually sell food at lower prices than formal markets and are closer and more accessible to consumers. They have other desired attributes including food freshness, food taste, selling livestock products from local breeds, vendors who are trusted and the availability of credit or other services.

Markets for livestock products are growing rapidly because of increases in population, urbanisation and shifting dietary tastes. These rapidly growing markets offer an opportunity for smallholder farmers who produce most of the livestock consumed in domestic markets and for all those involved in bringing food to informal markets and selling it. However, smallholder farmers and informal market sellers face rising standards for safety and quality. Our studies show that most consumers say they care about food safety and, what is more, they show it by stopping purchasing products in the wake of food scares about these products.

Food sold in informal markets often contains pathogens or substances that have the potential to cause harm (hazards). However, the presence of hazards does not necessarily mean these food products are harmful to human health. For example, studies in Kenya found milk was often contaminated with biological hazards (bacteria); but, because nearly everyone boiled milk before consumption, the risk to human health was low.

Our research shows the need to move from conventional, hazard-based approaches that assess the presence of hazards in food to newer, risk-based approaches that assess the likelihood of harm to human health. However, because of their cost and complexity, risk-based approaches have not been widely applied in the informal markets of developing countries. An important part of our research has been to adapt risk-based approaches for developing countries and build capacity in their applications.

The key messages from our studies include:

Informal markets have a major role in food security and food safety.

- The informal sector accounts for 39% of national gross domestic product (GDP).
- More than 80% of food is sold in informal markets.
- Informal markets are accessible and affordable to everyone.
- Informal markets involve many actors other than producers and consumers.
- Informal markets are unregulated and non-transparent, thus prone to activities that might compromise food safety.

Informal markets are not necessarily dangerous, nor formal markets safe.

- Informally marketed food is often safe for human consumption.
- Improper post-processing handling is one of the biggest challenges and largely depends on the prerequisites.
- Business-oriented attitudes are one of the major risks to food safety in informal markets.
- Some risks in both markets are underestimated as they do not cause immediate harm.

Hazards are common in informal markets but do not always translate into risks.

- Hazards are defined as agents likely to cause harm or damage to humans, other organisms or the environment in the absence of their control.
- Risk is the likelihood of that anticipated harm to occur, including the consequences for public health, ecology and the economy.
- The identification of hazards in animal-source foods does not estimate the impacts of the hazards in terms of human sickness and death, thus existing food safety regulation is often ineffective and anti-poor.
- Risk-based approaches brought new insights and are now standard for food safety issues in developed countries.
- Safe Food, Fair Food studies identified at least ten different hazards in food with different levels of risk to public health and local economies.

Greater stakeholder participation improves food safety in informal markets.

- Participation allows generating data for risk analysis at affordable costs for resource-limited countries.
- It proved to be particularly useful in exposure assessment to assess the real risk to public health.
- It supported risk communication during risk assessment.

- It was a feasible method to study social determinants of risk in traditional communities.
- There were some constraints in terms of time and lack of finances for implementation and follow ups and in balancing objectives of all stakeholders.
- The concept was understood differently by different stakeholders.

Farmers, traders and retailers are the *de facto* risk managers in informal markets.

- Contamination of food may occur at any stage in the food value chain.
- Risk pathway analysis identifies points where hazards occur from farm to fork and where risk is increased, reduced or eliminated along the way.
- Points where management is feasible can be identified and priorities can be set.
- Everybody handling the product, and financially benefiting from it, must take responsibility.
- Intervention is often simple but frequently lacks basic prerequisites.

Understanding values and culture is crucial for managing food safety in informal markets.

- Indigenous knowledge often contributes towards food safety.
- Eating food is not only for nourishment but also associated with cultural values.
- There are different cultural beliefs about risks associated with food.
- It can be difficult to change traditional practices that represent high risks.
- Some groups are more exposed to risk than others.
- Traditional risk mitigation strategies need further investigation.
- Cultural background must be considered in risk management and communication.

Efforts to improve food safety in informal markets should also be pro-poor.

- The poor are more prone to food-borne disease but cannot afford to fall ill.
- Risk-mitigating measures need training, skills development and prerequisites.
- Linking informal markets to formal markets could decrease local and domestic poverty.
- Impact assessment is needed in terms of economic losses and gains on risks that occur.

Understanding and managing food safety in informal markets requires a gender perspective.

- Men or women dominate or are excluded from different segments of the food value chain, and this varies by culture and geography.

- As a result, women and men get different benefits from informal food markets and are exposed to different risks.
- In addition to socio-cultural roles affecting health, men, women, the old, the young and other groups may have different vulnerabilities to different diseases.
- Informal food production, processing and marketing are of high importance to women's livelihoods and offer new opportunities.
- As agri-food chains change and evolve, the opportunities and risks also change.

1

INTRODUCTION

Delia Grace, Kristina Roesel, Kohei Makita, Bassirou Bonfoh, Erastus Kang'ethe, Lusato Kurwijila, Saskia Hendrickx, Cheryl McCrindle, Kwaku Tano-Debrah, Girma Zewde and Helena Matusse

Background

Why animal-source foods matter

In poor countries, livestock and fish feed billions. In East Africa, for example, livestock provide poor people with one-tenth of their energy and one-quarter of their protein needs. Fish account for more than half of the animal protein intake for the 400 million poorest people in Africa and South Asia. Meat, milk, eggs and fish are important sources of the micro-nutrients and high-quality proteins essential for growth and health. Studies in Egypt, Kenya and Mexico have shown strong associations between eating animal-source food and child growth and cognitive function, as well as better pregnancy outcomes for women and reduced illness for all.

Production and marketing of livestock and fish earns money for farmers, traders and sellers, many of them women. For example, in East Africa, almost half of rural incomes rely to some extent on livestock and fish. India has the largest dairy sector in the world, employing more than 100 million rural farmers. On the other hand, excessive amounts of animal-source food have been linked to heart disease. Animal-source foods are also important sources of biological and chemical hazards that cause sickness and death.

Why informal markets matter

Most of the meat, milk, eggs and fish produced in developing countries are sold in traditional, domestic markets, lacking modern infrastructure and escaping effective food safety regulation and inspection. By 'informal markets' we mean:

- markets where many actors are not licensed and do not pay tax (for example, street foods, backyard poultry and pastoralist systems);

- markets where traditional processing, products and retail prices predominate (for example, wet markets, milk hawking systems and artisanal cheese production);
- markets which escape effective health and safety regulation (most domestic food markets in developing countries).

Informal markets: a history of neglect and unbalanced interest

Much attention has been paid to the role of informal markets in maintaining and transmitting diseases but little to their role in supporting livelihoods and nutrition. Undoubtedly, hazards exist in informal milk and meat markets, including pathogens such as diarrhoea-causing *Escherichia coli*, *Salmonella* and tapeworm cysts. Severe acute respiratory syndrome came from – and avian influenza is maintained in – the wet markets of Southeast Asia. Concern over informal food has been heightened by the landmark Global Burden of Disease studies, which found that diarrhoea is among the most common causes of sickness and death in poor countries. Most of this is caused by contaminated food and water and as much as half is linked to animal pathogens or animal-source foods.

Food-borne illness and animal disease are of growing concern to consumers and policymakers alike. Consumers respond to scares by stopping or reducing purchases, with knock-on effects on smallholder production and informal market sellers. Policymakers often respond to health risk by favouring industrialization and reducing smallholder access to markets. These changes are often based on fear, not facts. Without evidence of the risk to human health posed by informally marketed foods or the best way to manage risks while retaining benefits, the food eaten in poor countries is neither safe nor fair.

Research on food safety in informal markets

For over a decade, the International Livestock Research Institute (ILRI) and partners (Annex 1) have been conducting research on food safety in informal markets to support intensifying livestock production by building capacity for better management of safety of animal-source food products. The ultimate goal is to maximize market access for the poor dependent on livestock and livestock products while minimizing the food-borne disease burden for poor consumers. A pillar of the research is building capacity for food safety in sub-Saharan Africa by adapting the risk-based approaches successfully used for food safety in developed countries and international trade to the domestic informal markets where most livestock products are sold: a methodology we call 'participatory risk assessment'.

Safe Food, Fair Food: an example of successful research targeting food safety in informal markets

Many of the research activities featured in this book were funded by the German Federal Ministry for Economic Cooperation and Development (BMZ) through the Safe Food, Fair Food project. The first phase of the project ended in 2011 and its main mechanisms were building capacity in risk analysis through postgraduate training linked to proof-of-concept studies, winning over key decision-makers through participation in project activities, raising awareness of stakeholders through workshops and generation and dissemination of research results on food safety in informal markets. Actively linking research with capacity building, proactively engaging with policymakers and use of participatory methods at community level provide mechanisms by which tools and results generated by the research will be used to promote better food safety management in informal markets in sub-Saharan Africa.

The project supported twenty-five graduate and postgraduate students from twelve different countries to conduct proof-of-concept studies on food safety. Among the students who have graduated, more than half are working in government food safety departments, holding positions as associated researchers or teaching at universities. Eight training courses were given, with more than seventy participants from academia and public institutions responsible for food safety.

Situational analyses of food safety in eight countries developed an up-to-date and user-friendly summary of the food safety situation in each country. National workshops were held in all countries, under the auspices of the risk assessment champions supported by the project. At these workshops, the concept of risk assessment for safer food and enhanced smallholder market access was shared with a variety of stakeholders. Preliminary results from the project and their implications for food safety were discussed. For a full list of publications, please see Annex 2: List of publications from the Safe Food, Fair Food project.

In January 2012, CGIAR launched a new research programme on Agriculture for Nutrition and Health. The programme has four components, one of which focuses on food safety in informal markets. Many of the approaches and methods pioneered in the Safe Food, Fair Food project have been incorporated in the major sub-component on food safety.

What we have learnt about food safety in informal markets

Informal markets are highly preferred

Our studies have shown that informal markets are the most important source of meat, milk and eggs for poor people in Africa and Asia and will continue to be so for at least the next decade. Informal markets often sell food at lower prices, but they have other desired attributes including food freshness, food taste, selling livestock products from local breeds, vendors who are trusted and the availability of credit or other services (Chapter 2).

Food safety matters to poor consumers

Our studies show that most consumers (48–97%) in informal markets say they care about food safety. They also show it in purchasing behaviour: for example, 20–40% of consumers switch to alternative meats in the wake of animal disease epidemics. Willingness-to-pay studies indicate that consumers will pay a 5–15% premium for safety-assured products and demand for food safety increases with economic development, rising income, urbanization, increased media coverage and education level (Chapter 2).

The situational analyses found that decision-makers, too, are increasingly concerned about food safety. The analysis identified key problems at different parts of the farm-to-fork value chain. The analysis also prioritized brucellosis, tuberculosis, salmonellosis and toxigenic *E. coli* infection as the most important food-borne diseases from the perspective of decision-makers and national experts.

Hazards don't always matter, but risks do

Hazards are all things that can cause harm. Bacteria, viruses, parasites, chemicals and fungal toxins in food all have potential to cause harm: they are hazards. Risk, on the other hand, is the likelihood of that harm to occur, including its consequences for public health and the economy. Our studies from many markets in eight countries show that food sold in the informal sector often contains hazards. Moreover, as value chains become longer and more complex, transport larger, more diversely sourced volumes of food and place larger distances between producers and consumers, so hazards tend to increase. Consumer and market value chain studies confirm the bulk of literature that suggests, in some contexts, a high level of disease in developing countries is associated with food. An assessment in Nigeria found a high risk from beef-borne pathogens and suggested beef-borne disease was costing Nigeria nearly US$1 billion per year.

However, a series of studies in informal milk and meat markets showed that although hazards are always common in informal markets, risk to human health is not inevitably high. Stochastic models based on data from a number of sites in East Africa showed that milk had many hazards but less risk (mainly because of consumer practices such as boiling which are effective at reducing hazards). In other studies, however, there is a clear link between consumption of foods containing hazards and increased illness. The message is that risk to human health cannot be assumed for informal markets: evidence is required (Chapter 4).

Perception is a poor guide for risk managers

Assessment is needed to understand the source of risk. For example, studies beyond the Safe Food, Fair Food project have shown that dairy cattle are the reservoir of cryptosporidiosis, a serious disease in people with HIV and infants. In Nairobi, risk was associated with vegetable consumption and not milk. Similarly in Vietnam, although pork in wet markets had high microbial loads, increased diarrhoea was associated with consumption of vegetables, not meat. Risk assessment allows actions to be targeted to evidence and not misleading perception, that is, directing scarce resources towards control or inspection of the actors, processes or steps in the value chain where most risk is created.

Studies by the Safe Food, Fair Food project in East and southern Africa came to the surprising conclusion that food sold in formal markets, though commonly perceived to be safer, may have lower compliance with standards than informally marketed food. This emphasizes that food safety policy should be based on evidence and not perception, and failure to do this may be prejudicial to the poor who dominate and rely upon informal value chains (Chapter 3).

Situational analyses showed that only a few of the public health problems were regularly tested and that most food in the traditional or informal sector was not inspected. Where some inspection occurred, it did not follow a farm-to-fork pathway approach, that is, inspection happened only at some points and in a sporadic fashion. In some countries, personnel have been trained in food safety and risk assessment procedures but training is more often oriented to developed country situations and not adapted to local needs or contexts. There is a lack of systematic, risk-based surveillance and inspection because of either lack of infrastructure and laboratory facilities or lack of skilled manpower. Another reason may be lack of a comprehensive approach and understanding of how to address these issues under conditions of poor consumer awareness and demand for remedies of such problems.

Draconian food safety policy makes things worse

The existence of a huge food sector that largely escapes regulation, the high level of hazards in food and the massive burden of gastrointestinal illness all suggest that current food safety policy is not working. In our situational analyses of food safety in eight countries, we found that stakeholders often blame insufficient legislation or lack of strict implementation for poor food safety. In recent years there have been several attempts to improve food safety but this 'command and control' method is less likely to work. Paradoxically, legislation can increase the level of risk. A study in Kampala, Uganda showed the importance of poor dairy farmers as risk managers and the paradoxical effects of conventional policy. Thirty practices were described which were used spontaneously by farmers that reduced risk. Moreover, farmers who had experienced harassment by authorities or who believed urban farming to be illegal used significantly fewer risk-managing practices.

Values and cultures are more important drivers of food safety than pathogens

A study in West Africa found that the Fulani believed milk was in its nature pure and could not be a source of disease. They boiled the milk they sold to customers but not the milk they drank themselves (Chapter 7).

Traditional food preparation methods can mitigate food-borne diseases

A study in Ethiopia showed the significant role of traditional fermentation in preventing staphylococcal poisoning (reducing the risk by 90%). In West Africa, anthropology studies contributed to understanding of the perception of risks related to milk. For example, if adulterated milk earns more money, women still consider the adulterated milk 'good'. On the other hand, cattle owners consider that if milk is heated, it is 'bad' and has no nutritional value. These findings have led to risk management recommendations.

Risk assessment can be applied in informal markets by using participatory methods

The lack of data is a challenge to understanding risks from animal-source foods. We found that the application of participatory methods in data collection allowed the rapid and inexpensive collection of data to fill gaps in information required for conducting risk assessment. Eight stochastic risk assessments have been conducted partly based on participatory data, showing this method is applicable to developing country food safety problems (Chapter 5).

Value chain mapping gives insight to product flows and dynamics and alerts to emerging problems

Several studies incorporated value chain mapping. This confirmed that the great majority of animal-source foods flow through informal value chains. Furthermore, several studies found value chains are lengthening in order to supply emerging urban and peri-urban markets, resulting in increased risk (Chapter 6).

Gender equity in Safe Food, Fair Food

Food is a gendered commodity and informal food production, processing and marketing are of high importance to women's livelihoods. Our research used gender-sensitive approaches in conducting research (Chapter 9). Of the twenty-five studies supported, eleven focused on products which are mainly managed by women (poultry, smoked fish, milk in West Africa and processed meat), seven focused on issues mainly managed by men (beef and game) and the remainder on products for which men and women were equally concerned.

Future activities and the way forward

We believe that food safety is a fixable problem. Our studies on milk in East Africa have shown that simple interventions can lead to substantial improvements in food safety. These interventions involved training, simple technologies (such as the use of wide-necked vessels for milk which are easier to clean), social approval, tests for food safety which can be applied by traders and consumers (for example, lactometers to check for added water) and certification of trained vendors (Chapter 4). Economic assessment of the Smallholder Dairy Project in Kenya showed that recognizing the informal sector and training and certification of informal milk traders led to benefits worth US$28 million per annum, thus showing the high potential impacts of better ways to manage food safety. This study and others focusing on the livelihood and gender benefits of smallholder value chains show the importance of multi-sectoral approaches to food safety that consider the incentives for change in a given value chain and the aggregate benefits available to the whole sector by way of rewards being paid for quality and spill-overs in terms of improved market function (Chapter 7).

Our work over the last decade confirms our hypothesis that food safety is an important and growing constraint to smallholder value chains because of its multiple burdens on human health, livestock production and product marketing. The new CGIAR Research Program on Agriculture for Nutrition and Health is an opportunity to bring new resources to tackle this problem. Some of the strategies that guide this programme will be:

Prioritization and systems understanding

Comparative risk assessment: We need to continue developing rapid, appropriate methodologies that can identify the food safety and zoonoses constraints to value chains and systems and the benefits of addressing these.

Risk and socio-economic assessment

Integrated measurement of multiple health and economic benefits and burdens is needed to raise awareness of the relative importance of problems and improve resource allocation. Social and economic determinants affect behaviour of both consumers and value chain actors and so are important drivers of food safety. Assessment of incentives at the individual, group and whole chain levels can lead to better risk communication and management.

Risk management

Risk factor assessment can give insights (often contradicting conventional wisdom) into food safety management and increase the effectiveness and equity of packages of interventions. A substantial part of the risk associated with informally marketed food can be reduced by relatively cheap and simple interventions which are compatible with the incentives faced by specific individuals or coalitions within value chains. Current regulations and inspections based on the presence of hazards rather than health risks to consumers are ineffective at assuring food safety and prejudicial to smallholder farmers and informal value chains. Risk-based approaches can lead to more effective and equitable food safety management.

Cross-cutting approaches
Integrated, multi-disciplinary or trans-disciplinary approaches to food safety can give added insights, increase ownership, improve effectiveness and generate efficiencies.

Organization of the book

The introductory part highlights the context of our research on food safety in Africa, the lessons learned about food safety in informal markets and opportunities for future research in this area. In Part 1, the key research messages are presented. Part 2 presents further details of twenty-five proof-of-concept studies. Our intention was to present key findings in a format that would appeal to both specialist and non-specialist readers.

Food safety is often considered a very theoretical topic, but it is indeed an issue of regular concern in sub-Saharan Africa. Safer food can generate both health and wealth for the poor, but attaining safe food production in developing countries requires a radical change in food safety assessment, management and communication.

PART 1

Food safety in sub-Saharan Africa

2

TAKING FOOD SAFETY TO INFORMAL MARKETS

Delia Grace, Kohei Makita, Erastus Kang'ethe, Bassirou Bonfoh and Kristina Roesel

Safeguard the informal market and you safeguard the society.

Edgar Mahundi, Tanzania

Key messages

- The informal sector accounts for 39% of national gross domestic product (GDP).
- More than 80% of food is sold in informal markets.
- Informal markets are accessible and affordable to everyone.
- Informal markets involve many actors other than producers and consumers.
- Informal markets are unregulated and non-transparent, thus prone to activities that might compromise food safety.

Background[1]

In developing countries, incomes are low, governments weak and enforcement of regulation poor. As a result, the informal sector is large, accounting for 39% of GDP. Previously undervalued, the informal sector is now recognized as an important provider of employment and engine of economic growth. During the 1970s and 1980s, the informal sector was widely defined as unregulated economic enterprises or activities. Recent definitions have expanded to include small businesses, employment without worker benefits or social protection (both inside and outside informal enterprise), own account workers, unpaid family workers (in informal and formal enterprises) and members of informal producers' cooperatives. In the food sector, informality has the additional meaning of escaping any systematic sanitary inspection and tax payment. In Africa, agriculture, petty trading of agricultural products and selling of food have always been largely informal activities.

By these definitions, most food in Africa is produced, processed and sold in the informal sector. For example, in Kenya, Uganda and Mali, raw milk produced by smallholders and sold by vendors or small-scale retailers accounts for an estimated 80%, 90% and 98% of marketed milk in each country, respectively. This is an important source of income not only for small-scale producers (for example, 600,000 farm households in Kenya) but also for intermediaries along the milk value chain such as transporters, hawkers and processors (365,000 intermediaries in Kenya). Our studies confirmed the importance of the informal sector: in Côte d'Ivoire, for example, 90% of milk is produced by smallholders and 80% passes through the informal sector. In South Africa, an estimated 70% of goats are consumed after home slaughter, which is legal. The meat is consumed at village level and seldom reaches the roadside vendors but goat meat provides an important cultural function as well as improving food security in rural areas.

Diversity and inclusion

Condemned as black market in developed countries, the informal sector is vital for the livelihoods of a large number of people in sub-Saharan Africa. However, most are not self-employed outside the formal economy or not on anyone's payroll because it is their wish or choice. Rather, their chances to be hired by an employer from the formal sector are very small and their work agreements are often of short duration with no legal right to be hired again.

Because regulations prohibiting the informal sector are rarely enforced, the sector is accessible to anyone trading anything. Entry is easy; in countries with high poverty rates, people lack sufficient funds for medical care or the formal education and qualifications which entitle them to work in the formal industry. The informal market allows them to make the best out of their limited assets. Producers and vendors do not need to open bank accounts to process cheques or wait for cheques to mature but get paid immediately; the market is 'ready'. At the end of the market day, the revenues (in cash or kind) go back to their families and communities.

Our studies on milk production in East Africa showed the importance of informal markets. Most milk is produced by smallholders who usually sell the surplus of an animal-source product such as milk after feeding their families first. Much of the excess is sold to neighbours and some to intermediaries or markets. This surplus, however, is subject to large fluctuation mainly related to seasonal factors such as rainfall patterns and, hence, feed availability. This excludes the farmers from supplying formal markets with consistently large and uniform quantities. In the informal market, there are no standards for sizes or units. Likewise, in South Africa, small-scale and subsistence farmers sell or barter their products (mainly milk, eggs, chickens and live goats or cattle for home slaughter) within the village or settlement. The formal markets, which are closely aligned to transport hubs, do not sell these products. Only in South Africa was there a marked crossover from the formal market with commercial farmers, wholesale (fresh vegetable or fruit markets or abattoirs) or retail (supermarket) outlets supplying informal traders. In other countries studied, the formal sector was much smaller and was not an important supplier for the informal sector.

In rural areas, where road infrastructure is poor, most large villages have set market days, allowing people to sell their products provided they meet the local market regulations. In addition to the business, market days serve as a social platform; the latest news is exchanged on current commodity prices, politics or gossip. Therefore, informal markets are vital for social life in areas with little media coverage. The fact that everyone is acquainted with everyone facilitates both vendors and consumers to purchase goods on credit and pay back the debts at individually agreed terms. In our study in Mali, we found that 'trust in the seller' was one of the most important criteria for judging the quality of food.

The demand drives the supply

The informal food market never seems to sleep (Figure 1). During the cold season in Nairobi, on the way to work in the morning, one stops at a roadside stall for a steaming cup of tea *masala*. Although they sometimes resemble proper meals, 'snacks' such as samosa, corn cobs or *nyama choma* (roast meat) are always available. In Abidjan, it is popular to eat *garba* or to meet with colleagues at a *maquis* during lunch break (Box 1). Once back home from work, it is more convenient to go next door to buy vegetables from *Mama mboga* than to drive into town to the supermarket.

FIGURE 1 Meat and vegetables being sold at night in Kampala, Uganda.

Source: ILRI/Kristina Roesel

BOX 1 EATING OUT IN ABIDJAN

A typical Ivorian *maquis* is a reasonably priced open-air restaurant under a thatched roof and usually open for lunch and dinner. The standard specials are local sauces (eggplant, peanut or okra) containing chunks of meat or fish accompanied by rice, bread or *attiéké* (grated cassava), as well as *kedjenu*, the national dish made of slowly simmered chicken or fish with peppers and tomatoes. *Garba* (fried tuna served with *attiéké*, onions and tomatoes) is usually eaten at a little hotel or restaurant locally referred to as *garbadrome*.

Every consumer is a penny pincher; it does not matter whether rich or poor. Informal markets provide every client with a wide range of products at a cheap price compared to shopping malls or supermarkets. Even labelled goods are sold at a snip and there is always room for bargaining. Moreover, informal markets offer traditional foods with no formal alternative: fermented milk in many African countries, smoked fish or local chicken. The latter are referred to as 'hard' chicken in southern and eastern Africa and *poulet bicyclette* in West Africa where they are equally popular. These chickens are much preferred over 'soft' chicken sold at formal fast food chains. James Oguttu explains why: 'The soft chicken simply does not fill you up!' However, 'hard' chicken is only available at informal markets (Figure 2). Similarly, traditionally smoked fish is so popular in Abidjan that it employs over 70,000 people and is even exported to the diaspora in Europe.

Informal markets can also supply cultural products which formal markets cannot, for example goats for ritual slaughtering in South Africa and fetishes used for traditional medicine or local customs, especially in West Africa. Many informal markets also sell medicines, both modern and traditional, of course without a licence. While these markets are convenient for some, they are vital to the poor. There is not enough to be spent on transport, hence enhanced access to markets leads to increased food security. Self-sufficiency is impossible in the overcrowded peri-urban sprawl in South Africa, but the informal vendor at the corner can provide food. There may be no electricity for cooking or refrigeration and no backyard livestock, but a bowl of cooked porridge and chicken giblets in tomato sauce fills the void at an affordable price. One plate in South Africa costs between US$1 and US$2 and can feed up to four people.

The *kadogo* economy in formal and informal markets

In East Africa, the breaking down of commercially available quantities into smaller, affordable units is called the *kadogo* economy, which allows access to food to even the poorest (Figures 3 and 4). According to Cameline Mwai, in Kibera, the largest slum in Nairobi, milk is even sold by drops and sugar by spoon for tea in the morning.

FIGURE 2 Anything can be found at the informal market. Vendors selling chickens at Quelimane Market in Mozambique (note the painkillers at the back and the clothes to the right).

Source: ILRI/Stevie Mann

Businesses in the formal sector have discovered this potential too. In the meantime, many products available in supermarkets are found in informal grocery stores: washing powder, cooking oil, instant coffee or milk powder in any imaginable size. Vegetable oil is available in packaging sizes ranging from 300 ml, 500 ml, 1 litre to 5 litres at prices between US$1 and US$5. Even if pockets are left with only 10 cents, small sachets containing 50 ml are the lowest-budget solution. Many of these products find their way to informal markets but this is rarely the case for perishable fish, livestock products and fruit and vegetables which continue to be sourced mainly from smallholder farmers. For these products, we can truly say that they offer food 'by and for the poor'. Unfortunately, high-risk practices seem to emerge from the *kadogo* economy in East Africa and put the most vulnerable of society at risk (Box 2).

FIGURE 3 A supermarket in Uganda with different packaging sizes of cooking oil for different budgets.

Source: ILRI/ Kristina Roesel

FIGURE 4 Women sell raw (unpasteurized) milk in small plastic bags at Nairobi's informal Dagoretti Market.

Source: ILRI/Brad Collis

BOX 2 THE OTHER SIDE OF THE *KADOGO* ECONOMY

A beautiful thing becomes a worse nightmare than AIDS in Uganda
Charles Onyango-Obbo, Daily Monitor Uganda, 10 April 2013

The Kenyans call it the 'kadogo economy'. And it is probably one of Africa's most revolutionary contributions to the world, because it solved the problem of how to turn 'poor' people into consumers of modern goods. The 'kadogo economy' is when traders break down the old minimum measure of, for example, a quarter a kilogramme of sugar, and sell it by the spoon. In this way, cooking oil that is KSh5,000 (US$2), and therefore unaffordable for a street cleaner in a small town, can now be bought for KSh50 (US$0.02) per table spoon – and that is affordable for the one tiny meal he has decided to fry in a month. That is why we must never ban coins. Coins are the currency in the 'kadogo economy'. But nowhere has 'kadogo' economics been as truly revolutionary as in the mobile telephone industry. In Uganda, there was a time when the cheapest airtime you could buy was for KSh5,000. At that price, we had a good number of mobile phone subscribers, but the explosion – and the mega profits – came when airtime units became available in KSh1,000 units, then KSh500, and downward. Subscribers quickly shot to over 10 million and never looked back. As always happens, the 'kadogo economy' dynamics that allowed hundreds of millions to get connected, have now become deadly. The 'kadogo' dynamics are putting lethal gin in the hands of children as young as three, yes three, and some alarmed voices are saying it could all but kill off a whole generation of children. . . . Because of the size, cost, and convenient and portable packaging, they [sachets of gin] are easy for children to get. In eastern Uganda last week I learnt that both old and young people carry them in pockets, and sell to children along as they return from school and, even, along village paths! . . . Along with the sachet enguli, good sources told me that drug peddlers have also got into the 'kadogo economy', and distributing the tiniest 'affordable' portions of drugs up-country where police are too few to catch them.

Read the entire article at www.monitor.co.ug/OpEd/OpEdColumnists/Charles OnyangoObbo/A-beautiful-thing-becomes-worse/-/878504/1743858/-/p51 sdx/-/index.html (accessed 9 July 2014).

Dustbin or biggest client of the formal market?

Particularly among the Safe Food, Fair Food project participants from West Africa, sentiments became apparent when discussing the question of how important informal markets are to formal businesses. If products have expired or do not meet export standards, such as sizes for fish or bananas, they are usually 'dumped' at informal markets to minimize losses. In South Africa, unsold fruit and vegetables from the fresh produce market, which should legally be trashed, are sold illegally to informal traders.

Developed countries in Europe benefit from informal markets in sub-Saharan Africa, especially in West Africa, by exporting milk powder processed from surplus milk. The milk powder is reconstituted at informal markets by adding water, taking advantage of the poor distribution policies in developing countries. However, while these goods compete with the milk products produced by local farmers, they provide cheap food mainly for urban consumers.

In Kenya, trimmed off-cuts from export slaughterhouses and blood turned into 'cake' are sold at informal markets as animal feed especially for pigs. Offal, too, is particularly popular among the Luo people, one of the biggest ethnic groups in Kenya, as Cameline Mwai reports: 'When they leave Nairobi to go home for the Christmas holidays, the offal market in the capital city collapses'.

In South Africa, commercial farmers are not supposed to sell their products informally. Cattle, sheep and pigs are slaughtered at licensed abattoirs; eggs and milk are sold through wholesale companies or directly to supermarkets. However, informal vendors are often supplied directly by commercial farmers as it is legal for them to have retail markets for small volumes of produce. Offal from slaughtered animals and chickens is sold at the abattoirs directly to consumers, who may be informal vendors or intermediaries who sell it on. Cooked offal is a traditional delicacy in South Africa and is fortunately very affordable (Chapter 28). Heads and feet of chickens are another traditional delicacy that are now being sold to informal vendors by poultry wholesalers and supermarkets. Assuming that inspection is comprehensive, this is a crossover from the formal to the informal market and has the advantage of promoting both food safety (it is slaughtered and inspected at licensed abattoirs and the cold chain is maintained) and food security (it is affordable and accessible to low-income or poor consumers). This delicacy, previously a waste product of poultry slaughter, is also now being exported to neighbouring countries in southern Africa. Vendors of street food, who are often criminalized, are thus among the legal customers of commercial farmers. Many of them purchase all their animal-source ingredients, such as broilers, eggs, milk or packaged meat cuts, in a supermarket before preparing it for their clients in the street (Chapter 26).

Constraints in informal markets

There is a perception that informal food sales compromise the health of consumers and that there is a danger of a crossover to formal markets. As the preceding paragraph describes, the opposite has in fact been found: poverty, joblessness, lack of infrastructure and expensive transport have resulted in a huge market for affordable and accessible food. Thus, the major supplier has gradually become the formal market as the volumes and price cannot be matched by informal producers. Also, the consumer is very choosy and will go for the best product at the available price, and thus competition in the market is improving the quality and safety of food sold in informal markets. The cell phone revolution and television have possibly had a major impact on how consumers think about food, as even the poorest recognize a need for cleanliness (Chapter 26).

Discrepancies in supply and demand were often reported, and they were often brought on by the season. In Mali, there is a shortage of meat and milk from March to June when the herders take their animals on transhumance to the south. In Ethiopia, supply exceeds demand during the seven periods of fasting among Orthodox Christians who comprise about half of Ethiopia's population. During these fasting periods, the milk prices collapse.

Informal markets are the primary source of income for many people in sub-Saharan Africa. Therefore, competition is very high, often resulting in illegal activity. Many of the Safe Food, Fair Food studies observed the adulteration of milk (Chapter 12, 13 and 18) to increase the volume of milk that generates profits. In South Africa, vendors of ready-to-eat chicken are threatened by the constantly smouldering conflict at the taxi ranks (Chapter 26) and require the protection of the municipality authorities. In Kenya, inspectors of the city council collect taxes (approximately US$ 0.35) from each vendor on a market day in order to spend it on waste disposal. During their tour, they confiscate meat which is visibly very dirty. None of the vendors can afford to throw their produce away and this renders the inspectors prone to corruption.

Fewer regulatory constraints mean better access to markets and increased income. On the other hand, no regulations at all might result in compromised quality of food products. Apart from diseases that cannot be detected if there is no inspection, actors are often untrained and, as presented in many of the Safe Food, Fair Food studies in this book, are unaware of good hygiene practices when handling food. However, many of those who are aware lack the right pre-requisites, such as clean tap water, constant power supply and waste disposal, which were frequently mentioned in all of the study areas. The lack of storage and cooling facilities often result in high losses or practices that jeopardize food safety. Meat is sold at discount prices even though it was not refrigerated for several days, or milk is left in the sun for most of the day. Others favour day-to-day slaughter on demand to compensate for conservation problems such as lack of electricity for refrigeration. At the same time, this is a useful management practice reducing the risk of food-borne disease. Many traders have found ways and means to manage risk by using traditional methods or common sense (Chapter 6) because they lack the right support for a safe working environment. Our studies found that many of the people supplying and working in informal markets are quite knowledgeable about good practices and how to supply safe and quality products. These attitudes are entry points for further improving practices.

A short note on the plastics industry

In sub-Saharan Africa, everyone is part of the informal market: small-scale and commercial farmers, small-scale butchers and big abattoirs, street vendors and supermarkets, cooperatives and intermediaries, rich and poor consumers, municipalities and government departments. The list can be increased by many more: traders of fertilizer and fodder for primary production, public transport and its fuel suppliers and mechanics in order to carry goods to the market, intermediaries facilitating access to markets, municipalities providing electricity and water, and the plastics industry. This connection might seem absurd until one realizes how much plastic is involved in all kinds of markets (Figure 5). If milk, vegetable oil or potable water is sold in small quantities for consumer convenience, it is packed in small plastic bags. If you buy eggs at the market, they are carefully packed in a plastic bag. Whereas clean water seems to be lacking in street markets, plastic bags are abundant and most of the time they do not cost a thing. However, plastic bags are one of the major pollutants as well as a hazard for animals (Figure 6).

FIGURE 5 A market near Khulungira village near Dedza in central Malawi. Buy one bundle of onions and get a plastic bag for free.

Source: ILRI/Stevie Mann

FIGURE 6 Peri-urban Accra with humans and animals crowding in the middle of plastic bags.

Source: Joy Appiah

BOX 3 MAURITANIA BANS PLASTIC BAG USE: ANIMALS RISK DEATH BY EATING PLASTIC BAGS, THE GOVERNMENT SAYS

BBC News, 2 January 2013

Mauritania has banned the use of plastic bags to protect the environment and the lives of land and sea animals. More than 70% of cattle and sheep that die in the capital, Nouakchott, are killed by eating plastic bags, environment ministry official Mohamed Yahya told BBC Afrique. Plastic bag manufacturers could be jailed for up to a year. Plastic makes up a quarter of 56,000 tonnes of waste produced annually in Nouakchott, official statistics show. Mauritania's Organization of Consumer Protection head Moctar Ould Tauf said he welcomed the ban, Efe news agency reports. It was of 'particular importance' given the negative impact of plastic bags on the environment, animals and marine species, he said.

Environment Minister Amedi Camara said that nearly all of the plastic package waste is not 'collected and is found in the natural environment – land and sea – where they are sometimes ingested by marine species and livestock, causing their death'. The government, local non-governmental organizations and the UN Programme for Development (UNDP) have been promoting the use of new biodegradable bags, the Mauritanian Information Agency reports. Anyone using, manufacturing or importing plastic bags could be fined or sentenced to a year in prison, Mr Camara said. Several African countries, including Rwanda, have already banned the use of plastic bags.

Read more at www.bbc.co.uk/news/world-africa-20891539 (accessed 9 July 2014).

Note

1. Grace D, Makita K, Kang'ethe EK and Bonfoh B. 2010. Safe Food, Fair Food: Participatory risk analysis for improving the safety of informally produced and marketed food in sub-Saharan Africa. *Revue Africaine de Santé et de Productions Animales* 8(S): 3–11.

3

INFORMAL MARKETS ARE NOT NECESSARILY DANGEROUS AND FORMAL MARKETS ARE NOT NECESSARILY SAFE

Kristina Roesel, Delia Grace, Haruya Toyomaki, Cameline Mwai and Fanta Desissa

> *No matter how black a cow is, the milk is always white.*
>
> *Malawian proverb*

Key messages

- Informally marketed food is often safe for human consumption.
- Improper post-processing handling is one of the biggest challenges and largely depends on the prerequisites.
- Business-oriented attitudes are one of the major risks to food safety in informal markets.
- Some risks in both markets are underestimated as they do not cause immediate harm.

For Western travellers, local markets are a way of getting a glimpse of the African way of life. Often, tourists gaze at the incredible choice of anything that is sold here, from buckets to bikes, clothes to calabashes, fish to fetish, groundnuts to goats, spices to souvenirs, pottery to pungent foods. Many are tempted to try it but eventually hesitate as food in the street is denounced as a source of diarrhoea, the ultimate holiday killer.

While travellers can afford to switch to alternative food sources from supermarkets or hotels, most of the local people cannot. Many do not even live anywhere near a supermarket and exchange goods with neighbours or at the farmers' market. Do these financial or distance constraints exclude them from safe food?

BOX 4 A JAPANESE ABROAD

Haruya Toyomaki

In September 2011, I visited Addis Ababa in Ethiopia to attend the final workshop of the Safe Food, Fair Food project and that was my first time ever visiting Africa. Before travelling to Addis Ababa, I stayed a few days in Nairobi, Kenya to learn about ILRI.

Visitors from developed countries to developing countries know that foods in developing countries are very risky and they are also taught something about it. For example, 'Do not drink tap water!'

I followed suit and prepared many things before my first visit to Africa: wet wipes to disinfect hands, a painkiller, an insecticide for the prevention of malaria and a digestive. I got vaccinated against yellow fever, rabies, tetanus, typhoid fever and hepatitis A.

Staying in Africa, I did not drink tap water and used bottled water to brush my teeth. I was careful to wash my hands before having a meal and I used wet wipes to disinfect my hands after washing them. At the beginning, I did not eat raw foods for a few days. But friends who accompanied me ate them and did not fall sick. These dishes and African fruit looked very delicious, so I decided to try them. And, of course, they were indeed very delicious.

In Addis Ababa, I went to a local restaurant. The restaurant sold *nyama choma* (roasted meat) which I had studied in Japan (Chapter 24) by analysing beef from Arusha in Tanzania. I enjoyed eating *nyama choma* because my study suggested that it brought no risk of falling sick from campylobacteriosis (although it contained risks of other diseases). The restaurant also sold raw meat which is a traditional Ethiopian dish. I refused to eat it, but Professor Zewde from Ethiopia enjoyed it. Of course, the Ethiopian professor was fine the next day.

Fortunately, I enjoyed Africa without any illnesses, as did six of my friends who accompanied me in Kenya. Ironically, of all people, Professor Makita, who is used to staying in Africa, suffered from a bad stomachache. I could not imagine feeling comfortable in African countries before this trip. However, African foods were so very delicious that I did not eat any foods which I brought from Japan. The best discovery of my trip was that I love rice very much!

Informal food is not as dangerous as generally perceived

Research from the Safe Food, Fair Food project shows that most of the food marketed informally may not be as dangerous as perceived by many people. In South Africa, the products investigated were generally found to be safe for human consumption; chicken sold at taxi ranks (Chapter 26) and other ready-to-eat meat in the streets mostly originated from formal retailers (Chapter 27) and offal from game farms even stands formal meat inspection prior to sale in the informal sector (Chapter 28). In Ghana, experiments and observation found that fish sauces were not a risk for listeriosis due to the good cooking practices. Likewise in Abidjan, even though shellfish contained both parasites and cholera germs, the risk of infection to people was very low.

In Kenya it was shown that beef from a typical local slaughterhouse is just as safe as meat from the local improved slaughterhouse which sells to the domestic supermarket (Figures 7, 8 and 9). In fact, even fewer microbes were found in the informally slaughtered meat. Referring to official threshold levels, they can both be considered safe for human consumption (Chapter 21). Although in Mozambique (Chapter 25), chicken from a local market showed slightly higher levels of microbes, they were still compliant with national standards, and hence safe for human consumption.

FIGURE 7 A typical slaughterhouse in Nairobi, Kenya.

Source: Cameline Mwai

FIGURE 8 A local improved slaughterhouse in Nairobi, Kenya. This type of slaughterhouse was found to be the most contaminated.

Source: Cameline Mwai

FIGURE 9 An export abattoir in Nairobi, Kenya. This type was found to be the least contaminated.

Source: Cameline Mwai

Our studies meticulously investigated whether microbes were found along the food chain. Products were sampled at the farm, intermediaries and retailers and from the products' environment (Chapter 16 and 32). If microbes were found in the raw product, they were either completely eliminated or their levels reduced to such low numbers that they would not cause disease, as shown in studies on shellfish from Ghana (Chapter 32) and Côte d'Ivoire (Chapter 34).

However, that does not apply to every product of animal origin, and milk is a particularly delicate case. Nutritious to humans and microbes alike, it proved to be the perfect hotbed of disease. In West Africa, milk is often consumed raw, a practice that dramatically increases the risk for milk-borne diseases such as tuberculosis, listeriosis or brucellosis (Chapters 16 and 19). In East Africa, where milk is commonly boiled or pasteurized, consumers think themselves safe, which could be a fallacy if it is done too long after milking. Some studies showed a high risk of milk containing bacteria that produce toxins causing fever and diarrhoea. While the bacteria are killed during heating, their toxins survive (Chapters 12 and 13).[1]

Milk is often fermented in Africa. This is an excellent preservative technique but it can also decrease risk if adequately done and post-processing contamination is avoided. In Ethiopia, it decreased the risk of *Staphylococcus aureus* 15-fold but in Ghana it did not reduce the *Listeria* risk. Another study done in northern Ghana showed that 48-hour fermentation eliminated all microbial pathogens; however, this milk was too sour for the consumers.[2]

But dangers do lurk in informal markets

A common concern in our studies was that most of the food that was initially safe ended up being contaminated after processing (Figure 10). If food is thoroughly heated and consumed right away, most microbiological hazards can be eliminated. That applies to most of the germs that were in the product all along (for example, bacteria in milk and tapeworm cysts in raw meat) and to contaminants that were introduced to meat, milk and fish because food handlers did not wash their hands. In Tanzania, the ingredients for roast beef and vegetable relish are normally kept on the ground which is obviously dirty. The setting is more complicated in Dar es Salaam where ready-to-eat meat is prepared outside in a hotter and dustier environment than Arusha, where the climate is cool and food prepared inside. Cooling facilities are lacking all over, with the result that in Ethiopia, for example, cheese and raw milk are sold in the open for the entire day and the seller of *kitfo* (traditional raw minced meat), who normally eats the leftovers at night, falls ill.

Sometimes the problem is not knowledge, but the financial incentives to sell products. Safe Food, Fair Food participants recalled a butcher who stored meat he did not sell during slaughtering day in a refrigerator. Every day he added some leftovers and at the end of the week he sold the meat to customers at a discount price, even though he knew that his neighbourhood had experienced several power cuts during the previous week.

FIGURE 10 Damp smoked fish in Côte d'Ivoire is normally sold wrapped in newspaper of unknown origin, which could be a source of contamination.

Source: Yolande Aké Assi Datté

In the dairy industry in West and East Africa, it seems to be common practice to add water to milk in order to sell larger quantities. Adulteration of milk is not only criminal as the consumer gets less of what he paid for (Figures 11 and 12), but if the water is dirty, the sellers put their customers at risk of falling sick (Chapters 12, 14 and 18). However, this trader is no more criminal than companies adding melamine to milk powder destined to feed babies.

But formal is not always safe . . .

Food in the formal sector is usually bought and consumed without too much concern. Not many customers question the quality of food at Pick n Pay in South Africa, Shoprite in Tanzania, Sococé in Côte d'Ivoire or Nakumatt throughout Kenya; products are properly canned or bottled, labelled with an expiry date, stored in a clean and shiny environment and are more costly than food sold on the street. Most likely, and different from informal markets, customers will not find eggs with cracks as they are excluded from sale. However, the exception proves the rule.

It is not only that canned chicken sold at a leading up-market supermarket chain in South Africa for more than US$8 can be spoiled prior to its expiry date

FIGURE 11 A milk collector uses the alcohol test to check the freshness of raw milk.

Source: Fanta Desissa

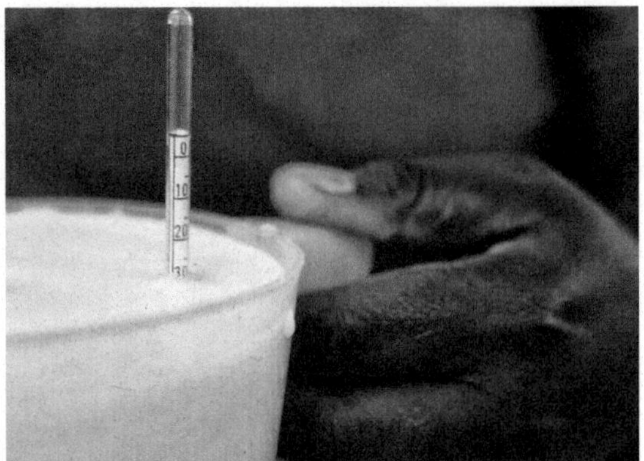

FIGURE 12 Using a lactometer to test milk for adulteration in Kenya's informal market.

Source: ILRI/Dave Elsworth

and, subsequently, the smell of the open can is simply not bearable. It also seems to be a common practice among supermarkets to deliberately sell products to the informal market at a bargain price once they are past their expiry date. Apart from 'overdue' products, formally marketed items can be prone to hazards as well (Figure 13). In 2008, melamine was discovered in formally marketed milk from China. Melamine is a chemical compound which is illegally added to food or feed products to increase the apparent protein content, a practice which presents serious health problems.[3] Previous studies in Kenya found that compliance with standards was no better for pasteurized milk in the formal sector than for informal sector raw milk hawked from door to door; a similar result was found in studies in India.

In 1997, 200 people in Abidjan fell sick from salmonellosis due to contaminated hamburger beef prepared and stored in bulk (Chapter 17). An incidental finding in a study in Tanzania showed that milk sourced from informal milk shops, but formally processed, pasteurized, homogenized and packed in pouches, was free of the pathogen under investigation (*Staphylococcus aureus*) but harboured another potential cause of disease, *Bacillus cereus* (Chapters 13 and 18).

What the formal rejects the informal eats

If products destined for export are rejected on the international market, they simply return to the domestic market. Failure to meet quality criteria, such as uniform sizes and weights, on international markets does not automatically render a product unsafe. But what if sub-Saharan Africa suddenly receives second-best goods? During the 1990s, the United Kingdom beef industry went through hard times due to the occurrence of 'mad cow' disease. The English beef originally destined for Durban,

FIGURE 13 This can of chickpeas bought from a supermarket in Germany was opened before its expiry date and its contents were found covered with mould.

Source: ILRI/Kristina Roesel

South Africa was rejected there, relabelled and shipped to Maputo, Mozambique. This way, the problem was simply taken back to the informal markets. In one of our studies, we found that milk rejected by a cooperative in Mali was not destroyed but taken home and, presumably, consumed by the women sellers.

Conclusion

It is wrong to generalize and assume that informal markets are unsafe *per se*. Surprisingly, there is not enough evidence to make strong statements about the safety of formal and informal markets. What we do know from case studies is that food from informal markets is often safe and food from formal markets is often not safe.

Notes

1. See also Donkor ES, Anin KG and Quaye J. 2007. Bacterial contamination of informally marketed raw milk in Ghana. *Ghana Medical Journal* 41(2): 58–61.
2. Akabanda F, Owusu-Kwarteng J, Glover LRK and Tano-Debrah W. 2010. Microbiological characteristics of Ghanaian fermented milk product, *nunu*. *Nature and Science* 8(9): 178–187.
3. World Health Organization. 2011. www.who.int/topics/melamine/en (accessed 9 July 2014).

4

HAZARDS DO NOT ALWAYS TRANSLATE INTO RISKS

Kristina Roesel, Delia Grace, Kohei Makita, Bassirou Bonfoh, Erastus Kang'ethe, Lusato Kurwijila, Saskia Hendrickx, Cheryl McCrindle, Kwaku Tano-Debrah, Girma Zewde and Helena Matusse

A cat in its house has the teeth of a lion.

Somali proverb

Key messages

- Hazards are defined as agents likely to cause harm or damage to humans, other organisms or the environment in the absence of their control.
- Risk is the likelihood of that anticipated harm to occur, including the consequences for public health, ecology and the economy.
- The identification of hazards in animal-source foods does not estimate the impacts of the hazards in terms of human sickness and death, thus existing food safety regulation is often ineffective and anti-poor.
- Risk-based approaches brought new insights and are now standard for food safety issues in developed countries.
- Safe Food, Fair Food studies identified at least ten different hazards in food with different levels of risk to public health and local economies.

Background

Unsafe food causes many acute and life-long diseases, ranging from diarrhoeal diseases to various forms of cancer. The World Health Organization (WHO) estimates that food-borne and water-borne diarrhoeal diseases taken together kill about 2.2 million people annually of whom 1.9 million are children. Food-borne diseases and threats to food safety constitute growing concerns to public health and local economies.

In countries where detailed attribution data exist, most of the burden of food-borne disease is the result of microbes being transmitted from animals to humans (zoonoses). For example, of the five most important germs causing disease in citizens of the United States of America, four have an animal reservoir and more than 80% of identified deaths from food-borne illness are caused by only three zoonotic pathogens: *Salmonella* spp., *Listeria monocytogenes* and *Toxoplasma gondii*. Poultry was the food most often implicated (25%) but beef, pork, shellfish and finfish were also important, each causing more than 10% of the total.

In the United Kingdom, a similar pattern is seen. There, food safety authorities have developed a method for estimating the relative risks associated with specific foods, dividing the number of cases due to a specific food (as derived from their outbreak database) by the estimated total servings of that food consumed in a year. Between 1996 and 2000, most illness was attributed to eating poultry (30%), complex foods (27%) and red meat (17%). The impacts of food-borne disease include fatalities in vulnerable groups (for example, malnourished infants and people with Human Immunodeficiency Virus (HIV)/Acquired Immunodeficiency Syndrome (AIDS)) and, in 2–3% of cases, severe and disabling long-term effects such as joint disease, kidney failure and disorders in the heart, eyes and brain. The latter chronic sequels, of which many policymakers are unaware, probably represent a greater health and economic burden than the immediate disease. Evidence is growing that in developing countries ill health can be not only a personal and household tragedy, but a major factor in causing and perpetuating poverty.

But hazards are not risks

Many studies focus on the identification of hazards in animal-source foods but do not estimate the consequences and impacts of the hazards in terms of human sickness and death. Without this information it is difficult for decision-makers to rationally allocate resources for risk management. Furthermore, identification of hazards has led to media scares and consequent loss of confidence in livestock products, resulting in dramatic drops in consumption with negative impacts on the livelihoods of those engaged in the food value chain and consumer nutrition. Hence the need for approaches which identify risk to human health rather than the presence of hazards and which include risk management methods appropriate for poor producers and other intermediaries.

For example, studies on milk in East Africa found that although zoonotic hazards were present in as much as 1% of household milk samples, infections in people were at least two orders of magnitude less common. While the small volumes of milk produced and handled per informal sector agent increased the risk of cross-contamination, consumers' widespread practice of boiling milk dramatically reduced the risk of disease.

A hazard is defined as any biological, chemical or physical agent that is reasonably likely to cause harm or damage to humans, other organisms or the environment in the absence of its control. Risk is the likelihood of that anticipated harm to occur, including the consequences for public health, ecology and the economy. Hazards can include, but are not limited to, microbial pathogens that cause food-borne illnesses with symptoms such as diarrhoea and fever, pesticides that cause poisoning or motor vehicles causing car accidents. Identification of hazards is the first step in performing risk assessment. As a rule, all Safe Food, Fair Food studies looked for hazards in informally marketed food (Table 1).

Physical hazards were not investigated, but these could be small stones in fish dried on the beach (see 'When tradition augments risk: fish processing in Ghana', Chapter 7) or glass splinters in a poultry abattoir, as Ana Bela Cambaza dos Muchangos from Mozambique explains. However, since very few abattoirs in Mozambique have glass windows, this is not very likely to occur and the risk for ingesting glass is therefore very low.

The following chemical hazards were identified in the course of our research:

- polycyclic aromatic hydrocarbons (PAHs) in traditionally smoked fish;
- veterinary drug residues in animal-source products;
- high fluoride content in water.

This group of hazards is particularly dangerous, as adverse health effects might not become visible immediately. While some chemical hazards, such as fungal toxins or pesticides, cause immediate disease or death, others such as fluoride in water might have a beneficial effect at a small dose (that is, healthy growth of bones and teeth), but long-term exposure to excessive levels can lead to tooth mottling in children or skeletal fluorosis in adults and children. This chronic disease is characterized by very stiff bones and joints and may even affect the spine (Chapter 10). PAHs in traditionally smoked fish proved to have both short-term effects on the women who prepare the fish in small shacks and long-term effects; they suffer from headaches, eye strain and fatigue and are at risk of getting cancer (Chapter 33). Veterinary drugs such as penicillin, accumulating in an animal's liver, might be ingested if withdrawal periods are ignored by producers and veterinarians. If consumed on a regular basis, people can subsequently develop allergies that might lead to a fatal allergic shock (Chapter 31).

The chemical hazards listed above were all identified. In Côte d'Ivoire, the levels of PAHs exceeded international standards by far and, given the regular exposure, imply high risk to public health (Chapter 33).

The majority of Safe Food, Fair Food studies focused on the identification of biological hazards, particularly bacteria:

- *E. coli* in water, milk, poultry and meat;
- *L. monocytogenes* in milk and fish;
- *S. aureus* in milk and meat;
- *Brucella* spp. in milk;
- thermophilic *Campylobacter* in beef;
- *Vibrio* in shellfish;
- life-cycle stages of a lung fluke (a parasitic worm) in shellfish;
- *Bacillus cereus* in milk.

TABLE 1 Synthesis of identified hazards, assessed risks and critical control points in the Safe Food, Fair Food project.

Country	*Student*	*Product*	*Importance of product*	*Gender aspect*	*Hazard*	*Risk*	*Where in the value chain*	*Critical point*	*(Indigenous) risk management in place*	*Innovations*
Côte d'Ivoire	Kouamé-Sina, Sylvie Mireille	raw milk	social, nutrition, livelihood	no	*E. coli, S. aureus, Enterococcus,* antibiotic residues, added water	high in retail milk	farms, collecting points, selling points (retail)	udder cow, mixing at farm, handling, no hand washing	fermentation, boiling	*Bifidobacterium* inhibits pathogen growth if fermented
Côte d'Ivoire	Youbouet Bassa Antoine	raw milk	social, nutrition, livelihood	no	*Bacillus cereus*	high in milk	farms, collecting points, selling points (retail)	mixing at farm, handling	boiling and cooling, fermentation	n/a
Côte d'Ivoire	Traoré, Sylvain Gnamien	fresh crabs and shrimp	livelihood	yes: women sell them	*Vibrio cholerae, parahaemolyticus, alginolyticus,* trematodes *(Paragonimus)*	low	retailers	cross-contamination with other products	cooking effective	n/a
Côte d'Ivoire	Aké-Assi, Yolande	smoked fish	economic, livelihood	yes: women smoke and sell it	polycyclic aromatic hydrocarbons (PAH)	moderate to high in smoked fish, unknown during smoking process	processing	smoking	none in place	reduce fatty fish, reduce heat, selective energy source (tree species)

Ethiopia	Desissa, Fanta	raw milk	nutrition, economic, livelihood	no	*S. aureus*	moderate	farm/ production (mastitis)	udder health, long lag time between harvest and processing, pooling of milk from different sources	fermentation, boiling	standardize, dairy cooperative
Ethiopia	Amenu, Kebede	water	livelihood	no	*E. coli*, fluoride	high	farm/ production	farm hygiene, handling, water pollution and contamination	smoking containers, fermentation, etc.	rain water harvest
Ethiopia	Spengler, Marisa	water, milk, raw milk products	livelihood	no	*E. coli*, coliforms (faecal contamination), total aerobic counts	high	farm/ production, transport, storage and bulking point (milk collection centre), traditional raw milk products	cross-contamination during milking, processing and handling at every step of the food chain, contaminated water	fermentation	n/a
Ghana	Appiah, Joy	raw milk	nutrition, economic, livelihood	yes: women sell and consume it	*L. monocytogenes*	moderate	farm/ production, retail market	retail	proper boiling of milk before fermentation or retailing	education, lobbying for communal pasteurizer to be installed on milk market

TABLE 1 Continued

Country	*Student*	*Product*	*Importance of product*	*Gender aspect*	*Hazard*	*Risk*	*Where in the value chain*	*Critical point*	*(Indigenous) risk management in place*	*Innovations*
Ghana	Bomfeh, Kennedy	smoked fish	nutrition, economic, livelihood	yes: women process and sell it	*L. monocytogenes*	low	processors, retail market	post-processing	well-cooked before consumption	education
Kenya	Mwai, Cameline	beef in slaughter-house	economic, livelihood	no	*E.coli* O157:H7	moderate	slaughter	abattoir workers, lack of good hygiene practices at slaughterhouse	none in place	participation at slaughterhouse level
Kenya	Kago, John	beef at butcher	economic, livelihood	no	*E.coli* O157:H7	moderate	transport, butcher (retail)	drivers, loaders, butchers, lack of personal hygiene, butchery hygiene	some good but some bad practices that lead to cross-contamination	participation of transporters, loaders and butchery attendants
Kenya	Kabui, Kevin	milk	economic, livelihood	no	coliforms (faecal contamination)	high	collection centres	farm hygiene, handling	none in place	testing quality-based payment scheme
Kenya	Ndongo, Flavien	milk	economic, livelihood	yes: women are producers	*Brucella* spp.	low	production/ market	handling of aborted material	boiling	cooperatives safest

				(occupational exposure, revenues)						
Mali	Koné, Bognan Valentin	meat, milk: small ruminants	social, livelihood, market	yes: women sell and consume it	multiple pathogens	potential	production, processing, consumption	recontamination (milk), not heating, taking back rejected milk	roast meat, fermented milk for home consumption, boiled milk for dairy unit	cooperative dairy unit, Choukouya (nutritional benefits > health risks)
Mali	Sow, Ibrahim	milk: cows/ small ruminants	social, livelihood, market	yes: women sell and consume it	*Brucella* spp.	low	production	recontamination, handling aborted materials	raw milk, fermentation	dairy unit/cooperative
Mozambique	dos Muchangos, Ana Bela Cambaza	poultry	nutrition (urban, periurban population rely on chicken meat due to the availability and low price compared to beef)	yes: producers and processors are mostly women	*E. coli* type 1, coliforms (faecal contamination)	potential to moderate	during processing in informal abattoirs	scalding, washing, packing	washing of carcasses in the final stage but not effective	use of petrifilms standardized in the lab, risk analysis as tool for food contamination evidence

TABLE 1 Continued

Country	*Student*	*Product*	*Importance of product*	*Gender aspect*	*Hazard*	*Risk*	*Where in the value chain*	*Critical point*	*(Indigenous) risk management in place*	*Innovations*
South Africa	Molefe, Margaret	animal-sourced products	policy	no	veterinary drug residues in food	potential	regulatory bodies (enabling environments)	fragmented government responsibilities complicate the implementation of policies for food safety		n/a
South Africa	Oguttu, James	prepared chicken	economic, livelihood	yes: mostly women sell the chicken	environmental contamination, *S. aureus*	moderate	processor, consumer (environmental contamination)	the most likely source of contamination is the environment and not the hands of the vendors as samples from human hands were positive for environmental contaminants rather than faecal contaminants	good basic hygiene practices (short finger-nails, protective clothing, keeping food covered and over fire, no handling with bare hands), sales on demand (no stocking of meat)	the focus group discussions motivated the sellers to start working as a group to combat pest animals
South Africa	Heeb, Alexander	prepared meat:	economic, livelihood	yes: most	environmental contamination,	low	initially safe but post-	processor and consumer level	cooking (consumer)	n/a

		beef, chicken and game		street vendors are women and were addressed in this study	*S. aureus*		process contamination to inadequate prerequisites and handling practices			
South Africa	Ramrajh, Shashi	game offal	nutrition	yes: the study worked with neigh-bouring primary school	multiple pathogens	low	processor, consumer	post-processing	hygienic slaughter and processing	game offal was not previously used for human consumption in this area
South Africa	van Zyl, Erika	biltong	economic, livelihood	no	environmental contamination	moderate	processor, consumer	poor handling		n/a
South Africa	Qekwana, Nenene	goats for cere-monies	social	no	multiple pathogens	potential to moderate	consumer	lack of knowledge, inspection	cook quickly after slaughter	n/a
Tanzania	Kilango, Kaiza	milk	economic	no	*S. aureus, Bacillus cereus, E. coli*	moderate	retail	udder hygiene, post-harvest and post-process handling	boiling; clot on boiling practice	registered collection centres
Tanzania	Mahundi, Edgar	beef at butcher and in bars	economic	no	thermophilic *Campylobacter*	high	retail	butchers' hygiene	cross-contamination	n/a
Tanzania	Toyomaki, Haruya	beef and chicken in bars	economic	no	thermophilic *Campylobacter*	low	retail	cooking and preparation	cross-contamination	n/a

The presence of microbes alone is not necessarily dangerous. On the contrary – depending on the severity of the disease (a cold is less severe than pneumonia) – the danger lies in the number of microbes able to cause disease, whether the food contains this infectious level and whether the person ingesting it is healthy or more vulnerable to disease. People who are more vulnerable to disease are the young, old, pregnant and immunocompromised (HIV-positive): the so-called 'YOPIs'. Pregnant women, for instance, are twenty times more likely than other healthy adults to acquire listeriosis.[1] In pregnant women, listeriosis might result in miscarriage or severe disease in the new born (Chapters 16 and 32).

Most of the investigated microbial hazards were identified. Some studies, for instance in Côte d'Ivoire, showed that particular microbes were present in 64% of the milk and roughly 13% of the people consuming it associated it with gastrointestinal disease (Chapter 17). The same milk contained *Bacillus cereus* strains that were multi-resistant to antibiotics commonly used for the treatment of animals and humans (Chapter 18). The consumption of this milk might not cause immediate illness but long-term effects may become visible when people later suffer from respiratory or urinary tract infections and antibiotic treatment loses effectiveness.

E. coli is a microbe that regularly inhabits the intestines of mammals and humans. It therefore indicates faecal contamination when detected in food. *E. coli* was found in high levels in poultry in Mozambique, yet the levels were still below the national threshold levels and said not to cause disease (Chapter 25). While most of the members of the *E. coli* family in animals and humans do not necessarily cause disease, some do. Investigations of beef carcasses in Kenya showed that even though levels were not high at the abattoir (Chapter 21), the long time lag between dressing and sale allowed the microbe to multiply on the way to the butchery and into the food at the ready-to-eat restaurant (Chapter 22), thus eventually exposing many people to risk of disease.

Almost 23% of the boiled milk in Tanzania was highly contaminated with *S. aureus* (Chapter 13) and even though otherwise-healthy people suffer from self-limiting diarrhoea or vomiting, YOPIs are more likely at risk when consuming the milk. In Ethiopia, the level of *S. aureus* in boiled milk was zero, which seems to be good news. However, this could be a fallacy as some strains of these microbes are able to produce a toxin which cannot be destroyed through heating. Milk tested prior to boiling contained high levels of the bacteria, suggesting that even though they were eliminated during boiling, the notorious toxin might still be present in the boiled milk, thus exposing many consumers, in particular the most vulnerable, to risk (Chapter 12).

Some other microbial hazards were not identified at all (brucellosis in peri-urban Nairobi, Chapter 15) or were found at very low levels (thermophilic *Campylobacter* in Tanzania, Chapter 24 and *Brucella* spp. in Mali, Chapter 19), even though they were present elsewhere in the countries. Others appeared in the raw product but not in the thoroughly cooked end product, that is, shellfish in Côte d'Ivoire (Chapter 34) and smoked fish (Chapter 32), suggesting the risk to consumers is low even though hazards were initially present.

The magnitude and occurrence of risk largely depend on the mode of food preparation and consumption, for example whether it is eaten raw or processed. One Safe Food, Fair Food study showed that traditional techniques such as fermentation of raw milk can reduce the risk of disease by 97%. Bacterial growth is inhibited by increasing acidity which, if the milk is fermented long enough, is likely to render a risky product into safe food at low cost (Chapter 12). In contrast, another Safe Food, Fair Food study in Ghana showed that the level of microbes was relatively low in naturally fermented milk compared to raw milk (Chapter 16). It seemed from the study that this was caused by inadequate fermentation and cross-contamination from unfermented milk through the use of containers. In another study in Ghana, extended fermentation was found to eliminate most pathogens.[2] However, in this case, the disease risk was much higher as only very few microbial cells are needed for infection and fermented milk was consumed every day (in contrast to raw milk that was consumed once every two weeks).

These examples show how commonsense management, which focusses on controlling the level of zoonotic hazards in milk and other animal-source foods, may not have much effect on decreasing the risks to human health, whereas other approaches that focus not on the hazard but on the risk to human health can be more fruitful.

Risk analysis is a promising approach to improving food safety

Faced with this complex challenge of high levels of hazards in informal food, but little understanding of the risks these represent to human health, along with the empirical evidence that small-scale food production and processing offer an important pathway out of poverty and that existing food safety regulation is often ineffective and anti-poor, new approaches are needed.

Historically, hazards associated with livestock and animal-source foods were managed through 'command and control' regulation involving inspection and production, transformation and sale backed with litigation in the event of harm. This approach was increasingly unable to deliver food safety, as demonstrated by highly publicized tragedies (such as the *E. coli* outbreak in Germany in 2011 in which 53 people died[3] and the bovine spongiform encephalopathy epidemic in the United Kingdom in early 2000). This led to a shift in approach from compliance with procedures enforced by external inspection to self-management of risk by empowered organizations. Risk-based approaches brought new insights and are now standard for food safety issues in developed countries, as well as being the basis of rules governing international trade in food products, and are endorsed by the Food and Agriculture Organization of the United Nations (FAO), the World Organization for Animal Health (OIE) and WHO.

One of the first risk-based methodologies was Hazard Analysis and Critical Control Points (HACCP), a structured approach to assessing potential hazards, deciding which control points are critical to safety, monitoring these and taking specified remedial action in the event of deviations from these control points.

HACCP is widely recognized as an effective and economically efficient approach to food safety control in food processing operations, predominantly because it is based on risk assessment and process control rather than end-product testing; it is starting to be applied to traditional food production systems in developing countries and preliminary results are encouraging. Microbial risk assessment (MRA) is an emerging tool for evaluating the safety of food and water supplies; it takes a systems and pathway approach ('farm to fork'), allowing an assessment to be made of the health risk to the population of interest from specific pathogens, foods or combinations of both.

For the last decade, risk analysis has convincingly dominated food safety and trade in animals and animal products. It offers a science-based, structured, transparent method for answering the questions that matter to policymakers and the public alike: Is this food safe? Is the risk big and important? What efforts are appropriate to reduce the risk? Risk analysis has three components: risk assessment, risk management and risk communication (Figures 14, 15 and 16). The first step – risk assessment – provides both an estimate of harm and the probability of harm occurring.

Having identified and characterized the hazard, it needs to be assessed to what extent the consumers are exposed to the hazard. This helps to understand the 'real risk' associated with the presence of a harmful agent. By assessing the concentration of hazards in food and the number of people who handle the contaminated product, and by determining the frequency and quantity of consuming this food, it is possible to evaluate the risk to individuals and groups of people in a particular

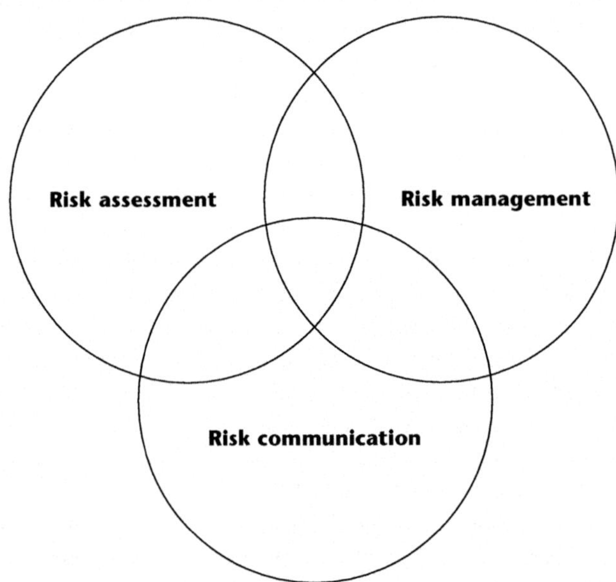

FIGURE 14 Risk analysis framework of the Codex Alimentarius Commission.

area. The data based on evidence eventually allow public health authorities to set threshold levels of contaminants in food such as 'accepted levels of protection'.

To be useful, risk assessment must be followed by action to mitigate those risks which are unacceptable to stakeholders. Risk management uses pathway approaches ('from stable to table') and probabilistic modelling to identify critical

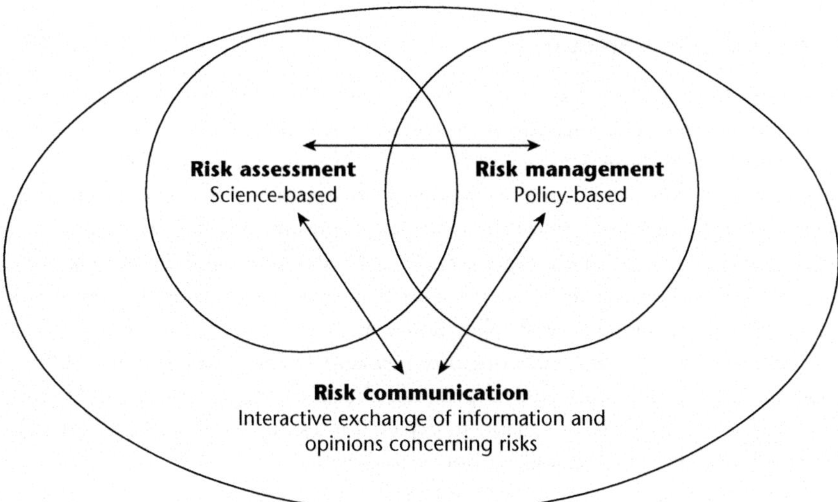

FIGURE 15 Risk analysis framework of the World Health Organization.

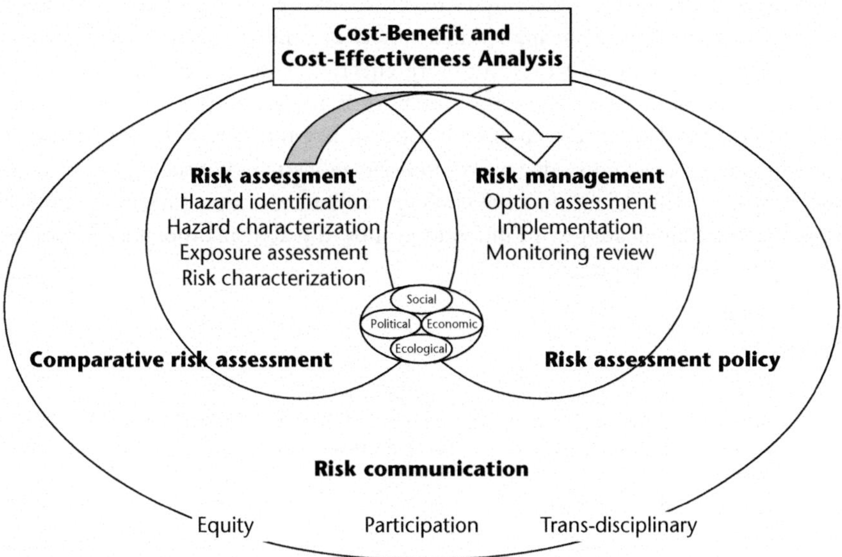

FIGURE 16 Risk analysis framework of the Safe Food, Fair Food project.

control points and apply strategies to remove or minimize risk (Chapter 6). The third and integral component of risk analysis is risk communication: the iterative process of communicating risk to those affected by it and incorporating their feedback into risk assessment and management. Risk analysis offers a new approach to managing food safety. Not only is it more effective at decreasing risks, but it can also be a bridge joining food safety and livelihood concerns (Chapter 8).

Criticisms of risk analysis

Like all dominant ideas, risk analysis is not without its critics. These vary from those who think risk analysis is a sound methodology but requires some improvements, to those who regard it as deeply flawed and liable to abuse. In the latter category are some citizens' groups who oppose a particular industry or decision and frequently criticize the methods and results of risk assessment. They argue that risk analysis is rather quantitative and reductionist and doesn't take into account people's legitimate concerns, and that information emerging from risk assessments is meaningless or invalid. Some go even further, believing that risk assessment is part of a conspiracy organized by agro-business. While many of these concerns are refutable on technical grounds, this does not address the underlying fears and concerns that lead many to reject, for example, vaccines, genetically modified food, pasteurized milk or fluoridated water.

This is partly a problem of lack of trust in authorities and is symptomatic of exclusion of stakeholders from decision-making and power. Based on previous analysis and research, incorporating participatory methodologies can improve stakeholder engagement in risk analysis. Since their introduction in the 1970s, participatory methods and techniques have become central tools for community development and have been applied in a variety of contexts and sectors. They are promoted on the basis that they are more effective, more sustainable, less costly and more ethical in their inclusion of the poor in the planning and decisions that affect them, and have been extensively used in livestock research. Sophisticated participatory tools acknowledge power imbalances, vested interests and incentives, and employ methods such as stakeholder analysis, outcome mapping, power mapping and triangulating with different groups to better incorporate viewpoints while preventing capture of the agenda.

Notes

1. www.cdc.gov/listeria/risk.html (accessed 9 July 2014).
2. Akabanda F, Owusu-Kwarteng J, Glover LRK and Tano-Debrah W. 2010. Microbiological characteristics of Ghanaian fermented milk product, *nunu*. *Nature and Science* 8(9): 178–187.
3. www.rki.de/EN/Home/EHEC_final_report.pdf?__blob=publicationFile (accessed 9 July 2014).

5

CAN PARTICIPATION IMPROVE FOOD SAFETY?

Kristina Roesel, Delia Grace, Kohei Makita, Bassirou Bonfoh, Erastus Kang'ethe, Lusato Kurwijila, Saskia Hendrickx, Cheryl McCrindle, Kwaku Tano-Debrah, Girma Zewde, Helena Matusse, Kennedy Bomfeh, Fanta Desissa, Yolande Aké Assi Datté, Sylvain Gnamien Traoré, Joy Appiah, Flavien Ndongo, Marisa Spengler, Sylvie Mireille Kouamé-Sina, Kaiza Kilango, Antoine Bassa Yobouet, Ibrahim Sow and Kebede Amenu

A fault confessed is half redressed.

Key messages

- Participation allows generating data for risk analysis at affordable costs for resource limited countries.
- Participation proved to be particularly useful in exposure assessment to assess the real risk to public health.
- Participation supported risk communication during risk assessment.
- Participation was a feasible method to study social determinants of risk in traditional communities.
- There were some constraints in terms of time and lack of finances for implementation and follow ups.
- It was difficult to balance multiple objectives of all stakeholders.
- The concept was understood differently by different stakeholders.

Participatory risk assessment in informal food value chains

In developed countries, risk analysis plays a great role in understanding risks in food and reducing food-borne diseases. Although there are always challenges in risk assessment even for these countries, risk analysis has become the gold standard for assessing food safety risks to human health. Risk assessment in developed countries benefits from a lot of records and information; increasingly, dose–response relationships (the probability of illness given the amount of microbes which a person ingests) are available and, in this case, risk can be assessed using public source data supplemented with surveys of hazards and consumption.

In developing countries, food-borne disease is a huge problem. Diarrhoea is the second largest cause of child deaths, following pneumonia. Risk analysis can be a powerful tool to reduce the burden of food-borne diseases in these countries too. However, lack of resources to generate public data and the predominance of informal markets, where information is even scarcer, have been great challenges. The Safe Food, Fair Food project used participatory methods in risk assessment of informally marketed foods to generate necessary data in the analysis at affordable costs for resource-limited countries.

Our research used established frameworks but adapted them to the context of developing countries by incorporating participatory thinking and approaches. The main framework used was MRA by the Codex Alimentarius Commission which

BOX 5 PARTICIPATORY TOOLS

A tool that we often start our group work with is proportional piling (Figure 17) to assess the changing herd composition in the course of one year. Using counters such as beans or pebbles to represent all the cattle (or other relevant species) in the village, you can find out what proportion stays in the village and what proportion leaves as well as the different reasons for herd exit. These could be sales, gifts or death. If death is among the reasons for exit, piling continues to investigate the reasons for death (for example, accident, starvation or disease). This activity can be continued for specific diseases and can help in identifying disease incidence and causes of mortality. Nevertheless, caution is required when interpreting the results as farmers usually describe signs of disease and do not provide confirmed laboratory test results.

Generally, this exercise is very well perceived by livestock farmers, partly because we do not ask the livestock keepers about the number of animals kept or their herds in particular, details that farmers are normally not comfortable discussing for various reasons. However, for best results, it is advisable that this exercise be used if the management practices are the same among the members of the focus group.

Other very informative and well-perceived tools in participatory epidemiology are the seasonal calendar and geographical mapping. Whereas the former captures temporal variations of disease or other production constraints, such as rainfall patterns, the latter visualizes village infrastructure including (animal) health care facilities, water sources or grazing areas and helps to identify institutional gaps or potential sources of infection and cross-contamination.

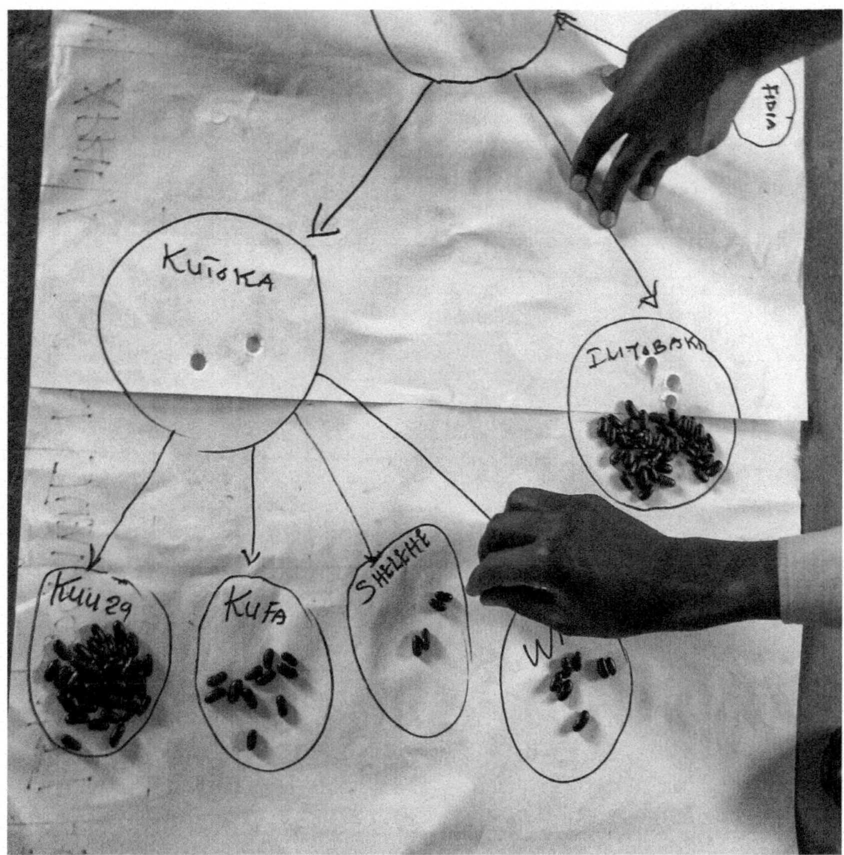

FIGURE 17 Proportional piling of herd exit in Tanzania.

Source: Mahmoud El Tholth

has been established by WHO and FAO as the world reference institute for food safety. The Codex Alimentarius framework consists of hazard identification, hazard characterization, exposure assessment and risk characterization. Participatory methods proved particularly useful in exposure assessment (Figure 18).

An outline of our approach for participative risk assessment is:

1. Identify and characterize hazards and dose–response relationships by literature review.
2. Understand the logic of exposure to a risk by using the fault tree approach (Figures 19 to 22).
3. Describe quantitative value chains (flow of commodities from production to consumption) by using rapid rural appraisals, a participatory technique and a conventional epidemiological survey (Figures 23 to 26).

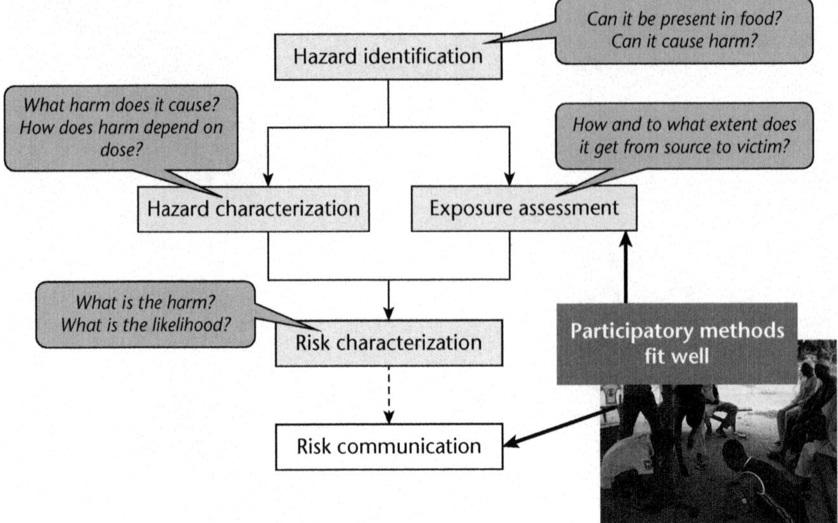

FIGURE 18 Risk assessment framework of the Codex Alimentarius Commission.

Source: Adapted by the Safe Food, Fair Food project

4. Quantify the contamination and bacterial growth by epidemiological survey and literature review (Figure 27).
5. Quantify risk mitigation practices along value chains by using rapid rural appraisals and interviews.
6. Develop risk models integrating parameters obtained through Steps 1 to 5 and run by computational algorithms, such as Monte Carlo simulation (Figure 28 to 31).
7. Identify the variable that influences the result the most by performing a sensitivity analysis.
8. Collect more biological samples for the variable identified as the most sensitive to reduce uncertainty of the risk estimated. The risk would be reduced most efficiently by a control option targeted to it.
9. Recommend areas where risk can be reduced most efficiently, based on modelling and qualitative assessment.

In addition to risk assessment, participatory methods were applied in studying social determinants of risk mitigation in traditional communities. People in rural Mali bought milk from sellers they trusted (Chapter 20) whereas for people in East Africa, price was the most important attribute when they bought milk. Such understanding of social determinants is useful in disseminating key messages for an intervention (Chapter 8). In the course of our research, the results of the risk assessments by participatory methods and their usefulness in food safety risk analysis in informal markets were presented to government stakeholders.

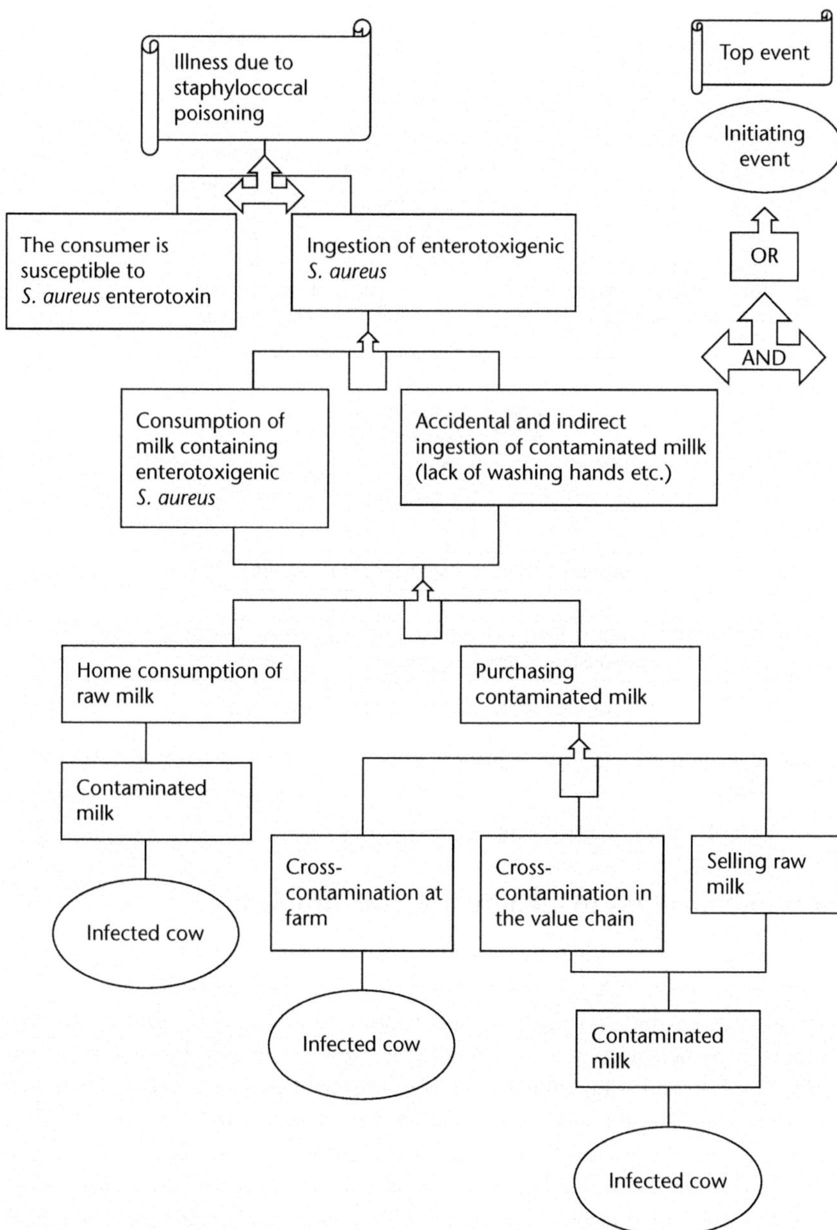

FIGURE 19 Fault tree showing events leading to staphylococcal food poisoning in Debre-Zeit, Ethiopia.

Source: Desissa (2010)

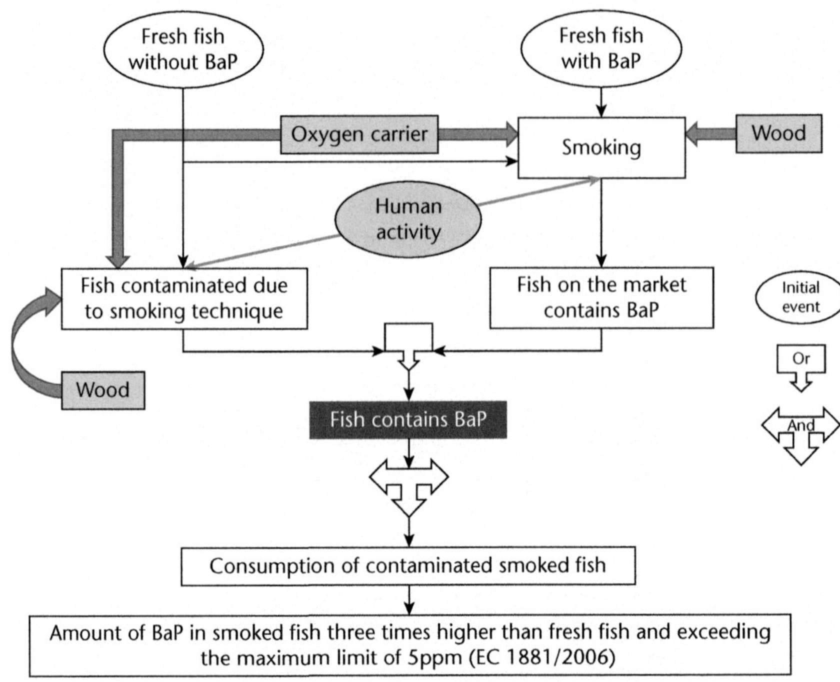

FIGURE 20 Fault tree for polycyclic aromatic hydrocarbon in smoked fish in Abidjan, Côte d'Ivoire.

Source: Yolande Aké Assi Datté (unpublished manuscript)

Participation helps to identify the 'real' problem

Many of our researchers felt that time was a major constraint when using participatory methods for risk assessment. However, it is undeniable that participatory methods can gather information much more rapidly than formal surveys. Moreover, participation was found to have many advantages. Raising awareness (on both sides) while obtaining data on consumption behaviour and food handling practices, as well as the analysis of food samples, was found to be very useful in order to get the 'big picture' (Figure 32). Participatory methods facilitate the quick generation of data on consumption and production habits directly from the people who can be used for risk assessment and identifying supply channels at the same time.

Alexander Heeb and Nenene Qekwana argue that education is the key to food safety as it changes people's perceptions. This, however, is only achievable by listening and talking to the people and through observation. The bottom-up approach of participation allows identification of the 'real' problem of the people most affected. Many of the Safe Food, Fair Food studies showed that much of the investigated food was contaminated due to poor sanitary prerequisites, poor

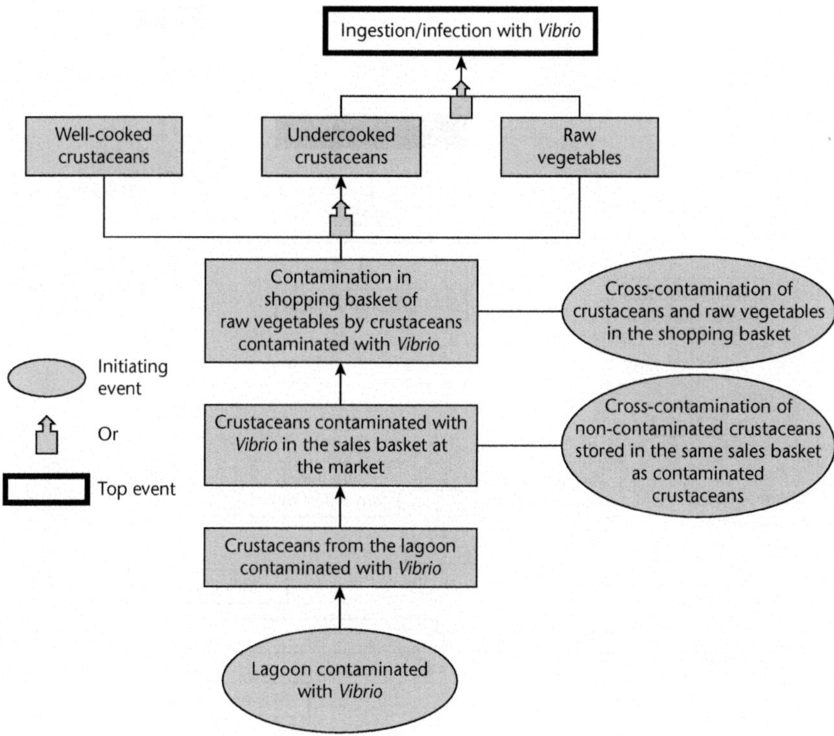

FIGURE 21 Fault tree for *Vibrio* spp. in shellfish in Abidjan, Côte d'Ivoire.

Source: Traoré (2013)

personal hygiene or faulty preparation practices. Participation also makes it possible to benefit from indigenous knowledge for risk mitigation (Chapter 7).

Participation works through hands-on experience, not theoretical or technical knowledge (Box 6). In trypanosomiasis projects in West Africa, extension personnel carry out microscopic examination of blood smears from cattle in the field. When they find the blood parasite, they show it to the cattle owners to give them an idea about the disease-causing microorganism in the blood of their animals. This way, the farmers who have seen their cattle wasting but never visualized the culprit become more aware of how small microbes are or what they actually look like. They will understand much better why teams of researchers come with cars and lots of strange equipment and keep them away from work for a whole day to sample all their cattle.

Participation is by nature including, not excluding, and defined as 'the action of taking part in something'.[1] In participatory learning and development, we often define different levels of participation from being present by order (a low level of participation) to actively taking charge (a high level of participation). Group discussions proved to be opportunities for participants to speak freely about

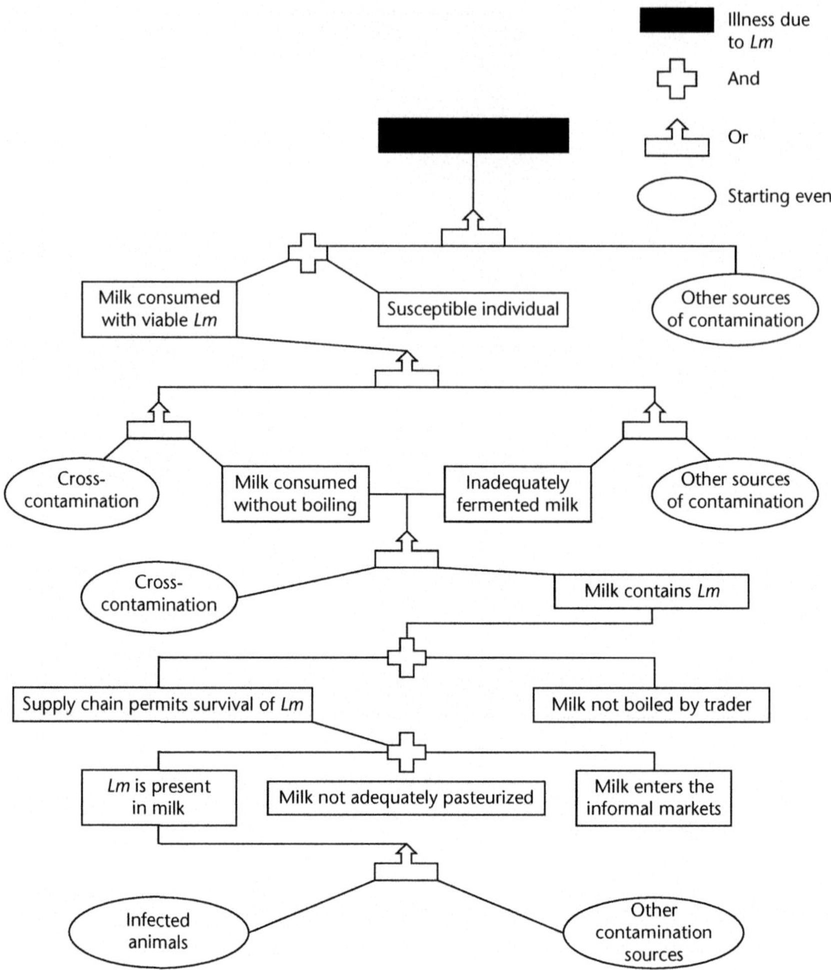

FIGURE 22 Fault tree showing events leading to ingestion of *Listeria monocytogenes* in Ashaiman, Ghana.

Source: Appiah (2012)

anything they wanted to say; they felt included and gained self-confidence to speak up. Since the participants spoke in front of their peers, their answers could be validated, and since the facilitator moderated the discussion, the concept proved to be a good negotiation and mediation tool. The contributions of stakeholders to improve their own situation created ownership and increased effective management of risks. Joy Appiah from Ghana assumed that there would be little resistance to risk management when recommendations were developed during discussion among the participants. He also took advantage of techniques such as mapping a seasonal calendar for disease in cattle in his study area (Figure 33). The

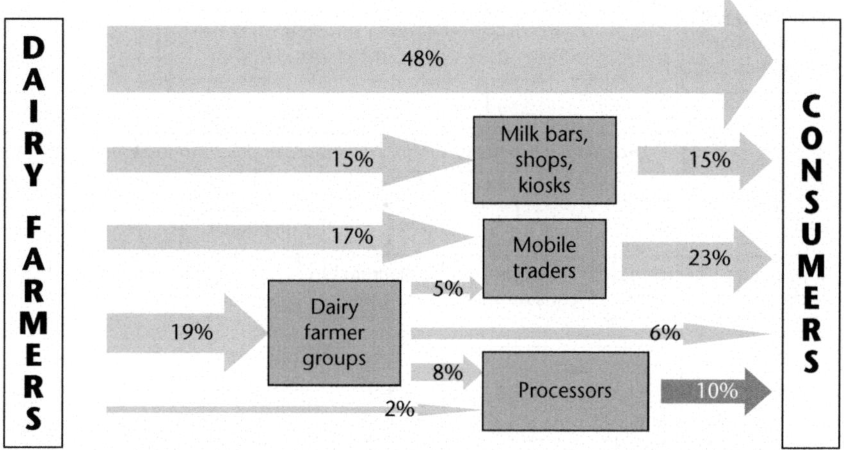

FIGURE 23 Channels of smallholder milk marketing and their relative volume in the East African Community.

Source: ILRI/Amos Omore

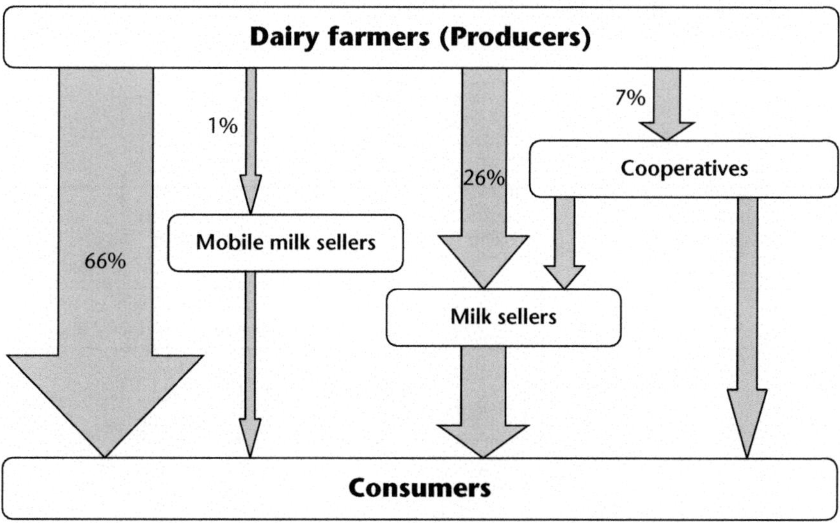

FIGURE 24 Channels of smallholder milk marketing and their relative volume in Kasarani, peri-urban Nairobi, Kenya.

Source: Ndongo (2009)

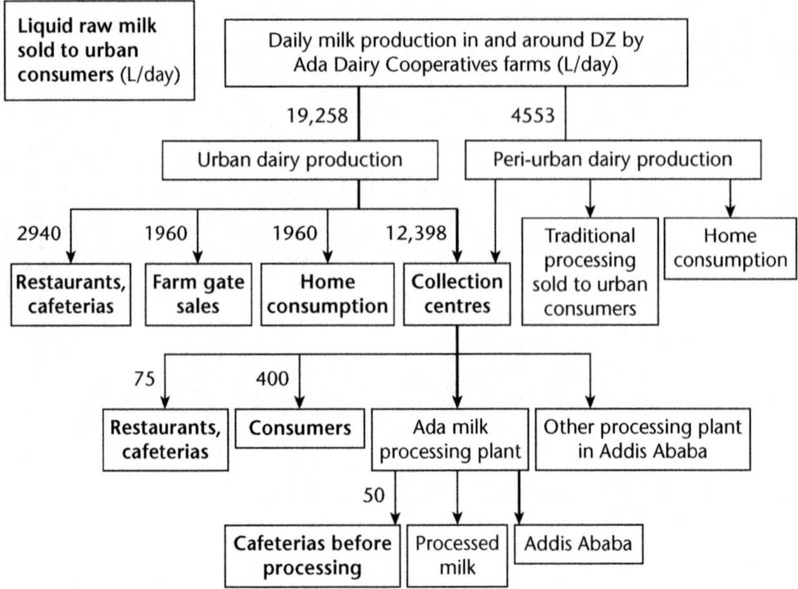

FIGURE 25 Daily milk production in Debre-Zeit, Ethiopia.

Source: Desissa (2010)

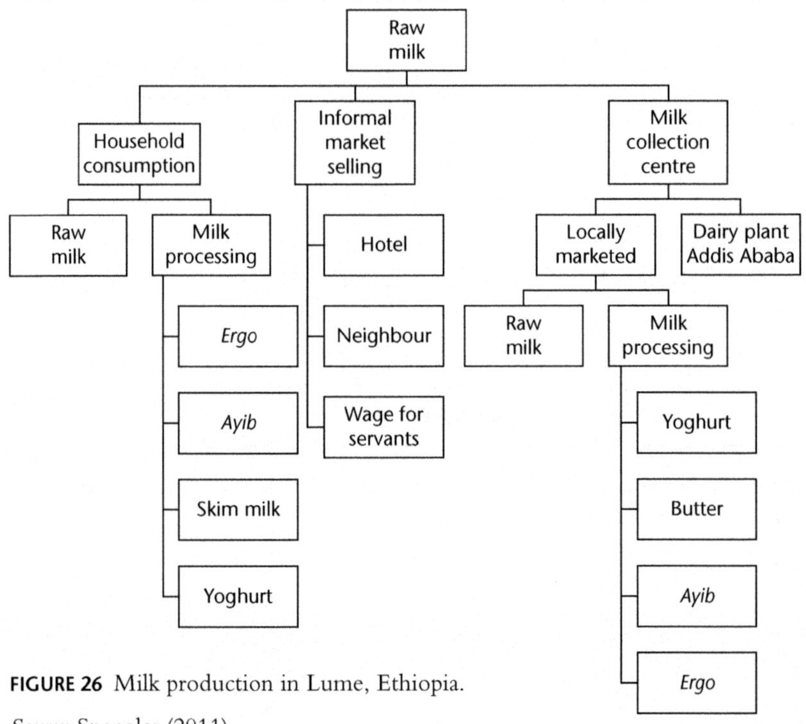

FIGURE 26 Milk production in Lume, Ethiopia.

Source: Spengler (2011)

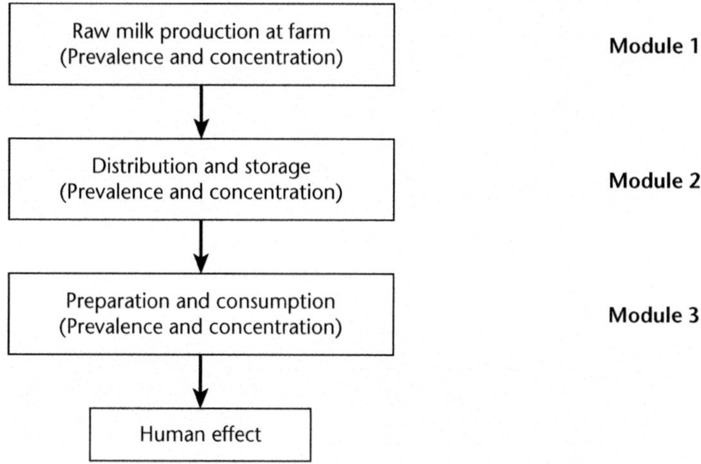

FIGURE 27 Pathway to describe milk contamination by pathogens.

Source: Sylvie Mireille Kouamé-Sina (unpublished manuscript)

activity revealed that disease in cattle was most common with the onset of the rains. Farmers attributed this to their animals eating 'too much fresh grass' but not with disease caused by microbes.

Another advantage of participatory methods, as compared to literature review or laboratory analysis only, is the physical presence of the researcher at the study sites. Apart from the social acceptance among participants, the researcher is able to verify the validity of responses obtained during interviews (for example, 'Do you wash hands prior to milking your cow?' or 'How many times a day is manure removed from the cow shed?'). Animal welfare concerns that would not have been noticed without the actual observation can be addressed, too. Nenene Qekwana, who investigated ritual slaughter practices in South Africa, explains how free-roaming animals are caught, how bulls are wrestled down and how they are eventually killed by stabbing a spear in the heart. However, this can be inhumane and a form of torture to the animal if not done properly.

Observation allows identifying 'risky' habits that otherwise would not have been reported and can help in disease control planning (Figures 34 and 35). That was the case in Kasarani in peri-urban Nairobi, where Flavien Ndongo observed risky practices that exposed people to brucellosis. In his study area he did not find brucellosis in milk. However, if it were to be introduced to the area from elsewhere in the country, high-risk behaviour in Kasarani implied risk to public health. Unfortunately, poor compliance with existing regulations was also observed. For instance, blood from abattoirs was let into a river at night even

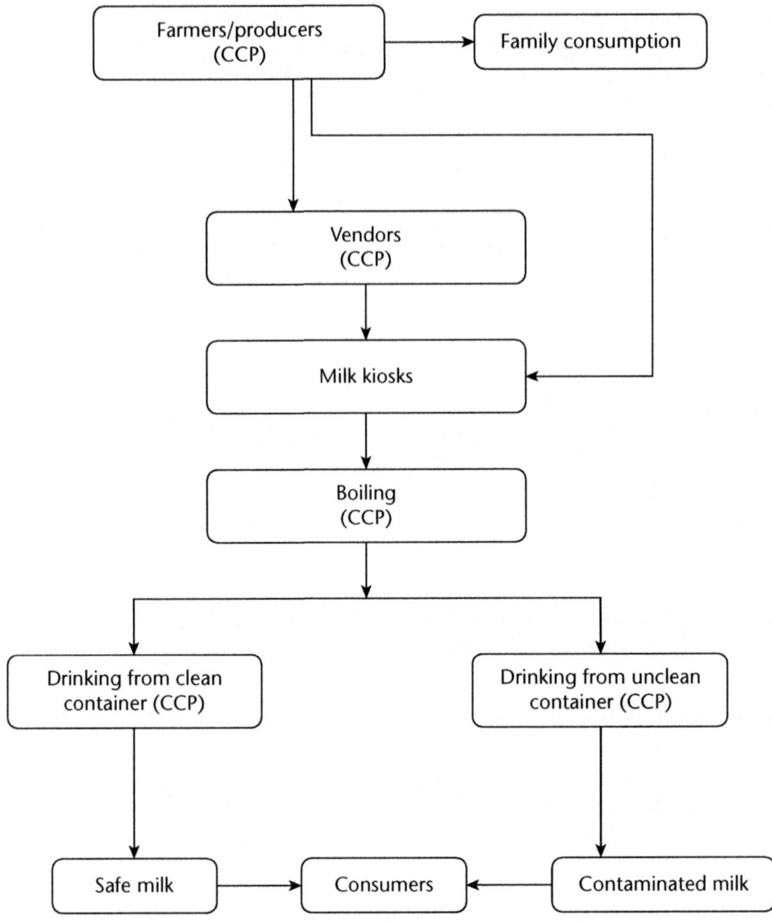

FIGURE 28 Risk factors from milk production to consumption.

Source: Kilango (2011)

though a collection tank was in place. Quarrels with neighbouring businesses were leading to illegal activities.

Participation brings about changes in practice

Many participatory tools were used in the Safe Food, Fair Food project. The main participatory tools are visual, including seasonal calendars for diseases, village maps, chapati (or Venn) diagrams showing the importance of institutions, ranking, rating and matrix scoring. We also used more conventional approaches in participatory ways, including one-to-one interviews (either completely open or in a structured form using interview guides), on-site observations using checklists, workshops, trainings, focus group discussions and cooking experiments (Box 7).

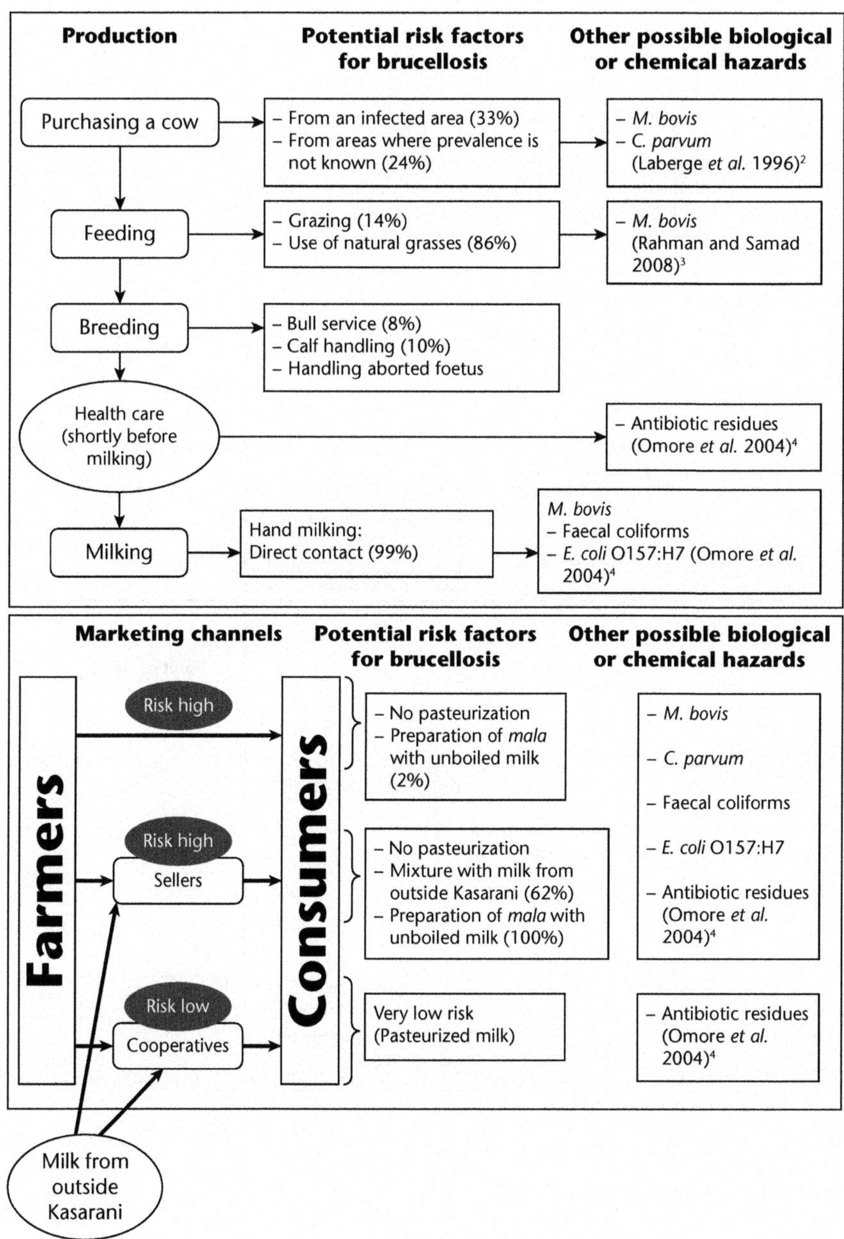

FIGURE 29 Risk factors for brucellosis.

Source: Ndongo (2009)

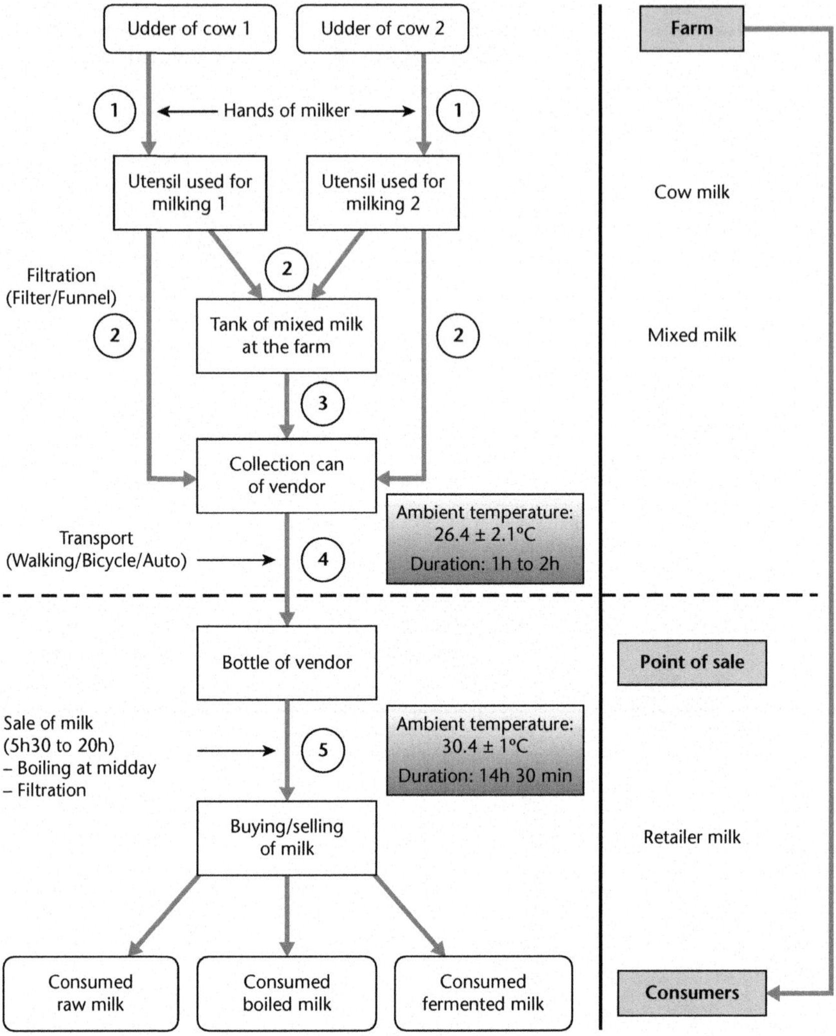

FIGURE 30 Risk factors during production, distribution and sale of raw milk in the informal sector in Abidjan, Côte d'Ivoire.

Source: Antoine Bassa Yobouet (unpublished manuscript)

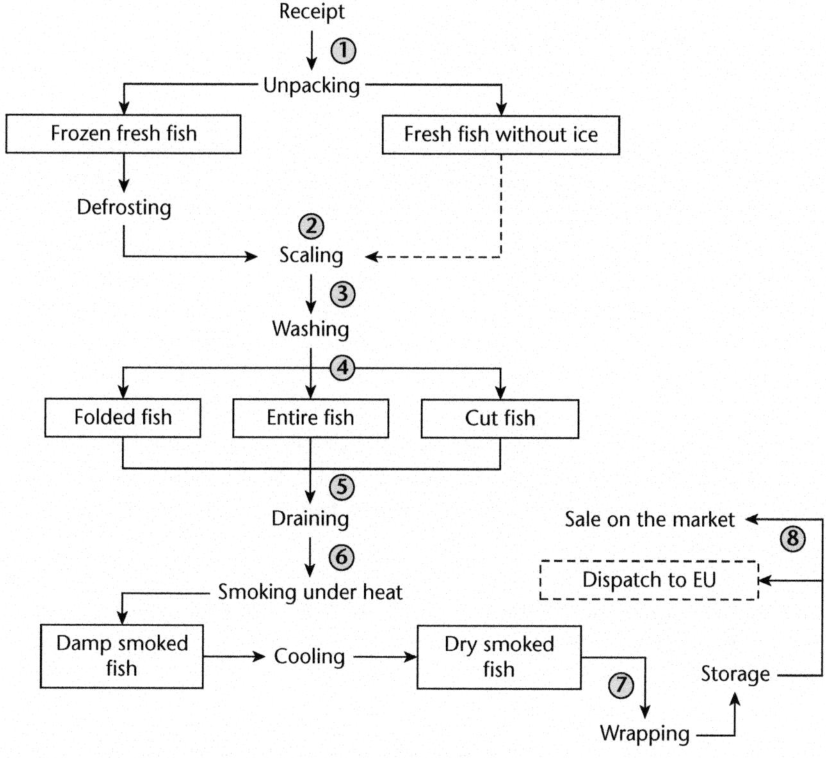

FIGURE 31 Risk factors during the traditional smoking of fish in Côte d'Ivoire.

Source: Yolande Aké Assi Datté (unpublished manuscript)

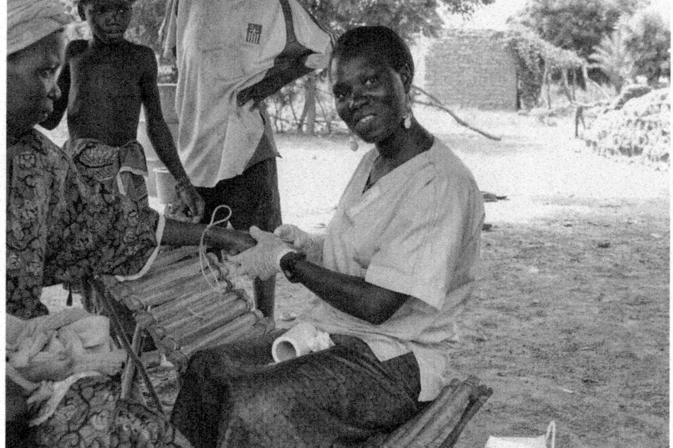

FIGURE 32
Sampling of blood at a health care centre to test for brucellosis.
During sampling, information was also collected on animal husbandry, milking and food handling practices in order to identify risky habits.

Source: Ibrahim Sow

BOX 6 HANDS-ON EXPERIENCE

To aid disease reporting in South Africa, farmers have been taught to use a score card to help them identify diseases from symptoms the cattle are showing. The score cards contain short phrases or pictures and the farmer checks abnormalities (i.e. temperature, ticks, vomiting or diarrhoea). As cell phones are all over, they call or text Dr Shashi Ramrajh whose diagnosis is based on assessing the score cards. She then tells the farmer what medication to get from the health care worker who is provided with a pharmaceutical kit. However, 'there is little point in educating farmers when they do not have drugs or equipment to use. If I train farmers on the use of thermometers, then I should be able to give them one so they are able to put their training into practice,' Ramrajh argues. She is aiming to provide farmers with basic tool kits containing drugs and treatments for wounds, which can be added to as training is provided. However, this will require funding, which Ramrajh currently does not have.

Source: *New Agriculturist*, November 2011. www.new-ag.info/en/focus/focusItem.php?a=2303

FIGURE 33 Participants set up a seasonal calendar to describe the movement of their animals and disease occurrence.

Source: Joy Appiah

Key informant interviews proved to be excellent tools to get acquainted with the informants and to establish trust, which was crucial for later microbiological sampling as many participants feared fines. Moreover, by answering questions, the respondents actually challenged their own behaviour. Sylvie Mireille Kouamé-Sina reported that consumers interviewed in Abidjan who used to drink a lot of raw milk later came to prefer pasteurized milk after they considered the risks associated with drinking raw milk. In South Africa, venison offal from commercial game

FIGURE 34 Livestock and humans sharing the same water source (and pathogens).

Source: Kebede Amenu

FIGURE 35 Industrial effluent discharged into a water body in Lume, Ethiopia.

Source: Marisa Spengler

BOX 7 LEARNING BY COOKING

Kennedy Bomfeh

The ability of *Listeria monocytogenes* to survive domestic cooking was tested by contaminating smoked fish (tuna, mackerel and herrings), *koobi* (tilapia) and sundried sardines with a control organism and using the fish to prepare two kinds of soups commonly consumed in Ghanaian homes: light soup prepared with tomatoes, garden eggs (eggplant), onions and pepper as the major ingredients and groundnut (peanut) soup, prepared with groundnut paste, tomatoes, onions and pepper as the major ingredients (Chapter 32).

The recipes for the soups and methods of preparation were recorded during informal focus group discussions with some young women (average age 24 years) who were involved in food preparation in their homes. At the end of the discussions, the preparation steps, average cooking times and regular ingredients often used for making the soups were agreed upon and used for experimental cooking in the laboratory.

Freshly smoked fish (tuna, mackerel and herrings), *koobi* and sundried sardines were then deliberately heavily contaminated with a control organism. Although *Listeria monocytogenes* generally occurs at low doses in foods, this high level of contamination was selected to assess possible outcomes in worst-case scenarios. The soups were prepared by some women from the focus group according to the method agreed on in the focus group discussion. Cooking started at the same time for all the soups. Total cooking times were 45 minutes for light soup and 75 minutes for groundnut soup, with respective average boiling temperatures of 99.2°C and 106.5°C. The experiment was repeated twice at five-day intervals (that is, three separate cooking experiments in total).

Immediately after each cooking, the fish were removed from the soups and prepared for the detection of the *Listeria monocytogenes* control organism. In both types of soup, it survived in at least one sample of each fish product, suggesting that at high levels of contamination, the pathogen could still be present in fish used to prepare the soups, and could thus present a risk to consumers.

farms used to be discarded, despite passing primary meat inspection. However, it is now used as food after Shashi Ramrajh interviewed key stakeholders living near game farms and found evidence of a market and demand for offal in the local communities (Chapter 28).

Focus group discussions, although not always considered a participatory tool, proved to be very fruitful in various ways. The answers are most likely honest as they are verified by the rest of the group. Sometimes, even more information is revealed than anticipated. In the case of a study in Pretoria (Chapter 26), street vendors of chicken came together for the first time during the survey and, after initial reservations, talked and discussed freely. The discussion helped to establish contacts for future networking and encouraged group spirit. Following the meeting, the vendors formed an association to deal with issues such as pest control.

Focus group discussions with South African policymakers from different departments, all directly related to public health but with overlapping responsibilities (Chapter 31), were difficult to organize due to busy schedules. They also turned out to be very frustrating when the participants became aware of the importance of exchange and communication between the departments. The very same frustration proved to be a catalyst; weaknesses were identified and possibilities to collaborate on a technical level were eventually evaluated.

In Mali, group discussions had an immediate effect when farmers exchanged knowledge about breeds, supplementary feeding in the dry season and how to handle abortions or stillbirths in cattle. At the same time, risk factors could be identified. In Tanzania, farmers learned about testing possibilities and treatment options for milk (Chapter 13).

Participatory tools were usually complemented by individual but anonymous questionnaires. These were helpful to obtain individual data on consumption and husbandry practices as well as symptoms of disease. In Mali, a woman reporting fever and joint pain and handling aborted material from cattle was later found to have contracted brucellosis (Chapter 19). In Côte d'Ivoire, people suffering from a chronic cough were examined for tuberculosis at local tuberculosis centres. Lung flukes transmitted by shellfish consumption, however, can cause the very same symptoms and were thus investigated at the tuberculosis centres. The flukes could be ruled out, but it was interesting to see that more than three-quarters of the patients with chronic cough also tested negative for tuberculosis; this surprising outcome calls for more in-depth studies to reveal the cause of chronic cough.

Edgar Mahundi recalled that when he gave feedback to the authorities, they closed a butchery which sold spoiled meat. The butchery's entrance had a sign announcing '*Cheap beef sold here*' and many people queued in front of it. Following the study, local health inspectors started inspecting the butchery once a week. Ana Bela Cambaza dos Muchangos reported a similar incident in Mozambique. However, one of the poultry abattoirs that had been closed twice before was shut down again while she conducted her survey. After this, the owner of the butchery asked to participate in one of the training workshops to get advice on how to improve the sanitation of the butchery. Today, university students are taken there for presenting best practice examples of local abattoirs.

Often, the initial research questions raised by the students later developed their own dynamics. Many of the students received inquiries from farmers, butchers or vendors who wanted to participate in training on food safety, complying with the project's finding that training (especially on prerequisites) is crucial for safe food. In Tanzania, the farmers now want a platform with agricultural officers to improve the quality of their products. However, this is still not implemented, thus risking the trust and motivation of the participants.

Follow-up visits and funding are vital to make participatory interventions last. When John Kago made a second visit to an abattoir in Kenya which he had previously surveyed, he observed that the attendants had put effort into cleaning the working surfaces. Cameline Mwai, who held workshops in an export abattoir, reported after a follow-up visit to the abattoir six weeks later that workers were still not provided with soap and paper tissues. The owner stated that 'it was stolen anyway'. Hot water was only accessible to the meat inspector.

The challenge: balancing multiple objectives and perceptions

The Safe Food, Fair Food participants considered funding and time limits to be the main constraints to using participation as a technique for risk assessment. Despite all the advantages, one-to-one interviews and focus group discussions take at least two hours, excluding all the time used for preparation of questionnaires and checklists, and actually getting to the meeting venues which are sometimes in remote rural areas (Figure 36).

To meet a considerable number of stakeholders at government level seems to be impossible because of their busy schedules. But even *nyama choma* sellers in Arusha are very busy men; every hour they spend talking to someone and not

FIGURE 36 'No hurry – *doni doni*!' When using participatory techniques in Mali, the researcher needs to set aside time for socializing over several rounds of green tea!

Source: ILRI/Kristina Roesel

selling roast beef, they lose money. Edgar Mahundi failed to organize group discussions with vendors due to insufficient funds. However, he interviewed the pub owners while they were working. He found that participatory methods were often not so successful for traders and businessmen, partly because they are often very busy but also because they don't always want to discuss their business in a group consisting of their competitors! In such cases, interviews with key informants when they are at leisure may be more useful.

When dealing with government officials, lunch and free accommodation seem to be 'incentive' enough in the Republic of South Africa. Further northeast, it is common among government officials to claim 'expenses' for attending meetings, which is obviously their job. The former term 'allowance' has been replaced by the Latin *per diem*, meaning per day. They actually get paid twice for the same thing. Of course, the underlying problem is that governments often do not have sufficient money to pay them a proper salary, and often no money to allow them to work in the field effectively. As a result, the project often had to fill this gap. But when projects have to pay officials to be part of research for improving things for everyone, why should someone wonder that the beef or chicken vendor wants to be remunerated as well?

There are also ethical issues around participatory processes which are not always addressed; people should not be forced into taking part in interviews or activities aimed at obtaining information from them. The concept of participation and its advantages for all the parties involved must be clearly explained prior to the survey. In one of the Safe Food, Fair Food studies, milk sellers in Tanzania refused to participate because they believed that contamination could only happen at the farm level. They had no idea about the possibility of re-contamination of food due to bad handling practices and were afraid that their shops would be closed down. Therefore, finding participants sometimes proved to be a challenge. Others were simply not present in the study area during the survey, depending on the season. For instance, the Fulani herders in West Africa moved their cattle to a different location in the dry season, whereas crop farmers were not available right after the onset of the rains as they were busy planting their fields.

Funds must be available to avoid students using their own resources such as private cars. The lack of expertise to organize meetings, workshops and trainings in terms of logistics was also found to be a challenge and could be integrated in preparatory training of future proof-of-concept studies. Language posed another obstacle; the participants of a survey might speak English or French but mostly it was not their first language. If a researcher did not speak the first language of the survey participants, it was hard to establish trust. Translators were able to help in most cases although some information might have been lost because they did not have the technical background for in-depth explanations. Language was mainly a challenge when working with local ethnic groups such as the Ovahimba in southern Africa (Chapter 27) and the Fulani in West Africa. The latter also do not like to talk to women, something which complicated work for Sylvie Mireille Kouamé-Sina in Côte d'Ivoire. Shashi Ramrajh also reported initial reservations because of her being a woman. In Mozambique, gender was not a constraint, but Ana Bela Cambaza dos Muchangos lost her camera when she visited a local market. The vendors mistook her for a health inspector who wanted to fine them or close down their food stalls. Similar experiences were reported in all studies, suggesting fear of authorities or competition. In South Africa, where Nenene Qekwana wanted to interview a vendor's customer, the vendor refused because he thought the researcher would 'steal' his clients.

Ignorance and attitude were issues at some points. The consumers' association in Maputo was not interested in a follow-up workshop where preliminary results were presented. The management of a Kenyan export abattoir considered themselves 'beyond HACCP', even though the carcasses there were found to be contaminated. The abattoir was stage-managed whenever there were audits and during the study and everyone was preoccupied with International Organization for Standardization (ISO) certification.

The different perceptions about what participation is and what it is not need to be discussed. The social construction of participating groups must be taken into consideration in order to follow the right protocol. Permission needs to be obtained from government departments, the village heads and individuals. In the studies carried out in West Africa, it was observed that if the chief was present during an interview, everybody gave the same answer. On the other hand, it was not possible to manage the assessed risks without the support of the traditional authority. Valentin Koné legitimately asked 'How do you tell the 80-year-old chief who has never fallen sick from drinking raw milk to start boiling his milk? After all, we will be the main contact person instructing and guiding his local community when risk management interventions will take place.'

Interviewed consumers may under- or over-estimate their daily intake of the investigated food, thus posing a level of uncertainty. Fortunately, this can be modelled using computer software. However, researchers always have to be aware that they are only exposed to the participants' lifestyles to a certain extent. Joy Appiah recalled that in Ghana, people are ashamed of poverty so the researcher would be directed to 'best practice' farms. This is unfortunate as solutions are most urgently needed in poverty-stricken areas. Flavien Ndongo suspected that the extension worker facilitating the survey also took him to the 'best' farmers as he was surprised not to find any evidence of brucellosis in Kasarani (Chapter 15). The longer the food chain and the more the individuals in it, the greater the likelihood of risk and the need for objectives to be balanced (Figure 37). Therefore, multi-disciplinary teams are needed to assess the risk and its increase or decrease along the value chain.

Conclusion

One of the key innovations of our approach was to add 'participation' to 'risk analysis'. Indeed we coined the phrase 'participatory risk analysis' to describe this new method of assessing, managing and communicating food safety in informal

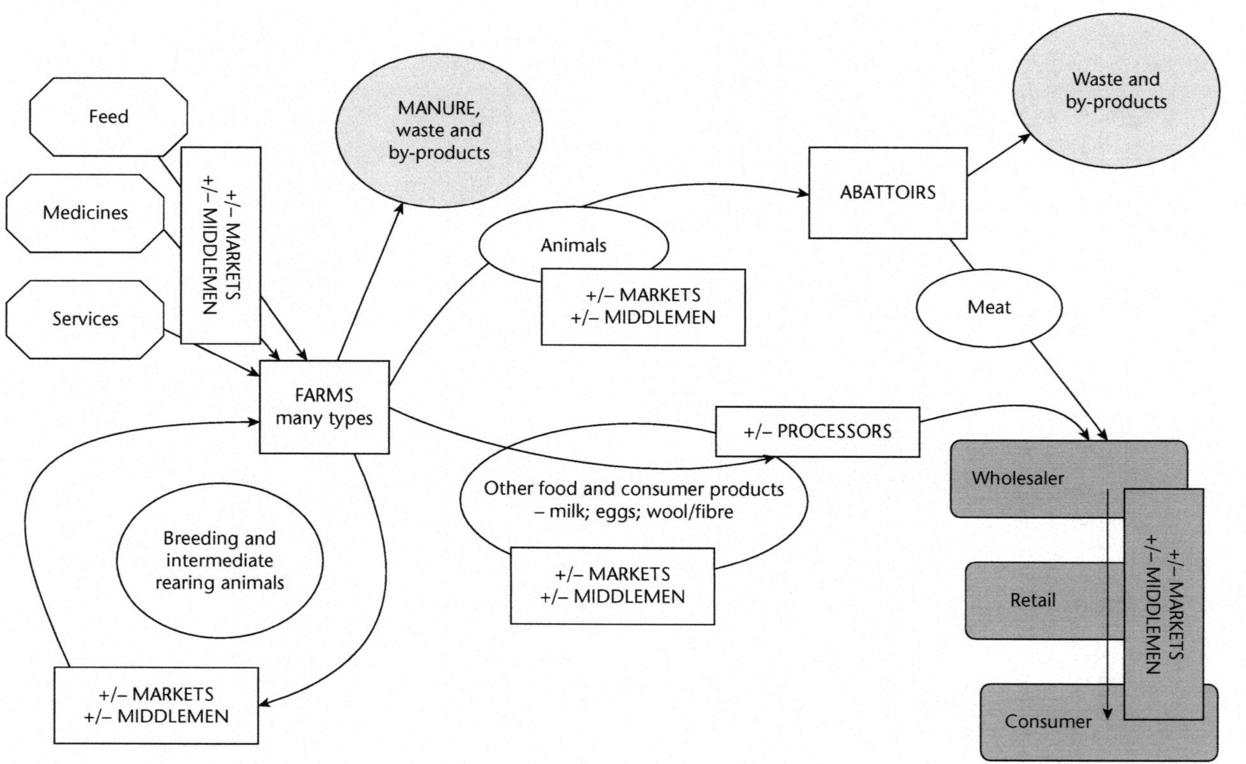

FIGURE 37
Multidisciplinary and complex value chain approach for the benefit of public health.

Source: Nick Taylor, University of Reading, and Jonathan Rushton, Royal Veterinary College

markets. Our general conclusion was that, compared to conventional risk analysis, participatory risk analysis was faster, feasible, friendly, inexpensive and easy to carry out.

Notes

1. http://oxforddictionaries.com/definition/participation (accessed 9 July 2014).
2. Laberge I, Griffiths MW and Griffiths MW. 1996. Prevalence, detection and control of *Cryptosporidium parvum* in food. *International Journal of Food Microbiology* 32(1–2): 1–26.
3. Rahman MM and Samad MA. 2008. Prevalence of bovine tuberculosis and its effects on milk production in Red Chittagong cattle. *Bangladesh Journal of Veterinary Medicine* 6(2): 175–178.
4. Omore A, Staal S and Randolph T. 2004. Overcoming barriers to informal milk trade in Kenya. In: *Unlocking human potential: Linking the informal and formal sectors*. A conference held by the Expert Group on Development Issues (EGDI) and the United Nations University–WIDER, Helsinki, Finland, 17–18 September 2004.

6

FARMERS, TRADERS AND RETAILERS ARE RISK MANAGERS

Kristina Roesel, Delia Grace, John Kago, Fanta Desissa, Marisa Spengler, Kebede Amenu, Joy Appiah, Kennedy Bomfeh, Cheryl McCrindle, Cameline Mwai and Alexander Heeb

> *Sometimes very simple messages and measures can have a big impact on health protection. [These] Five Keys to Safer Food have already contributed to the prevention of food-borne illness and deserve to be communicated more widely.*
>
> *Margaret Chan, Director General, WHO*

Key messages

- Contamination of food may occur at any stage in the food value chain.
- Risk pathway analysis identifies points where hazards occur from farm to fork and where risk is increased, reduced or eliminated along the way.
- Points where management is feasible can be identified and priorities can be set.
- Everybody handling the product, and financially benefiting from it, must take responsibility.
- Intervention is often simple but frequently lacks basic prerequisites.
- Risk pathway analysis is used to establish individual HACCP systems in formal and informal markets alike.
- More consumer-level studies are needed to evaluate to what extent consumers are exposed to hazards in foods.

BOX 8 THE MEAT ON MY TABLE: THE JOURNEY

John Kago

At dawn, most of the workers at the slaughterhouses in Kenya are busy at work. They have to start as early as 0400 hours to ensure that there are sufficient carcasses ready for the transporters and the butchers at 0500 hours. However, most of the slaughtering is done between 0530 and 0800 hours.

The butcher needs to buy carcasses at different places. Dagoretti is a complex of four slaughterhouses and supplies the bulk of the beef that is consumed in the capital city, Nairobi (Figure 38). Sourcing animals for slaughter is done by businessmen, most of whom do not own meat retail outlets. They have specialized in delivering the live animals to the abattoir from various sources, sometimes from as far as 300 kilometres away. The butchers then buy the live animals from these businessmen and pay the slaughter fee to the abattoir owners. Some of the businessmen sourcing the live animals pay for slaughtering the rest of their animals and then later sell the carcasses in quarters or halves to different small-scale butchery owners.

Eldoret is an example of a fast-growing town in Kenya. It is located 310 kilometres west of Nairobi. One major slaughterhouse there was built during the colonial days in the 1940s. There are three more small slaughter slabs in the area. Live animals are sourced by the butchery owners from the surrounding farms. A few of the major butchery owners may also sell quarters or halves of the carcasses to minor meat outlets.

FIGURE 38 Meat at one of the four slaughterhouses in Dagoretti that supply the city of Nairobi.

Source: John Kago

BOX 9 SLAUGHTERHOUSE PAST ITS PRIME

John Kago

> *The Eldoret slaughterhouse was built to serve the population surrounding the town in the 1940s but since then, the town's population has grown significantly. The slaughterhouse built for the Kenya Meat Commission is under the municipal council of Uasin Gishu district. It clearly shows that it has seen better days.*
>
> *Inspector in charge*

The meat transporters are major stakeholders in ensuring the safety of the meat (Figure 39). Most of the butchery owners do not transport their own meat but meat transporters are contracted to deliver the carcasses to the retail outlets and charge according to the distance and weight of the meat. The mode of transportation may be by bicycle, motorbike or motor vehicle mounted with boxes that have been approved by the veterinary officer. The boxes are mandatory and usually made of corrugated iron sheets or aluminium. Most of the boxes have two compartments: one for the meat and the other for the intestines and tripe. The boxes have no coolers. They are a familiar sight on the busy roads of Kenya's cities. The transporters are usually contracted by many butchery owners and thus heap many carcasses in the boxes at a go. The carcasses are offloaded at the butcheries en route and transport may take between 30 minutes and four hours under ambient temperatures of 18–20°C.

Loading and offloading may be done by the same person and clothes are rarely changed in between. Some slaughterhouses have their own staff for loading and offloading and at the butchery it may be done by the attendant. The butcheries are strategically located near the consumers or close to traffic hubs. Usually, a rail is mounted on the walls and carcasses are hung on hooks made of iron or stainless steel. A wooden log is used as a board for chopping the meat with a machete prior to weighing and selling it to the consumers. The meat may stay at the butchery for one or two days until it is sold. Some of the butcheries have freezers to store leftover meat. Intestines and tripe may be sold along with the meat but most of the time the same equipment is used for both. Wiping the equipment with a dishcloth is the only means of cleaning. Once a day, the equipment and working surfaces are cleaned with soap and cold water. The chopping board is scoured by scraping off pieces of meat and is then lubricated again with fat from fresh meat.

FIGURE 39 A private transporter who delivers meat to butcheries in highly populated or frequented areas.

Source: John Kago

Background

Food-borne diseases are the result of ingestion of food contaminated with micro-organisms or chemicals. The contamination of food may occur at any stage in the process from production to consumption ('farm to fork' or 'stable to table') and can result from environmental contamination, including pollution of water, soil or feeds. 'The ordinary udder flora, inflammation of the mammary gland, the milker and the environment are the main sources of microbes in milk and milk products', Marisa Spengler describes. 'When milk leaves the udder of a healthy cow, the amount of contamination is very low and usually not health-impairing. The risk of contamination increases along the production chain as the milk moves towards the end consumer.'

'Food safety is not only sensitive in terms of public health', Kaiza Kilango explains. 'It also has to be seen from an economic point of view. Whose budget should be used if an outbreak occurs? If the source of contamination is clear, it is much easier to delegate management and enforce allocation of financial means. The data also enable a fast and efficient response in the case of an outbreak.'

Objective parameters are already in place. Total bacterial counts in milk reflect its storage temperature and the time elapsed since milking, as the bacteria naturally occurring in milk as well as pathogens will multiply quickly if the milk is not cooled. They might cause spoilage and possibly pose risks to human health. Coliform counts in milk indicate the level of hygiene, since these bacteria mostly live in the intestinal tracts of people and animals and thus their presence in food is a sign of faecal contamination. East African countries have already harmonized standards for some products including milk (see www.eac-quality.net).

The magnitude of risks and hazards can be quantified for each point from farm to fork by laboratory analysis of food specimens. Participatory methods complement the process as they help to explain why activities either increase or reduce the risk. As high-risk behaviour – such as the consumption of raw milk in West Africa – increases risk among certain parts of the population, it will be possible to develop means of communication adapted to individual groups. This is called risk targeting and is an important part of risk analysis.

Figures 40 and 41 show how the bacterial load in milk in Ethiopia increased between the farm level and pasteurization. While boiling seemed to eliminate the microbes, interviews and observations revealed that certain factors, such as the pooling of milk, increased the risk of contamination. In Tanzania one Safe Food, Fair Food study showed that milk was only pooled at kiosk level and found to be contaminated, thus rendering all efforts by farmers and vendors useless (Chapter 13).

In Kenya, beef was found to be contaminated at every step from the abattoir (Chapter 21), during transport and at the butchery (Chapter 22), with the highest

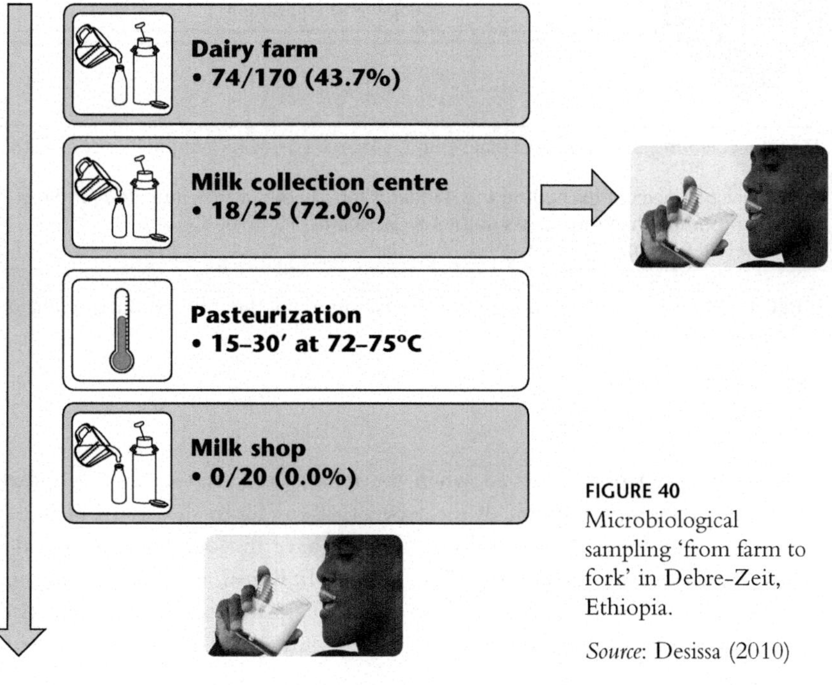

FIGURE 40 Microbiological sampling 'from farm to fork' in Debre-Zeit, Ethiopia.

Source: Desissa (2010)

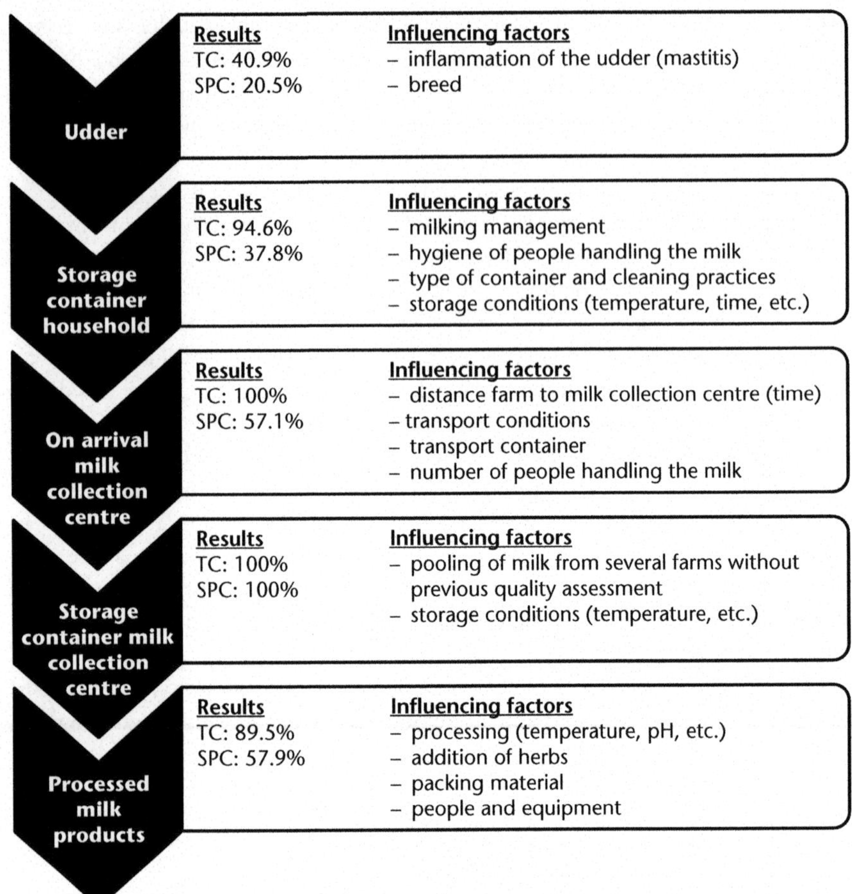

TC: total coliforms, SPC: standard plate count, CFU/ml: colony forming units per millilitre

Results given in percent **exceeding** the standards for sale of raw milk intended for direct human consumption in most parts of the UK. Standards: TC < 100 CFU/ml, SPC ≤ 20,000 CFU/ml

FIGURE 41 Microbiological sampling and risk factors along the milk production chain in rural Ethiopia.

Source: Spengler (2011)

levels of contamination observed when the meat was closest to the consumer. Fortunately, cooking or frying of meat eventually reduced the risk, but highly contaminated raw meat is not a good thing to have in your kitchen or fridge because it can contaminate other foods or objects. In Kenya, we found some good practices in place but they were not likely to be adequate because other practices were missing. A box separating tripe and meat is only useful in combination with adequate cooling. It is also necessary to avoid the cross-contamination that can occur as a result of heaping several carcasses in the same box.

Analysis of risk pathways helps to understand the whole process. At farm level, feeds, faeces, bedding material and soil may transfer bacteria into the food (Chapter 18). Improper cleaning of utensils, use of poor-quality water to clean the udder and equipment, and poor personal hygiene of the milk handlers are all examples of potential sources of contamination and disease (Chapters 10 and 11).

Traditional interventions lead to substantial improvements

Food safety has long been tackled by using traditional methods and common sense. It is in every culture's interest to develop practices and customs that reduce the risk of falling ill. Many farmers and traders use traditional ways and means to increase the shelf life of their products, to manage risk and hence to reduce the risk of food-borne disease. Milking is done early in the morning and butchers source meat from abattoirs in the early hours of the day. Many favour the day-to-day slaughter and sales to compensate for conservation problems such as lack of electricity for refrigeration. Drying, curing and smoking are still used to conserve animal-source products, and numerous Safe Food, Fair Food studies showed that risks due to bacterial hazards were highly reduced by heat treatment, such as thorough cooking of fish and meat or boiling of milk.

One Safe Food, Fair Food study showed that traditional techniques, such as fermentation of raw milk, can reduce the risk of disease by as much as 97%. Bacterial growth is inhibited by increasing acidity and if milk is fermented long enough, it is likely to render a risky product into safe food at low costs (Chapter 12). Ethiopian farmers store raw milk in containers smoked with branches from the African olive tree (*Olea europaea* ssp. *cuspidata*), locally referred to as *ejersa* (Figures 42 and 43). The smoke is said to enhance the taste of the milk and is supposed to have antimicrobial effects (Chapter 11). However, traditional risk management is less likely to develop where foods or hazards are relatively recent.

Consumer studies show consumers' level of exposure to the real risk

The path does not end at the milk shop or the butchery; we also need to investigate modes of preparation of the food and consumption habits and frequencies. Safe Food, Fair Food studies showed that thorough cooking or boiling eliminated lung fluke stages in shellfish (Chapter 34), bacteria in fish (Figure 45) (Chapter 32), pathogens in chicken (Chapter 24) and contaminants in meat (Chapter 27) and milk (Chapter 14). In Mali, communities eat meat from animals that died of disease because they can only afford to buy live animals for certain ceremonies (Chapter 20). However, they always cooked the meat for at least an hour and had never associated eating meat with disease.

FIGURE 42 In Ethiopia, containers for storing raw milk are smoked with branches from the African olive tree.

Source: Kebede Amenu

FIGURE 43 *Ejersa*, the African olive tree.

Source: Kebede Amenu

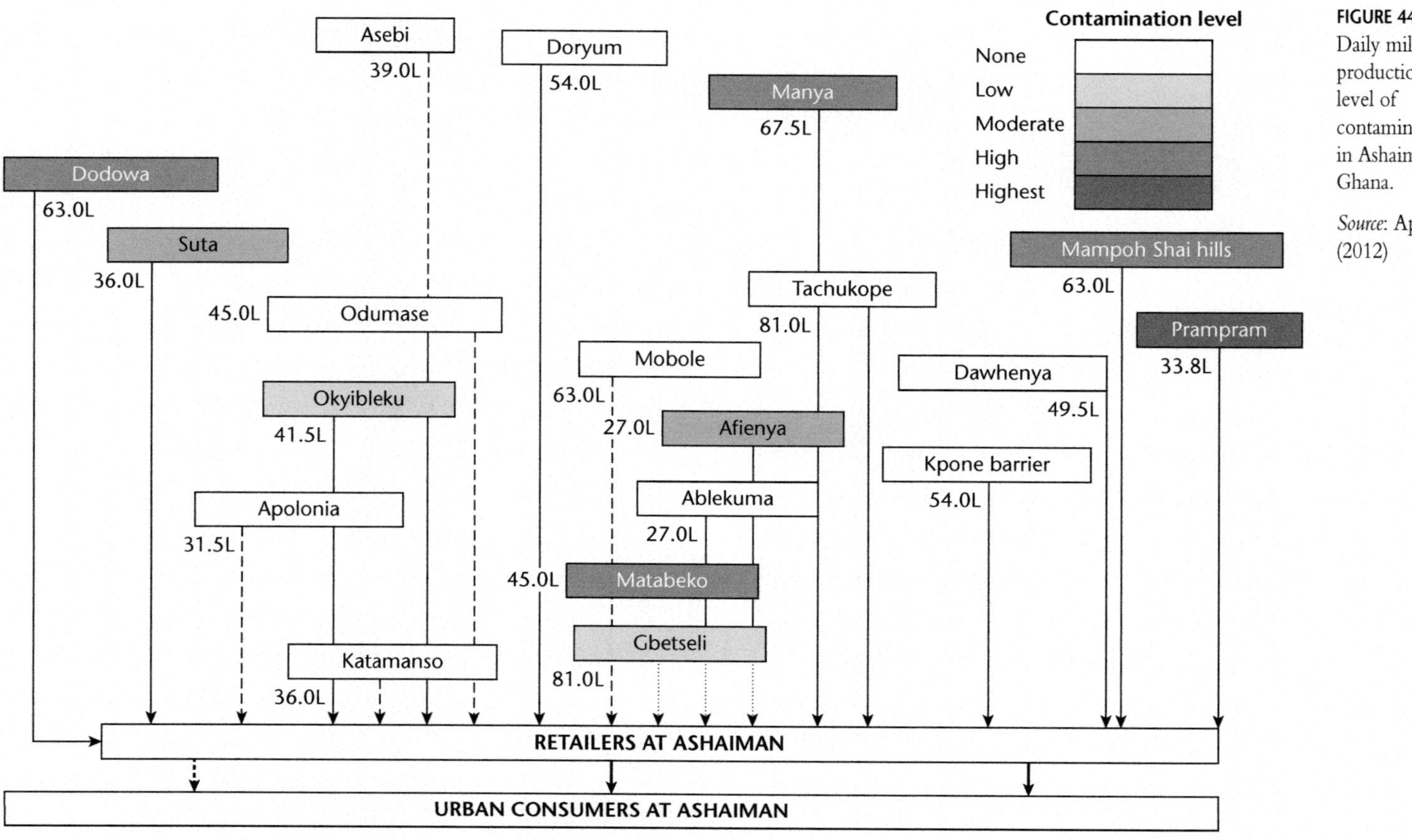

FIGURE 44 Daily milk production and level of contamination in Ashaiman, Ghana.

Source: Appiah (2012)

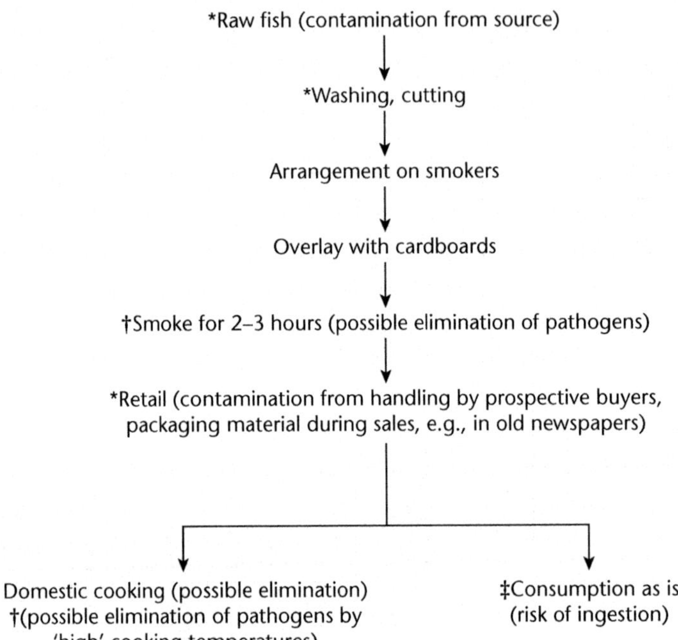

FIGURE 45 The evolving risk of ingestion of *Listeria monocytogenes* in smoked fish in Ghana.

Source: Bomfeh (2011)

On the other hand, risks are higher where animal-source products are consumed raw, such as raw meat in Ethiopia (Chapter 7) or raw milk in Côte d'Ivoire and Mali. A study in Ghana found that even though the people studied did not drink a lot of raw milk, they consumed half a litre of unboiled fermented milk daily and thus were exposed to some degree of risk (Figure 44) (Chapter 16).

Participatory risk assessment using HACCP

The assessment of risks along the food value chain allows determination of where risks can be managed most efficiently by identifying critical control points (CCPs). These are points, steps or procedures at which intervening techniques can be applied and where a hazard can be eliminated or reduced to an acceptable (critical) level, thus reducing the risk of ingestion. The most common CCP is cooking. An essential characteristic of a CCP is that people should be able to set limits within which the process stays (for example, boil for at least 30 minutes). However, most of those in the informal market do not have set limits; rather, they work by estimates and 'guesstimates'.

The research question of the Safe Food, Fair Food team in South Africa was whether it was possible to use participatory risk assessment within a food chain approach using HACCP and prerequisites for hygiene and sanitation.

The HACCP system (Box 10) is a scientific, rational and systematic approach to identification, assessment and control of hazards during production, processing, manufacturing, preparation and use of food to ensure that food is safe when consumed.[1] The system is applied following a logic sequence:

1. Assemble the HACCP team.
2. Describe the product.
3. Identify the intended use.
4. Construct the flow diagram.
5. Confirm the flow diagram on-site.
6. List all potential hazards and conduct a hazard analysis.
7. Determine CCPs using a CCP decision tree (www.who.int/foodsafety/fs_management/en/intro_haccp_figures.pdf).
8. Establish critical limits for each CCP.

BOX 10 THE CONCEPT OF HACCP

From outer space

The acronym HACCP, which stands for Hazard Analysis and Critical Control Point, is one which evokes 'food safety'. One cannot write about the HACCP system, however, without giving credit to those who conceived it, that is, the Pillsbury Company, together with the National Aeronautics and Space Administration and the United States Army Laboratories at Natick, who developed this system to ensure the safety of astronauts' food. In the thirty years since then, the HACCP system has become the internationally recognized and accepted method for food safety assurance. While it was originally developed to ensure microbiological safety of foodstuffs, it has been further broadened to include chemical and physical hazards in foods. The recent growing worldwide concern about food safety by public health authorities, consumers and other concerned parties, to a great extent due to WHO's advocacy in this field, and the continuous reports of food-borne outbreaks have been a major impetus in the application of the HACCP system.

Source: www.who.int/foodsafety/fs_management/haccp_intro/en/index.html

9. Establish a monitoring system for each CCP.
10. Establish corrective action for deviations that may occur.
11. Establish verification procedures.
12. Establish documentation and record-keeping.

The Safe Food, Fair Food studies have proved participation to be a good technique for investigating food value chains and it can be combined with qualitative (presence of a hazard) and quantitative methods (that is, level of bacterial load). The results can be used as a basis for audit checklists, guidelines and better explanation through visualization (Figures 46 and 47).

In general, HACCP can work well for large, formal organizations where people are used to a lot of record keeping. However, it is quite impractical for most of the small, informal sector businesses where processors and sellers may be illiterate. We recommend a modified HACCP which takes into account the core principles but does not require complicated procedures.

Even where organizations aspire to have or require a HACCP plan, for it to be effective, a strong foundation of safety-related prerequisites is essential. Such programmes are not specific to a single product, as is the case with CCPs. Instead, they serve to control the environment in which processing occurs. Prerequisite programmes include the implementation of good manufacturing practices, sanitation standard operating procedures, recall programmes, employee hygiene and training, product labelling and coding, facilities design, equipment maintenance and equipment calibration.

WHO prevention programme: *Five Keys to Safer Food*[2]

WHO identified the need to communicate a simple global health message, rooted in scientific evidence, to educate all types of food handlers and ordinary consumers. *Five Keys to Safer Food* is a global health message which explains the basic principles that individuals all over the world should know to ensure safe food handling practices and prevent food-borne diseases. The *Five Keys to Safer Food* and associated training materials were developed to provide countries with materials that are easy to use, reproduce and adapt to different target audiences.

Translated into 67 languages (including Kiswahili, Tswana and Zulu), mainly on initiative from countries, the *Five Keys to Safer Food* message serves as the basis for health promotion campaigns and educational programmes in more than 100 countries and is used to train food handlers in restaurants, canteens, street and market places, small processing businesses, hospitals, health care centres, schools and at home. Recognized as an international reference source, the message is also extensively used in emergency situations to prevent and control outbreaks of diseases such as cholera.

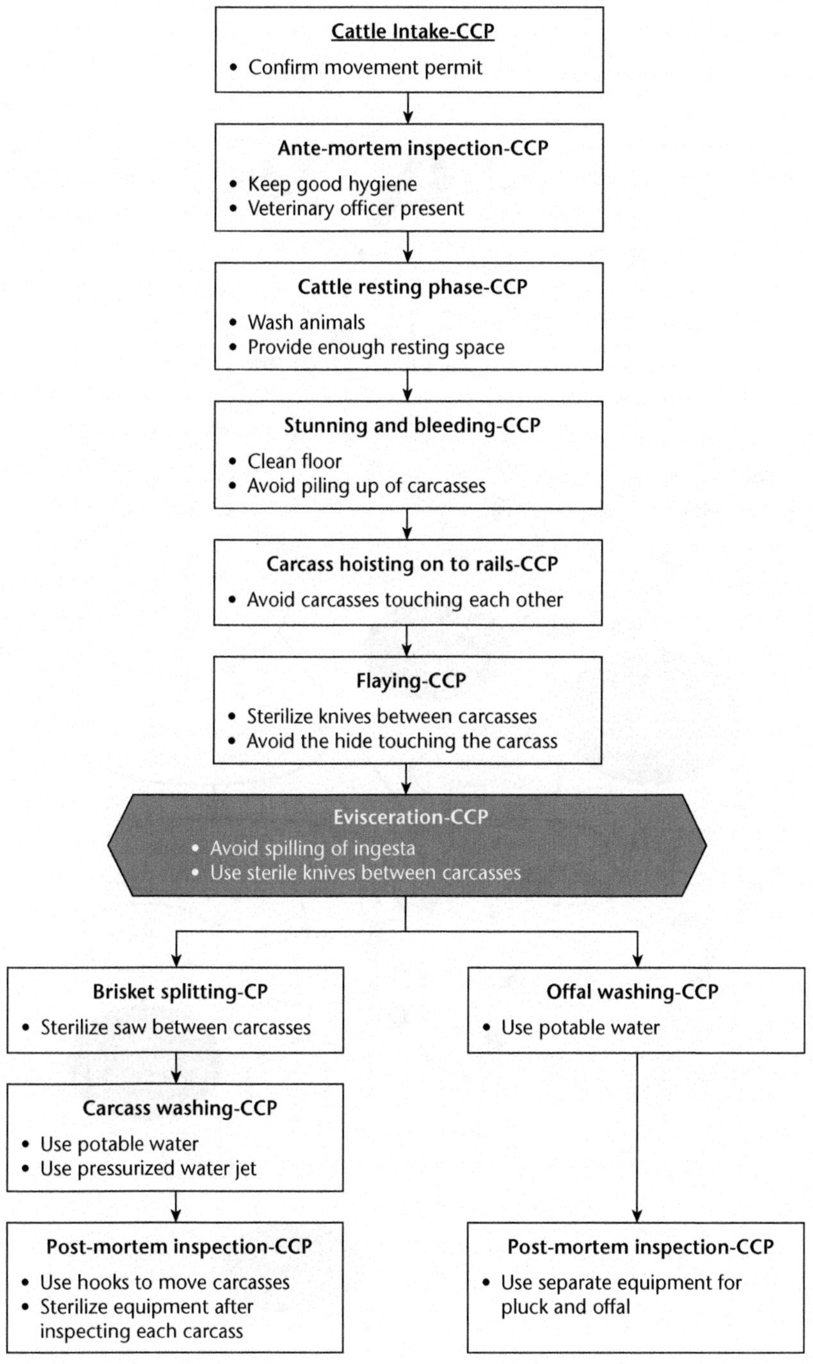

FIGURE 46 HACCP model developed for a Kenyan abattoir.

Source: Mwai (2011)

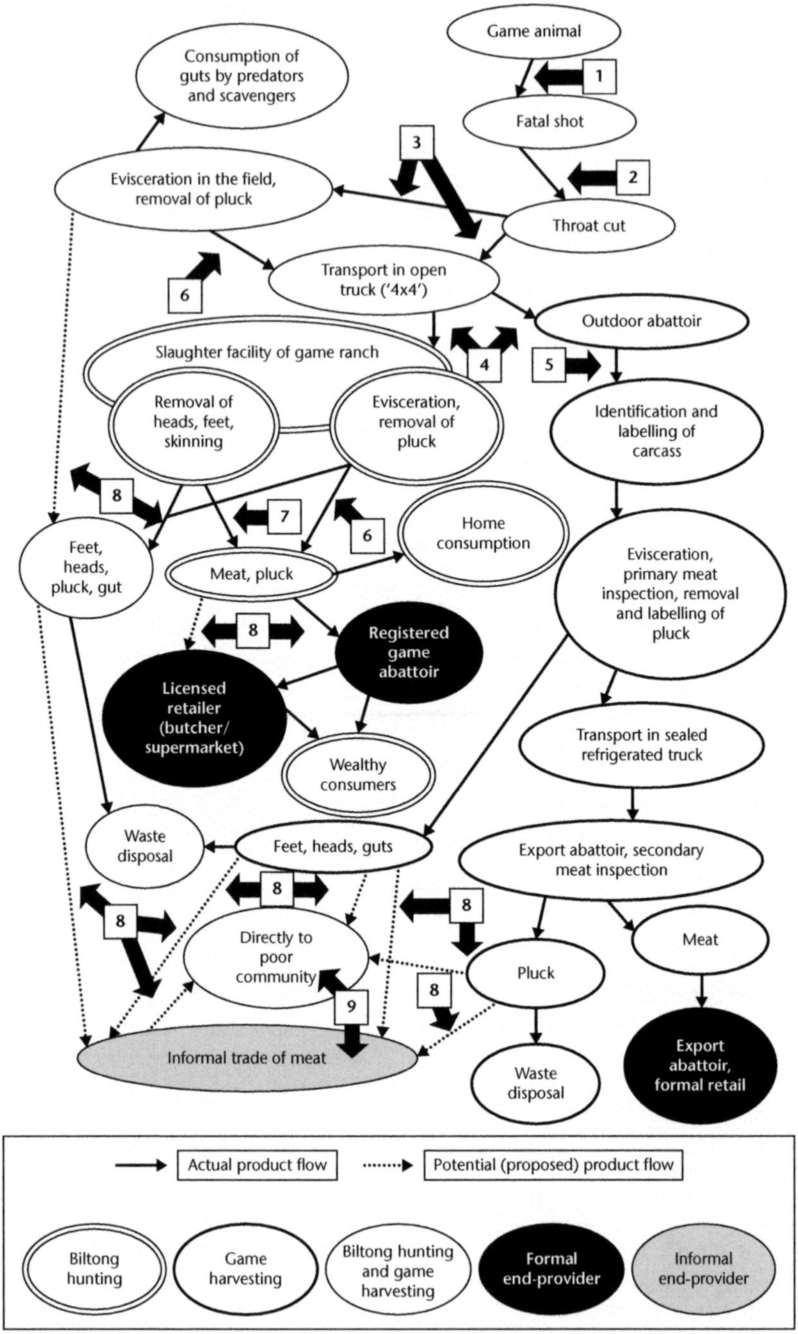

Game animal
1
Fatal shot
2
Throat cut
3
Consumption of guts by predators and scavengers
Evisceration in the field, removal of pluck
6
Transport in open truck ('4x4')
Outdoor abattoir
4
5
Slaughter facility of game ranch
Removal of heads, feet, skinning
Evisceration, removal of pluck
Identification and labelling of carcass
8
7
6
Home consumption
Feet, heads, pluck, gut
Meat, pluck
Evisceration, primary meat inspection, removal and labelling of pluck
8
Registered game abattoir
Licensed retailer (butcher/ supermarket)
Wealthy consumers
Transport in sealed refrigerated truck
Waste disposal
Feet, heads, guts
Export abattoir, secondary meat inspection
8
8
8
Directly to poor community
Meat
Pluck
8
9
Informal trade of meat
Waste disposal
Export abattoir, formal retail

Actual product flow
Potential (proposed) product flow

Biltong hunting
Game harvesting
Biltong hunting and game harvesting
Formal end-provider
Informal end-provider

FIGURE 47 Critical control points for the antelope game meat value chain in South Africa.

Source: Heeb (2009)

BOX 11 EDUTAINMENT: LEARNING BY EAR

The *Learning by Ear* programme (www.dw-world.de/dw/0,,11908,00.html) of the German international broadcaster *Deutsche Welle* examines the challenges that young Africans face and engages listeners in an informative and entertaining way. The programme is a lively mix of in-depth reports, radio dramas and feature stories that provides listeners with an opportunity to get the necessary skills to succeed in Africa today and to discover a whole new world of knowledge. It is particularly popular among the youth who can identify with the actors in the plays. This way, even sensitive topics such as awareness of diarrhoeal diseases and HIV/AIDS are heard. *Learning by Ear* is available in six languages (English, Kiswahili, French, Hausa, Portuguese and Amharic) during various broadcasting times on different frequencies.

Source: www.dw-world.de/dw/article/0,,3564140,00.html. The programme is supported by Germany's Federal Foreign Office.

The five keys to safer food are:

1. Keep food clean.
2. Separate raw and cooked food.
3. Cook food thoroughly.
4. Keep food at safe temperatures.
5. Use safe water and raw materials.

WHO actively promotes the dissemination of the *Five Keys* message and its adaptation to the local level, and to this end has developed the following educational materials:

- The *Five Keys to Safer Food* poster which contains the key message, specific instructions and explanations as to why the safety measures are important.
- The *Five Keys to Safer Food* manual which suggests ways to communicate the message.
- The *Train the Trainer* course targeted at women.

Notes

1. WHO. 1997. Introducing the Hazard Analysis and Critical Control Point system. www.who.int/foodsafety/fs_management/haccp_intro/en/index.html (accessed 9 July 2014).
2. WHO. 2011. Prevention of food-borne disease: Five keys to safer food. www.who.int/foodsafety/consumer/5keys/en/index.html (accessed 9 July 2014).

7

UNDERSTANDING VALUES AND CULTURE IS CRUCIAL FOR FOOD SAFETY MANAGEMENT

Kristina Roesel, Delia Grace, Antoine Bassa Yobouet, Sylvain Gnamien Traoré, Sylvie Mireille Kouamé-Sina, Yolande Aké Assi Datté, Valentin Bognan Koné, Flavien Ndongo, Ibrahim Sow, Kennedy Bomfeh, Cameline Mwai, John Kago, Kaiza Kilango, Kebede Amenu, Marisa Spengler, Fanta Desissa, Joy Appiah, Haruya Toyomaki, Kevin Kabui, Edgar Mahundi, James Oguttu, Shashi Ramrajh, Margaret Molefe and Alexander Heeb

Si le lait est chauffé, la laitière sera tarie – If the milk is boiled, the dairy runs dry.
Fulani in Mali

BOX 12 A CASE STORY FROM MALI: RAW MILK DOES NOT HARM

Antoine Bassa Yobouet, Sylvain Gnamien Traoré, Sylvie Mireille Kouamé-Sina, Yolande Aké Assi Datté, Valentin Bognan Koné, Flavien Ndongo and Ibrahim Sow

Cinzana is a rural area in central Mali with more than 36,000 people living in at least 72 villages. Milk plays an important role in the livelihood of the people and is a fundamental part of good relationships (Figure 48). When visitors come to a home, the first thought is to offer them raw milk to show respect and consideration. When a bad event occurs in a family, the children are offered raw milk to receive God's blessing. Raw milk is also drunk during wedding ceremonies and other traditional rituals.

People think that raw milk gives them strength and good health and according to their perception, milk is not associated with any problems. They believe that 'you will never get sick if you drink raw milk'. The quality of milk is judged by its colour, taste and odour. But even more important to the consumer is the level of faith and trust in the seller.

Usually, milk is consumed raw soon after milking. Additional milk is fermented, a traditional way to preserve it, which can also reduce the level of some microbial hazards. The milk is collected in a container and kept in the house for 24 hours. In the local language, the product is referred to as *non-non koumou*.

Cheese is also consumed in Cinzana. To prepare it, a goat younger than three months is slaughtered and the content of the stomach (containing rennin) is mixed into the raw milk. The blend is then kept in the house for 24 hours. After the milk is coagulated, it is pressed in a cloth to remove the remaining liquid. The solid part is then dried under the Malian sun. In Cinzana, cows are normally milked by men while women milk the goats. Women are also in charge of fermenting and preparation of cheese.

FIGURE 48 An old man milking a goat in central Mali.

Source: Valentin Bognan Koné

BOX 13 WHEN TRADITION AUGMENTS RISK: FISH PROCESSING IN GHANA

Kennedy Bomfeh

Fish has long been recognized as an important part of Ghana's food basket. Being the cheapest source of animal protein, it is consumed throughout the country and is reported to contribute about 60% of animal protein in Ghanaian diets. The product also features prominently in family budgets, where it has been estimated to account for about 20% of household food expenditures and up to 26% in poor households. Accordingly, as of 2008, the annual average per capita consumption of fish in Ghana was estimated at 20–25kg, which at the time was about twice the world average of 13kg.

Fishing is therefore an important economic activity in the country. It is reported that as far back as the 1700s and 1800s, Ghanaian fishermen were actively involved in marine fishing along the coast of the country as well as in neighbouring Benin and Côte d'Ivoire. At that time, very simple and inefficient tools were used and catches were meant primarily to meet domestic demand. After the country achieved political independence in 1957, the government made significant investments in the fishing sector. These included acquisition of fishing technologies (such as vessels for industrial-scale fishing) and infrastructural developments (such as the construction of a harbour and a boatyard) that were deemed to be important for the rapid development of the sector. These encouraged individual participation in the fishery trade and introduced mechanized and efficient ways of fishing, which together contributed to making Ghana a major fishing nation in West Africa.

While the government made capital-intensive commitments, traditional rulers (chiefs) in most fishing communities ensured adherence to cultural practices aiming at the sustainability of fishing activities. For example, fish were offered some protection from humans by a traditional decree; no fishing activities were allowed on certain days of the week or periods within the year. This is practised even today. While some may view this as a superstitious ritual, it does have a preservation sense: it prevents over-exploitation of fish stocks. But are humans, the eventual beneficiaries of all fishing activities, protected from the fish? Could fish be a vehicle for hazards that could make its consumption a risky endeavour? The answer, of course, lies in the safety of the products at the point of consumption, which in turn depends on the manner in which they were processed, distributed and prepared.

Whereas massive investments have been made to increase fishing capacity in Ghana, relatively little has been done for the processing of fish. The country still relies on the use of traditional methods, such as drying, smoking, salting and fermentation, to process fish, particularly for the domestic market (about 80% of fish landings in Ghana are processed traditionally). Since Ghana consumes more of its fish landings than it exports, any compromise on the safety of these products is most likely to affect the domestic consumer, especially given that the strict importation safety checks in international markets are non-existent on the domestic informal food markets where the products are mostly sold.

Sun drying, one of the traditional methods of fish processing in Ghana, involves very simple operations; fresh fish are rinsed in water and spread on the ground to dry under the sun. When dry (usually after three days, depending on weather conditions), the products are gathered into heaps with brooms, collected into baskets and are ready for the market (Figures 49 to 52). This method, although highly economical, is not without risk. By drying fish on the bare ground, several kinds of microorganisms, including pathogens, could contaminate the fish and end up on the consumer's plate – uninvited – if not eliminated during food preparation. Although dried fish is mostly cooked (possibly eliminating some pathogens), consumption of the product without heat treatment is not uncommon. Consumers could therefore be exposed to ingesting these harmful organisms and cooking will not remove hazards such as toxins or chemicals. A study in Ghana showed that coliform bacteria were found in sundried fish on the informal food market. These germs are mostly associated with unhygienic handling or contact of food with soil; sundried fish has gone through both. When sweeping dried fish from the ground with brooms, solid non-food materials, such as stones, splinters of glass and hardwood, and other potentially hazardous materials could be collected along with the fish. Ingestion of such physical materials has obvious health implications. Most consumers are also familiar with the unpleasant experience of biting into sand or stone when consuming sundried fish which has caused tooth loss in some instances.

Other methods of traditional fish processing also have food safety challenges. For example, studies have reported that the bacterial load of smoked fish is low immediately after processing, but increases as the product moves along the distribution chain and worsens on the informal food market due to improper handling. It is apparent that traditional methods of fish processing and handling in Ghana involve practices that could add to the food safety risks associated with foods sold on the informal market. Ironically, whereas campaigns are ongoing to promote the consumption of traditional foods in Ghana, efforts at ensuring their safety seem to be struggling to catch up. To ensure availability of fish (and foods in general) in Ghana to safeguard food security, traditional methods of food processing cannot be done away with. These methods should, however, be improved into forms that are affordable and easy to implement. For such improvements to deliver the best results, they should be developed with the indigenous people through participatory approaches. When this is done, the chief source of animal protein for most Ghanaians will receive an added key value – safety – with the welcome assurance that sundried fish, for example, can be enjoyed without losing a tooth.

FIGURE 49 Rinsing fresh fish.

Source: Kennedy Bomfeh

FIGURE 50 Spreading fish on the ground to dry.

Source: Kennedy Bomfeh

FIGURE 51 Sweeping dried fish from the ground.

Source: Kennedy Bomfeh

FIGURE 52 Dried fish gathered in a basket.

Source: Kennedy Bomfeh

BOX 14 SMOKED FISH IN PORT-BOUËT IS GOOD – BUT WOMEN, BEWARE!

Yolande Aké Assi Datté

The community of Port-Bouët has always been part of Abidjan in Côte d'Ivoire. When the country was under French rule from 1893 to 1960, Port-Bouët was a trading post. Most of the fishermen from the countries near the sea came to Port-Bouët to exchange their goods and many of them settled down, got married or moved with their families. Ever since, the Ashanti, Alladjan and Fati people have lived together peacefully.

While the men usually catch the fish, the women smoke and sell the fish to feed their families. Today, women still use the same technology as their mothers and grandmothers did in the past. Smoked fish is popular among the people of Abidjan but it is also exported. Women use the money they earn to send their children to school. Moreover, smoked fish is also important during cultural ceremonies in the local community such as weddings, funerals and baptisms. Smoked fish is consumed by everyone – old or young, male or female – as it is known to be very nutritious and rich in proteins, vitamins, minerals and fat to gain or regain strength.

During interviews with the women, however, I observed certain practices that could be risky when smoking the fish (Figure 53):

- They used branches from rubber trees, which contain a lot of resin.
- The temperature was very high.
- They used metal sheets to build their ovens.
- They smoked the fish for a long time.

To ensure safe production of smoked fish and therefore the economic benefits, we need ways of mitigating the risks which are in accordance with these women's ancestral traditions and hence acceptable to them.

BOX 15 MEAT CONSUMPTION IN EAST AFRICA: DOES CULTURE REALLY MATTER?

Cameline Mwai, John Kago, Kaiza Kilango, Kebede Amenu, Marisa Spengler, Fanta Desissa, Joy Appiah, Haruya Toyomaki, Kevin Kabui and Kennedy Bomfeh

Eastern Africa is a block of neighbouring countries comprising Burundi, Djibouti, Ethiopia, Kenya, Rwanda, South Sudan, Sudan, Tanzania and Uganda. It is one

FIGURE 53 Grid with fish at the end of the smoking process, Fanty village, Port-Bouët, Côte d'Ivoire.

Source: Yolande Aké Assi Datté

part of sub-Saharan Africa where the economy mainly depends on agriculture. Livestock are integral components of the people's livelihoods and play multiple roles and meat of different livestock species is consumed. However, the preparation and consumption of meat products are affected by cultural and social beliefs. Depending on the cultural group habits, both the type of product and the way it is prepared can be different. These practices might have positive or negative impacts on the safety of the meat products. Therefore, the identification of such practices can be a useful tool in assessing and managing the risks associated with these food products.

Raw is better: meat consumption in Ethiopia

In Ethiopia, meat is consumed cooked, semi-cooked or raw. Consumption of raw meat is widespread in both rural and urban areas. According to a legend, raw meat consumption started during the Italo-Abyssinian war in 1935. To avoid being spotted by Italian soldiers, the Ethiopians changed from cooking their meat to eating it raw. The notion was that lighting a cooking fire at night could reveal their ambush to the Italians. However, it is likely that the custom is much older than that (Figure 54). Today, the practice is carried out predominantly with the belief that raw meat consumption indicates strength and courage among young men. Red meat from the loins, diaphragm, hump and thighs is preferred. This is either consumed just after slaughtering or during the same day. Generally, consumers are aware of food-borne diseases that can be transmitted through the consumption of unwholesome meat. However, they have different perceptions of what 'unwholesome' meat entails. For example, some people do not consider infection with tapeworms through meat to be harmful (see Box 16).

Hot is tastier: *mshikaki* in Tanzania

In Tanzania, red meat is mainly sold in butcheries and either prepared by women for home consumption or sold as roast beef (*nyama choma* in Kiswahili) and skewer beef (*mshikaki*) by young men (Figures 55 and 56). In most Tanzanian towns, roast beef is sold in beer bars while skewer beef is sold in the streets at vendor stations or by hawkers. After being grilled, a piece of roast beef is taken from the grill and cut into pieces on a cutting board. It is then kept on a plate before being served with a stiff porridge (*ugali*), roast banana or alone. For eating, most of the consumers use their bare hands, washed with water of unknown quality. The price of roast beef is high compared to that of skewer beef, leading to most of the vendor stations being found in the densely populated peri-urban areas where low-income groups live. The operators of these stations are often people with minimal education and have neither official medical records nor health certificates. The skewer beef is mainly prepared in the morning and consumed in the late afternoon and evening and often left exposed to dust and flies.

FIGURE 54 Raw meat served with *injera*, Ethiopian pancake-like bread.

Source: ILRI/Apollo Habtamu

FIGURE 55 *Nyama choma* (roast meat) sold at local joints in Uganda.

Source: ILRI/Danilo Pezo

FIGURE 56 *Mshikaki* (skewer beef) sold by hawkers or at vendor stations in Tanzania.

Source: Edgar Mahundi

BOX 16 'TAPEWORM INFECTION IS NOT A DISEASE'

In a survey to assess the knowledge of tapeworm infection in central Ethiopia, the following conversation occurred between a researcher and a consumer named Abebe.

Researcher: 'Have you ever suffered from tapeworm infection?'
Abebe: 'Who told you that tapeworm infection is a disease?'
Researcher: 'Do you consider tapeworm infection to be normal?'
Abebe: 'A man without tapeworm is not really a man.'

BOX 17 PIPI THE CAT: THE MEAT INSPECTOR

Most meat is sourced from butcheries and on some occasions, animals are slaughtered at home. Most of this meat is inspected by veterinary meat inspectors but there are exceptions! There are 42 ethnic groups in Kenya. The Kikuyu, for example, traditionally believed that meat safety could be tested by feeding it to a cat before eating it. If the cat ate the meat, it was considered to be safe and *vice versa*. Covering a piece of meat with hot ashes and observing what happened was another common test: the meat was considered unsafe if it produced a 'pop' sound (suspected to carry anthrax). Visible dirt during slaughter was avoided by spreading clean banana leaves on the ground and placing the carcass on them. During skinning and dressing, the meat was often hung on trees or up in the huts to prevent it from getting dirty.

The preparation of African sausage (called *mutura* in Kikuyu, meaning 'to stuff the intestines') involves the use of fibres collected from banana trees. These fibres are used to tie the stuffed intestines at either end to avoid spilling the meat. The large intestines are first cleaned with water and then stuffed with boiled meat mixed with raw blood. The small intestines, however, are prepared by squeezing the dung out before roasting them. This is done mainly by men while women do the boiling and cooking of the other meat. Most of the meat is eventually eaten boiled, fried or roasted but some communities such as the Maasai eat raw meat and drink blood during certain occasions, especially initiation ceremonies when young men (*morans*) are entering adulthood. The kidneys of a cow are some of their favourite parts and eaten immediately after slaughter. Home slaughter is mainly done during traditional rituals, Ramadan or Christmas.

BOX 18 TRADITIONAL SLAUGHTER AMONG ETHNIC GROUPS IN SOUTH AFRICA

James Oguttu, Shashi Ramrajh, Margaret Molefe and Alexander Heeb

South Africa has more than twelve ethnic groups, each with its own way of producing food of animal origin. Different practices are applied during slaughter and for the preservation of meat and each of these ethnic groups also has its own way of assuring food safety. The law provides for the traditional slaughter of animals for religious and cultural purposes. In such cases, killing of animals is done by different methods such as using bare hands, stabbing the back of the neck, stunning, shooting on the forehead, or casting the animal down and slitting its throat. In some of these instances, the method of killing does not allow thorough bleeding. Traditional methods of killing animals may have an effect on the meat's quality; meat from animals that are insufficiently bled has a poor shelf life and is tough if not left to mature. There also may be issues when cultural practices clash with animal welfare standards!

Slaughter as practised by the Tswana, Ndebele, Pedi and Tswati
For celebrations such as weddings and funerals, these ethnic groups believe that a cow should be slaughtered at the celebrant's house. They believe that the flowing of the cow's blood will please the ancestors and bless the occasion. In the event of a death, the flowing of blood allows the deceased to depart in peace. The uncle of the deceased decides how the animal will be killed, either by plunging a knife through the back of its head or by shooting it. Where a knife is used, those present use their pocket knives which are cleaned with ordinary water. This is not recommended, as it could lead to contamination of the meat. The law recommends the use of knives that are sterilized for such slaughter.

Handling of slaughtered meat by the Ovahimba ethnic group of Namibia
The Ovahimba generally store meat without cooling it but keep it on the roof of their huts or hung on a tree, out of the reach of their dogs and other animals. In most cases, meat is not stored longer than overnight. If there are amounts of meat that cannot be consumed by the members of a clan within a reasonable time, they are usually given away to other clans in the area. From time to time, larger amounts of meat are dried by hanging them from the roof of a hut or on a tree. This procedure is therefore similar to that for making biltong. The Ovahimba prefer to eat meat that is well cooked or roasted instead of raw meat, therefore, the meat is always well done. A fireplace with wood is used as a source of heat (Figure 57). The meat is then served with spices and porridge. Seasoning is done prior to cooking or roasting the meat and may be

repeated during cooking. The water used for cooking is fetched from a tap situated about 1 km away and ferried in large containers that are carried by donkeys.

When asked how they would know if a piece of meat was no longer good for consumption, the Ovahimba explained that they would tell by the look and smell of the meat. Such meat, they stated, would be given to their dogs rather than being eaten. They claimed never to have fallen sick in any way after eating meat.

FIGURE 57 Himba by the fireplace.

Source: Alexander Heeb

Key messages

- Indigenous knowledge often contributes towards food safety.
- Eating food is not only for nourishment but also associated with cultural values.
- There are different cultural beliefs about risks associated with food.
- It can be difficult to change traditional practices that represent high risks.
- Some groups are more exposed to risk than others.
- Traditional risk mitigation strategies need further investigation.
- Cultural background must be considered in risk management and communication.

Sub-Saharan Africa is home to some 874 million people[1] living in 48 different countries and speaking more than 1,000 different languages. Most Africans adhere to either Christianity or Islam, but many also follow traditional religions. This multifaceted religious life has a strong influence on people's perceptions, motivations and practices, especially in the rural areas where knowledge is reverently transferred from one generation to another.

The Safe Food, Fair Food project included research from 25 students originating from twelve different countries and investigating food safety in eight countries in sub-Saharan Africa. All of them investigated food-borne hazards and risks by using participatory methods (Chapters 4 and 5). Even though many of them did research in their home countries, observations and interviews with stakeholders needed to be facilitated by translators and local authorities who were well known to everyone involved. The students all agreed that a high level of sensitivity and respect was needed when doing research in rural Africa.

The Safe Food, Fair Food team was very diverse, ranging from microbiologists and nutritionists to veterinarians and a social scientist. Participation took into account the social background of all the key actors related to the food product under study. This multidisciplinary approach followed the One Health concept to attain health for people, animals and the environment alike.

Indigenous knowledge contributes towards food safety

The population in rural areas of sub-Saharan Africa is often perceived as being less educated because many cannot speak English, French or Portuguese or do not know how to read and write. However, much knowledge in most African cultures is based on oral tradition. For hundreds of years, indigenous knowledge has been handed down from one generation to the next. Given that many of these cultural groups still exist today, it might be an option to consider their ways of dealing with risks associated with food.

All over Africa, fires are used to prepare meat. During the night, wild predators would not come anywhere near a fireplace to take the meat and throughout the day, meat on the fire scared off nuisance flies. In South Africa, a big pot used to be left on the fire, meat and vegetables were constantly added and the stew literally simmered for hours over hot coals. This is still practised today by both locals and visitors and is known as *potjiekos* (pot food). Long cooking times have proved to be one of the most effective and feasible ways of eliminating disease-causing microbes but it is not the best way of retaining nutrients. Moreover, cooking in iron pots has been associated with other health risks.

Solar energy is a rich resource in many areas of sub-Saharan Africa and sun-drying is an effective method of preserving meat by extracting water. The water in raw meat and fish serves as a medium for the multiplication of microbes. Thus, drying is one of the most common practices for preserving these food products, not only in Africa but elsewhere in the world. Sometimes, the food is impregnated with salt and spices that catalyse drying and add extra flavour. In South Africa, even today, meat from domestic animals is still sliced, dried and eaten as biltong. Fish from the great freshwater lakes in East and southern Africa is left in the sun for several days and then stored before being cooked in a sauce with tomatoes and onions. Along the coast in West and East Africa, fish is traditionally smoked over fire.

Storing food off the ground, eating food while it is still hot and washing hands before eating are well-known good hygienic practices. However, washing hands could pose a health risk if the water is not clean or if soap is not used. Increasing populations result in people and animals sharing the same sources of water (Chapter 10), leading to increased risk of people contracting water-borne animal diseases (Chapter 11).

Some traditional practices are still useful today for contributing to food safety. In eastern Africa, women separate 'bad' and 'good' milk, thus mitigating the risk of cross-contamination during pooling of milk. Additionally, they use locally produced pots made of unbaked clay to store their milk at home. These pots serve as a 'refrigerator' due to the cooling effect of evaporation. The women usually cover these pots with nets or a cloth to protect the milk from flies or dust.

Milk is particularly important to West and East Africans. In the rural areas, where cooling facilities are lacking, surplus milk is often fermented into sour milk, yoghurt and cheese. What is called *ergo* in Ethiopia is known as *maziwa lala* in Kenya and *féné* in Mali. Joy Appiah from Ghana noted that the fermentation of milk confers some safety for consumers as it produces acid which kills some of the germs in milk. However, the backslopping method (adding a portion of previously fermented milk as starter culture to initiate fermentation of a new batch) is a potential source of contamination. Sylvie Mireille Kouamé-Sina found that fermentation could not guarantee a uniform product and that acid was sufficient to inhibit growth of all pathogens (Chapter 17). Fermentation is not only used for milk and dairy products but also for the production of Ethiopian yeast-risen flatbread, *injera*, which is traditionally made out of flour from grains of the local lovegrass species, teff (see Figure 54).

Most Africans eat their food with bare hands, sharing the same plate with several people as part of their culture (Figures 58 and 59). With the absence of toilets and water for washing hands, there is a high risk of diarrhoeal disease, though not necessarily zoonotic. As Sylvain Gnamien Traoré from Côte d'Ivoire concludes, indigenous knowledge can improve food safety but traditional misperceptions can result in adverse effects.

Knowledge about food safety and risks

According to John Kago from Kenya, diarrhoea and stomach ache are the most common problems associated with food poisoning. However, not everyone associated this with disease-causing microorganisms in the food or poor hygiene. Cameline Mwai is from Kenya's Kikuyu ethnic group and she recalled that if her people eat outside their homes ('chips in town') and fall sick afterwards, they associate diarrhoea with food eaten somewhere else and mostly because of 'too much oil' rather than infectious disease. Therefore, they only eat food that is well done when they eat out. People in her home village slaughter and consume meat without prior inspection, which she considers ignorant behaviour, and she does not understand why they do not take advantage of her profession as a veterinarian.

In Tanzania, Edgar Mahundi reported that people were indeed aware of diseases being transmitted by eating contaminated meat. People in Arusha vividly

FIGURE 58 Kebede Amenu from Ethiopia uses his bare hands to eat *injera*.

Source: Antoine Bassa Yobouet

FIGURE 59 John Kago from Kenya and Kennedy Bomfeh from Ghana prefer to use cutlery to eat *injera*.

Source: Antoine Bassa Yobouet

recalled the 2007 outbreak of Rift Valley fever that killed more than 100 people who had eaten infected meat. They were also aware that too much meat can cause diseases such as gout, but nobody knew about campylobacteriosis being a hazard in the most popular dish, *nyama choma*.

Ethiopians love to eat raw red meat, Fanta Desissa states. Some know about the associated risks and take their own precautions by drinking *katikala*, a local liquor made of grains containing 75% alcohol, as they eat raw meat. Similar customs have been observed in Germany where people drink herbal liquor after a heavy meal as a digestive. In France, this small tot is called *eau de vie* (water of life), a clear, colourless, fruit brandy.

Marisa Spengler, a Safe Food, Fair Food participant from Germany, observed that in Ethiopia, most villagers considered raw milk to be 'good' and did not associate disease with milk consumption. Some of them did, however, but went to traditional healers or paramedics if they suffered from diarrhoea or fever. In her study area Siraro, diarrhoea and other gastrointestinal infections were among the top ten diseases; the cause remains mostly unknown but contaminated food and water are the likely culprits.

In East Africa, it is commonly known that milk should be boiled to prevent disease and fast deterioration, whereas in West Africa, boiling of milk is not widely practised. All Safe Food, Fair Food participants from Mali, Côte d'Ivoire and Ghana confirmed that boiling milk is a taboo (Chapter 20). There are more than 12 million Fulani, the traditional cattle herders, who are found everywhere from Senegal to Cameroon. Cattle occupy a central position in the society, with the Fulani often putting the welfare of their animals above their own. For the Fulani, milk cannot make people sick. The most dominant group in Mali are the Bambara, originally farmers. Nowadays, they keep some livestock, partly to use the organic manure for their fields and partly as a financial back-up for hard times. The Bambara often hire a Fulani to look after their livestock as they are considered to be 'real herders'. Therefore, they are largely influenced by Fulani practices.

Antoine Bassa Yobouet adds that if the Fulani suffer from diarrhoea after drinking milk, it is not called a disease because they drink the milk to prevent constipation in the first place. Those who get sick are simply not used to it or drank too much at once.

Sylvie Mireille Kouamé-Sina explains that others consume raw milk in the morning because they are normally in a hurry to go to work and thus do not have time to boil it first. They believe that 'plain milk' can cause 'malaria' although this is not because of the milk *per se* but the microbes it contains. These microbes may have been introduced into the milk during handling. For yet others, disease might be associated with food consumed at the same time as milk. 'Malaria' actually refers to the symptom of fever and is often linked to the bread that accompanies the milk. However, it is scientifically inconceivable that milk can transmit malaria. But linking it with this food-borne disease refers to the symptoms (vomiting, fever or headache) that are often experienced by those who consume milk of poor microbiological quality. This is a false and dangerous conclusion, as these symptoms are similar to those of diseases such as tuberculosis or brucellosis (Chapter 19) and treatment for malaria would not help.

In Ghana, Joy Appiah recalls farmers who usually report a surge in the prevalence of cattle diseases with the onset of the rains. They attributed it to the consumption of fresh grass. The majority of Ghanaian consumers surveyed mentioned diarrhoea as a usual and direct consequence of consuming raw milk. However, none thought that the consumption of unwholesome food could result in symptoms such as spontaneous abortions, stillbirths, premature births and even epilepsy, which were worryingly common among them. Furthermore, some others who had come to the conclusion that raw milk consumption could cause illness said their antidote was to consume it less frequently, oblivious to the fact that a single exposure might be enough for infection and consuming less milk is bad for their nutrition as well as the domestic dairy industry.

Some ethnic groups in South Africa believe that disease derives from a person but not from germs. They call it 'bad hand' and refer to witchcraft. Nenene Qekwana carried out research on traditional slaughter rituals in South Africa and explained that if people got sick from ritually slaughtered meat it was because the ancestors were not contented with the sacrifice. If people got sick after eating food at a funeral they associated it with the dead person being angry with somebody.

Some groups are more or less exposed to risks because of customs

Certain cultural and religious beliefs expose people to a higher risk because of certain practices, as in the case of Muslims who are found all over in Africa with higher numbers in the West. The end of the Ramadan fasting season is likely the

BOX 19 LACTOSE INTOLERANCE: A NATURAL HANDICAP

In Ghana, consumers associate diarrhoea with the consumption of raw milk. Even though bacterial infestation of milk might be one reason, it could also be lactose intolerance, as documented by Kretchmer (1972),[2] which is considered to be high amongst blacks (Scrimshaw and Murray 1988).[3] Lactose intolerance is the inability to digest lactose, a sugar found in milk. People who lack the enzyme required to break down this sugar in the digestive tract experience symptoms including abdominal pain, bloating, diarrhoea and nausea soon after drinking milk. Lactose intolerance is said to be a handicap. However, it is actually part of human evolution. In the past, milk was given to children only. After weaning, the number of enzymes digesting the milk sugar eventually decreased. This natural development became a handicap when adults started drinking milk or eating yoghurt, butter or cheese.

most important Islamic festival. Some 80–90% of Malians are Muslims and when the month of Ramadan is over, the entire country bustles with preparations for *la grande fête de Tabaski* (*Eid al Adha* or the Feast of the Sacrifice). After the morning prayer, thousands of male sheep are slaughtered in accordance with the rules in the Holy Qur'an. After the animals are slaughtered, the entire family takes part in preparing the big feast. The head of the family trims and dresses the carcass. The children help to cut the carcass into pieces and hang it off the ground. They will later leave the house to wander the neighbourhood giving meat to relatives or people in need in return for gifts for their own family. While the sheep is taken apart, the women gather in the kitchen and boil rice, chop vegetables and stir the stew with meat and offal. Several courses are served throughout the day and eating is the main activity, only interrupted by drinking glasses of green tea.

In theory, because of Islamic religious law, Muslims are not exposed to certain diseases of animal origin as they are not allowed to eat carrion, blood products or pork, all of which are considered dirty.[4] However, due to their customs, they might be at risk of exposure to other diseases (Figures 60 and 61). They also follow certain rules of etiquette that save them from hazards. Among Muslims, the left hand is reserved for bodily hygiene and considered unclean. Thus, only the right hand should be used for eating.

According to Ana Bela Cambaza dos Muchangos from Mozambique, Seventh-day Adventists are not allowed to eat fish that do not have fins and scales. The

FIGURE 60 In Mali, during the Tabaski festival that marks the end of Ramadan, thousands of male sheep are slaughtered and the testicles prepared. Are these two children at risk of exposure to brucellosis as they are in charge of preparing the testicles?

Source: ILRI/Kristina Roesel

FIGURE 61 Meat is hung for storage before being given to neighbours, friends and family members during Tabaski.

Source: ILRI/Kristina Roesel

Seventh-day Adventists are known for presenting a 'health message' that recommends vegetarianism and expects adherence to the kosher laws,[5] that is, abstinence from pork, shellfish and other foods that are said to be 'unclean'. Therefore, Seventh-day Adventists will most likely not suffer from infections with lung flukes which can be transmitted through consumption of shellfish, as investigated in Côte d'Ivoire (Chapter 34).

Religious rules and risks associated with food of animal origin are relatively easy to identify compared to thousands of customs practised on the level of ethnic groups or even families. The Maasai in East Africa are basically the counterpart of the Fulani in West Africa who believe that 'the true Fulani is the one who loves raw milk'. The Maasai believe that God has given all the cows to them only, so if anyone else has cattle, it is because at some time in the past they stole the animals from the Maasai. When the Maasai practise transhumance, their lives depend on their cattle. They live off the raw milk and even drink the blood from the live animal without killing it. This practice has also been witnessed among herders in South Sudan (Figure 62) and leaves them highly exposed to contact diseases such as anthrax, brucellosis and zoonotic tuberculosis.

Because of a lack of knowledge of the bacterial hazards associated with raw milk, many ethnic groups put the most vulnerable members of their communities at risk. Mothers in Ethiopia, Mali and Côte d'Ivoire mean well when they give their children and the elderly raw milk every day, so long as the family cow is

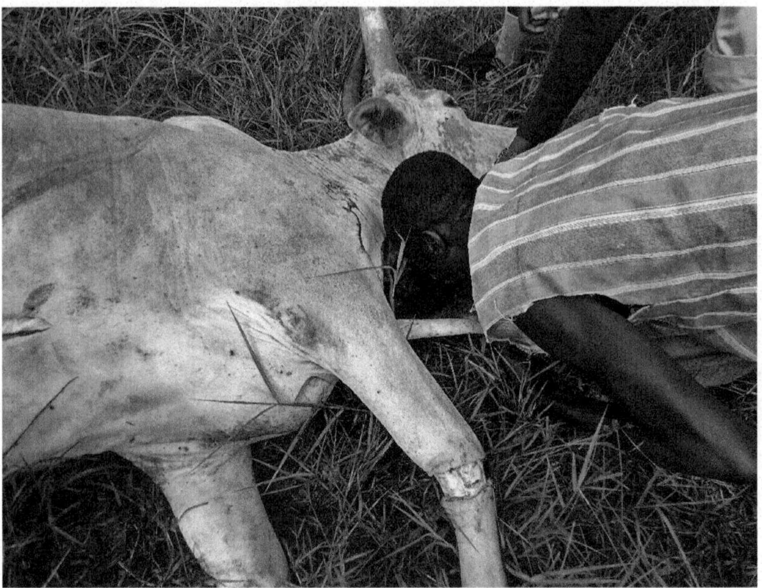

FIGURE 62 Herders in South Sudan drinking blood from cattle.

Source: Joseph Atia

lactating, as milk is considered to be a nutritious source of energy. In some ethnic groups in South Africa, it is the old women who get to eat the aborted foetus of an animal, whereas young women are forbidden to do so as it is said to cause abortion. These young women must also not eat eggs or cheese, as it is widely believed that doing so would cause them to enter puberty too early. Many of these eating habits seem to be related to fertility. In some ethnic groups in South Africa, if old men are 'struggling', they are supposed to eat red offal to improve virility. In West Africa, this feature is attributed to raw milk and raw crabs.

All these cultural peculiarities have to be considered when assessing, managing and communicating food-borne health risks. Assessing these risks is one big test which the participants of the project tried to tackle. After identifying them, ways and means of managing them need to be set up and implemented. Here another challenge arises: how do you convince an 85-year-old Fulani chief in Mali, who never suffered from food-borne disease, to suddenly change his beliefs and habits? After all, he is the key person in the village advising and leading the entire community.

Notes

1. The population of sub-Saharan Africa was last reported at 874,841,049 in 2011, according to a World Bank report published in 2012.
2. Kretchmer N. 1972. Lactose and lactase. *Scientific American* 227(4): 71–78.

3. Scrimshaw NS and Murray EB. 1988. The acceptability of milk and milk products in populations with a high prevalence of lactose intolerance. *American Journal of Clinical Nutrition* 48(4): 1142–1159.
4. Masri ABA. 2009. *Animals in Islam*. www.call-to-monotheism.com/animals_in_islam__by_al_hafiz_b_a__masri (accessed 9 July 2014).
5. Leviticus 11. www.biblegateway.com/passage/?search=leviticus%2011-11&version=NIV (accessed 9 July 2014).

8

CAN FOOD SAFETY BE PRO-POOR?

Kristina Roesel, Delia Grace, Ibrahim Sow, Valentin Bognan Koné, Cheryl McCrindle and Shashi Ramrajh

It is too late to fatten the cow on market day.

Zambian proverb

Key messages

- The poor are more prone to food-borne disease but cannot afford to fall ill.
- Risk-mitigating measures need training, skills development and prerequisites.
- Linking informal markets to formal markets could decrease local and domestic poverty.
- Impact assessment is needed in terms of economic losses and gains on risks that occur.

Background

While appreciation has grown of the high costs of food-borne disease, the costs of food safety are sometimes forgotten. Everyone wants improved quality but someone has to pay the price and those who cannot afford to may have to go out of business. The informal market can no longer operate in traditional ways. Urbanization, globalization, technological change and agricultural intensification are changing the way in which markets function. As markets evolve, there is a natural tendency for formal standards to become stricter and better enforced and for private-sector standards to proliferate. The costs of meeting standards will fall disproportionately on small producers as they need to change most. This 'retail revolution' is occurring more slowly in sub-Saharan Africa, but change is already evident. In Kenya, supermarket sales are growing at 18% per year and accounted for 20% of retail urban food by 2003.

Smallholder production is expanding but there is less evidence that smallholders are improving the quality and safety of food they sell. Indeed, many people think

BOX 20 HOW A DAIRY HELPS CHILDREN IN BAKAWÊRÊ TO ATTEND SCHOOL

Ibrahim Sow and Valentin Bognan Koné

Following his inauguration speech at the opening of a new dairy, the president of the dairy cooperatives, Alou Karagnara, decided to send his children and all of his nephews to school. His village called Bakawêrê is located about 17 kilometres away from the dairy and is home to people of the Djawambé ethnic group who are traditionally livestock keepers and normally do not take their children to school.

During his survey (Chapter 19), researcher Ibrahim Sow chatted with Alou, who said he had never thought that they could ever sell their milk through channels like the new cooperative and had never imagined speaking in front of a camera. In response to the question on what he regrets most in life, he said that he regretted not having learned how to read and write.

'What prevents you from sending your children to school?' the researcher asked. 'Nothing,' replied Alou. 'It was simply our tradition not to send our children to school. I had never been to one until the dairy organized training courses at a school. There, we learned about good breeding practices and their advantages.'

The dairy helped the community to improve productivity of their animals through better livestock management that included providing feed supplements. The supplements can be obtained from the dairy against interest-free credit. Access to marketing channels and additional jobs that have been created also helped increase the revenues of rural communities. Alou plans to send his children and nephews to school by bicycle as the nearest school is 10 kilometres away from their village.

PAFLACIN is the French acronym for *Projet d'appui à la filière lait de Cinzana* (project to support the dairy sector in Cinzana). The dairy was opened in 2008 with the aim to benefit five different groups: livestock owners, wives of dairy farmers, herders, unemployed youth and consumers. The project has set up six cooperatives to promote the collection and processing of milk, supply wholesalers, retailers and end consumers with pasteurized and fermented milk, and render technical and social services like loans to producers (Figure 63).

that smallholder farmers are unlikely to produce food of adequate safety and quality in the absence of incentives and support. The benefits of food safety are reaped by consumers, so there is a public health argument for helping smallholder farmers to improve their practices. Farmers who cannot meet standards will be excluded from the higher-value domestic and international markets starting to emerge in Africa. This raises the real possibility that unless something is done, poor

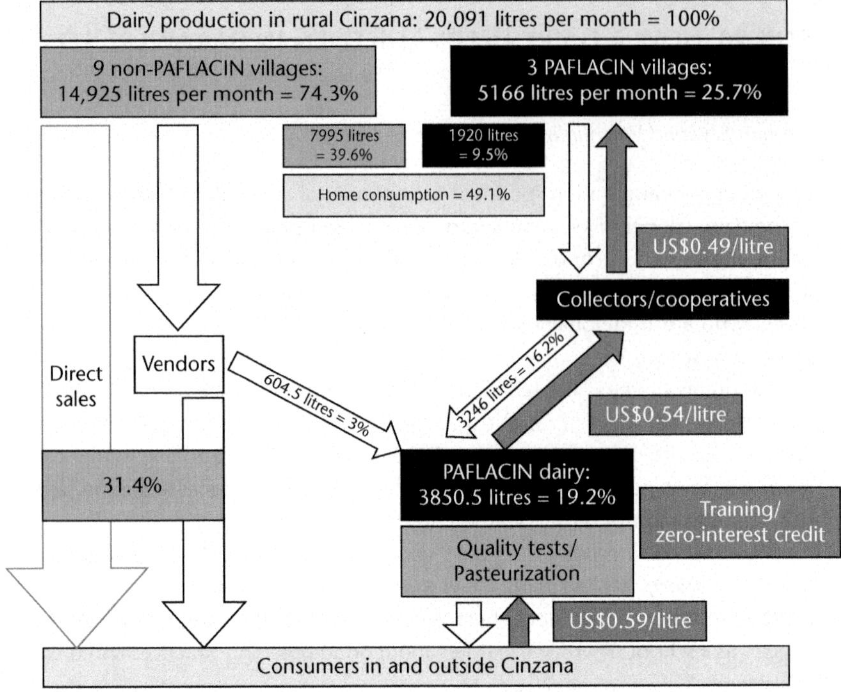

FIGURE 63 Dairy product flow with and without a formalized dairy farm.

Source: Sow (2011)

farmers will lose market share, miss out on opportunities offered by the Livestock Revolution and become increasingly marginalized.

As well as opportunities lost, the inability of the smallholder value chain to meet safety standards exposes participants to harassment from authorities. In Kenya, for example, the costs incurred by milk traders as a result of operating informally included bribes to police, discarded milk and confiscated milk cans; these amounted to 38% of the total market margins accruing to traders (total revenues less procurement costs). Unfortunately, there is little evidence that 'command and control' and harassing small-scale farmers and traders actually improves food safety. Indeed, it may make things worse. A study on peri-urban dairying in Kampala found that farmers who (incorrectly) believed that urban dairying was legal were more likely to carry out risk-mitigating procedures such as using metal milk containers and washing containers with hot water and disinfectant. This is only to be expected. Once something becomes illegal, there is a 'race to the bottom' and little reason for people to invest in good practices.

Risk analysis offers a new approach to managing food safety. Not only is it more effective at decreasing risks, but it can bridge food safety and livelihood concerns. The first component of risk analysis, risk assessment, generates an estimate of negative health impacts of a hazard as well as the likelihood of their occurrence. This information can then be compared with economic data on the costs and benefits of smallholder production and marketing (including externalities such as income opportunities for poor women or environmental degradation from abattoirs), and the costs and benefits of risk mitigation.

This allows decision-makers to set appropriate levels of protection based on evidence rather than anecdote and subjective preference. Moreover, the focus on a 'farm-to-fork' pathway approach allows the identification of risk mitigation points along the food value chain. This can help identify interventions that maintain market access for smallholders. Risk analysis is also compatible with the development aims of African governments as shown by a recent regional conference in which African countries, recognizing the importance of food safety and their limited capacity to assure it, called for a risk analysis approach and capacity building at national level.

Occasionally, it is said that in countries which are food-insecure, food safety cannot and should not be a priority. This attitude is being replaced with a more holistic perspective that sees food security and food safety as inter-dependent (Box 21).

The poor cannot afford to fall ill

Everyone is part of the informal market (Chapter 2). However, those supplying it are not there because they like operating informally but because they have to make a living. The poor not only dominate informal markets but are also the most vulnerable to disease. They only see a doctor if they cannot work anymore and this leads to a vicious cycle: they are not paid for the time they are not working and sometimes spend more than they can afford to receive treatment at a hospital. It is even worse if several members of the family are ill and not able to work. If they cannot afford medical care they are at risk of life-long disabilities or long-term debt. Moreover, not being able to work in the fields can result in food insecurity.

The WHO quantifies the burden of disease by using metrics such as disability-adjusted life years (DALYs). One DALY can be thought of as one lost year of 'healthy' life. The sum of these DALYs across the population, or the burden of disease, can be thought of as a measurement of the gap between current health status and an ideal health situation where the entire population lives to an advanced age, free of disease and disability.[1]

BOX 21 FOOD SAFETY AS PART OF FOOD SECURITY

Life expectancy is low in developing countries where food security is often seen as more important than food safety due to high levels of undernourishment in the population (Unnevehr 2003).[2]

DALYs for a disease or health condition are calculated as the sum of the Years of Life Lost (YLL) due to premature death in the population and the Years Lost due to Disability (YLD) for reported cases of the health condition: DALY = YLL+YLD.

By calculating these metrics, the WHO determined the two leading causes of disease burden to be infectious disease: lower respiratory infections and diarrhoeal diseases. In countries with good data, it is often the case that livestock and fish products are the foods most commonly implicated in food-borne disease. Given that people share 60% of their diseases with animals, that is not surprising. Moist, nutrient-rich foods such as meat and milk also provide a better environment for bacteria to grow than dry foods such as cereals or vegetables.

But as well as being implicated in making people sick, livestock and fish also contribute to good health through the nutrients they supply. In poor countries, livestock and fish feed billions and provide them with energy and proteins. Fish account for more than half of the animal protein intake for the 400 million poorest people in Africa and South Asia. Meat, milk, eggs and fish are important sources of the micro-nutrients and high-quality proteins essential for growth and health.

Prevention is better (and cheaper) than cure

Many of the Safe Food, Fair Food studies found post-process contamination to be a main problem for food safety in informal markets. Ironically, most of the measures that mitigated the risk of food-borne disease along the value chain did not require heavy investments.

There is agreement among the Safe Food, Fair Food participants that if hygiene were practised the poor would benefit. A study in Côte d'Ivoire showed poor hygiene leads to post-process contamination of milk. If European Union (EU) quality standards were implemented, 60% of the milk in the study area would have to be discarded per day. However, many stakeholders of informal food value chains seem to lack either training on good personal hygiene and good manufacturing practices or the prerequisites such as potable water and electricity to work in a sanitary environment. Sometimes they lack both. The situation is far from uniform. We found that many dairy farmers in Kenya and Tanzania observed good practices such as washing hands before milking and cleaning the udder of the cow, while dairy farmers in other countries often did neither.

Good hygiene practices are open to everyone and it is the responsibility of governments to provide adequate frameworks and preconditions. Children must be taught while they are still young that it is healthy to wash their hands with warm water and soap before eating. Keeping food covered and cool as well as thorough cooking must be promoted among mostly female vendors. However, campaigns like this need to be coordinated by government agencies and thus require collaboration and communication between departments that hold mandates related to food safety. There is often better success if messages are marketed in such a way as to make behaviour change socially desirable rather than just focusing on a health message.

A big problem in all the countries where we worked was the disconnection between policy and practice. In South Africa, government officials were reported to be too rigid on enforcement of regulations with no provision for training or skills development. In West and East Africa, existing regulations were reportedly not properly enforced. We argue that this is because the policies and regulations are often inappropriate and based on 'inspect and punish' rather than 'explain and support'. This is an area where participatory approaches to risk management can be much more effective than top-down measures.

Why do countries rely on imports rather than their own resources?

Mali is home to more goats and sheep than people. Eight million cows produce 300,000 litres of milk annually. However, the country still relies on imports, especially to meet the rising demand for milk by the growing number of urban consumers in the cities. This presents an opportunity for rural dairy farmers to benefit from new urban markets, if their produce is safe for human consumption and actually finds its way to the big cities.

The formation of cooperatives linked to dairy plants in rural areas, such as PAFLACIN in Cinzana in Mali, has had great benefits. Dairy farmers are able to pool their milk and supply it to the dairy plant which then sells it to wholesalers who supply the retailers in the urban centres. The women who are involved in most of the milk handling and trading are trained in milk hygiene and quality improvement. They learn to use lactometers to measure the density of milk and detect unfair and unsafe adulteration of milk. They do basic tests to assess the level of contamination of raw milk and they learn to pasteurize the milk, a practice that previously had been unknown and even condemned by the dairy farmers who are mostly Fulani to whom milk is sacred. However, work still needs to be done to address the bias of the women boiling milk for sale but not for home consumption. In addition, the set-up and running costs of cooperatives can be a challenge to this model of milk supply.

Cooperatives are one way to link informal with formal markets (Figure 64). Shashi Ramrajh found another way. With many years of experience as a veterinarian

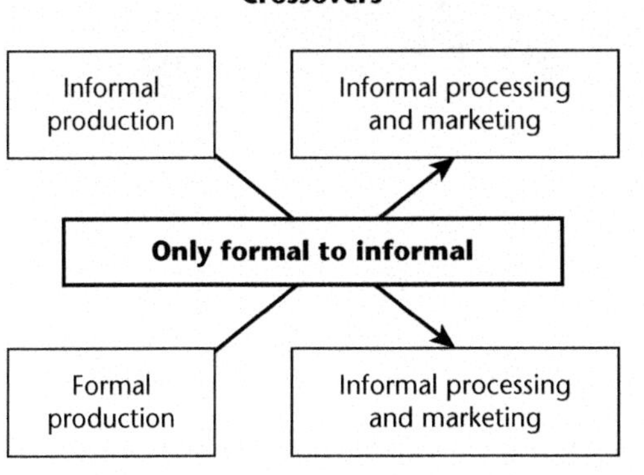

FIGURE 64 Crossovers only from formal to informal markets.

Source: Cheryl McCrindle (unpublished manuscript)

in KwaZulu-Natal in South Africa, she regularly supervises 'game harvests' at commercial game farms. Dozens of impala antelope are shot during the night and procured to the export abattoir following evisceration in the field and primary meat inspection. The meat is sold to end consumers who can afford it, the pluck (heart, liver and lungs) is processed into pet food and the tripe (intestines), head and feet are left behind for the vultures. Since the heads are still covered with muscle and tripe is also rich in protein, Ramrajh investigated whether there was demand for venison offal in local communities living next to game farms (Figure 65). It was found that

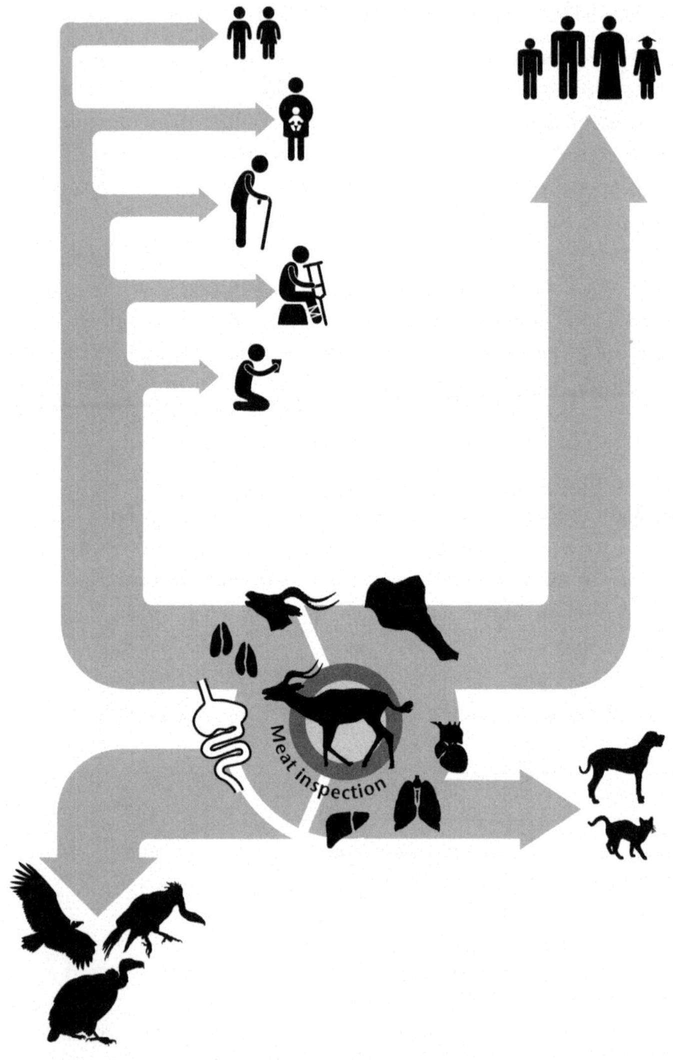

FIGURE 65 Feeding people instead of vultures.

Source: Shashi Ramrajh and Hubertus Schnorr (unpublished manuscript)

there was indeed demand for offal but until then, the game harvesters had not considered supporting their neighbours with animal-source protein that had passed meat inspection and was safe for human consumption (Chapter 28).

Recalling Edgar Mahundi from Tanzania who said 'Safeguard the informal market and you safeguard the society', more efforts for the benefit of the poor are necessary because they are the main producers and consumers in the informal markets. Fanta Desissa adds: 'With the key findings of the Safe Food, Fair Food project, we now have to go back and build capacity through training at all levels.'

Notes

1. www.who.int/healthinfo/global_burden_disease/metrics_daly/en (accessed 9 July 2014).
2. Unnevehr LJ. 2003. Overview. In Unnevehr LJ (ed.) *Food safety in food security and food trade*. 2020 Focus 10. Brief 1. Washington, DC: IFPRI. www.ifpri.org/sites/default/files/publications/focus10.pdf (accessed 3 August 2014)

9

GENDER ASPECTS OF INFORMAL MARKETS FOR ANIMAL-SOURCE FOOD

Delia Grace, Kristina Roesel and Kevin Kabui

BOX 22 WHY MY MILK?

Kevin Kabui

It is the dawn of a new day in one of the sleepy villages that dot the majestic and expansive Great Rift Valley in Kenya. Sharon Kibet, a middle-aged woman, wakes up, braving the cold morning to milk her two dairy cows and prepare her children for school. She warms some water and later heads to the makeshift milk parlour where the cows gather upon seeing her. She calls the first cow by name and, like a faithful servant, it heads to the parlour where she embarks on milking. She washes the udder with a cloth and the water she had warmed and proceeds to wipe off the excess water using her hands. She applies milking salve and starts milking. She repeats this with the other cow and thereafter, releases both to graze in the expansive pasture.

She sets part of the milk aside for breakfast while the rest is put in a yellow plastic 3-litre container ready to be transported to the milk collection centre which is less than half an hour's walk from her homestead. The dairy cooperative she belongs to has organized farmers around her area into dairy management groups, each with a maximum of 15 members. Each group constitutes a collection centre where farmers leave their milk awaiting transportation to a cooling plant about 10km away and onward to the processors in the big city. The transporters fill the milk from the collection centres into 50-litre aluminium containers. It takes two to three hours before they collect all the milk from the different collection centres and transport it to the cooling plant (Figures 66 and 67).

Various tests are carried out on the raw milk to check for adulteration or contamination before it is accepted. Some of the bulked milk is rejected and the farmers concerned will have to bear the losses. Unfortunately for Sharon, her milk was in one of the containers that were rejected. She will have to either painfully pour the rejected milk away or take it back home. It is particularly bitter for her that she does not get an explanation of whose fault it was that the milk went bad. She walks off wondering whether tomorrow will be a better day.

FIGURE 66 Milk delivered to the collection centre for bulking and transport to the cooling plant.

Source: Kevin Kabui

Key messages

- Men and women dominate or are excluded from different segments of the food value chain, and this varies by culture and geography.
- As a result, women and men get different benefits from informal food markets and are exposed to different risks.
- In addition to socio-cultural roles affecting health, men, women, the old, the young and other groups may have different vulnerabilities to different diseases.
- Informal food production, processing and marketing are of high importance to women's livelihoods and offer new opportunities.
- As agri-food chains change and evolve, the opportunities and risks also change.

FIGURE 67 Bulked milk being offloaded at the cooling plant.

Source: Kevin Kabui

Women and men in informal markets

Almost two-thirds of the world's 925 million poor livestock keepers are rural women, and women often predominate in urban agriculture, which fits well with their traditional care-taking and house-holding roles. Women often have greater involvement in keeping poultry and small ruminants and men in larger animals; dairying is an interesting exception where the roles of women and men vary dramatically between cultures.

Animal slaughter is also often differentiated by gender with women being responsible for killing poultry typically inside the home, but most slaughter of larger animals outside the home being done by men. Small-scale processing of animal products to make traditional products is frequently a woman's task while more modern, industrialized operations (such as dairy cooperatives) are often dominated by men, at least in managerial and ownership roles.

In Africa, the majority of perishable food, such as livestock and fish products and fresh vegetables, is sold in small-scale, traditional markets which may be called 'informal' or 'wet' markets. They are typically covered or open markets run by local or municipal authorities, which consist of tens to hundreds of small kiosks, tables or spaces on the floor where food and other products are sold. These markets often lack refrigeration, electricity, running water and proper waste disposal. In most cultures, both women and men can sell and buy in these markets but there are often gender differences depending on the products and place. They succeed in serving a broad range of customers with lower prices and at quality that is often equal to and sometimes superior to that of supermarkets.

Street food, whether sold by itinerant vendors or from pavement establishments, is another important part of the informal food sector. It is a source of inexpensive, convenient and nutritious food and is especially important for the poor who lack resources to prepare meals at home. In Ghana, for example, a study found that among the poorest quintile almost 40% of the total food budget goes to purchasing street food compared to just 2% in high-income households. Animal-source foods are among the most commonly sold street foods in most countries and often are derived from animals kept in cities. In most African countries, the majority of street food processors and vendors are women, while the majority of customers are men. As well as being one of the few livelihood strategies open to poor women, the street food sector is of great importance to the economy. In South Africa, it is probably the single largest informal sector employer, in Harare around 9000 people are involved in street food vending (of whom 81% are women) and in Ghana the street food sector employs more than 60,000 people and has an estimated annual turnover of more than US$100 million.

Almost everywhere in Africa, women are responsible for preparing and cooking food for consumption. This often includes acquiring the fuel needed for cooking, often wood, charcoal or animal dung. Pollution resulting from cooking over open fires or basic stoves has been linked to the deaths of 4 million people annually; women and children are most at risk.

Why does food safety research need a gender perspective?

Women have an important role in producing, processing, selling and preparing food. These roles may have negative and positive impacts on their health and may also lead to differences in health outcomes for men and women. While some of this difference is attributable to biology (for example, women are more prone to auto-immune diseases and pregnancy brings many risks to health), differences in health and nutrition states are also attributable to gender. In some cases, men or boys may experience worse health outcomes.

Gender refers to the socially constructed roles, behaviour, activities and attributes that determine the power relations between men and women. It is a central organizing principle of societies and often determines the processes of production and reproduction, consumption and distribution. Gender analyses take a close look at women's relationships with men and how these relations define women's roles, rights (access to and control of resources), division of labour, interests and needs. This analysis can help explain social determinants for undesirable health outcomes and hence help find ways to better prevent them.

Some of the questions which gender analysis can help answer are:

- How do the differing roles of women and men affect their exposure to hazards?
- How does the biology of women and men, young and old, healthy and sick affect their vulnerability to different diseases?
- As food systems undergo change and evolution, how might this advantage or disadvantage different women and men?
- How do women and men differ in their capacity to manage risk and how can we best enhance risk management?

The next sections set out some of the findings from our case studies especially relevant to gender considerations around food in informal markets.

Different roles for women and men

In our studies, we found that milk production in West Africa was often dominated by men. For example, in Ghana, men own the cattle and are responsible for milking, feeding and care; women and girls may assist with cleaning, collecting water and feeds. However, the women were responsible for the boiling and fermentation of the milk as well as its sale. This is true even for Muslim groups, where women's roles are often more confined.

Similarly, in Mali, local milk production is in the hands of the men, except for milk from small ruminants (Figure 68). Often, Fulani herders – who are considered the 'true cattle keepers' – are hired to take care of the animals at dairy farms of other ethnic groups. The milking of the cows is done by either the male Fulani herders or the male children in the family. The man as the head of the family hardly ever does the milking himself, and the women must not do it at all. However, the very moment the milk pours into the calabashes, it belongs to the women who take it to the market or prepare it for home consumption.

In one of the areas we studied in Kenya, informal urban smallholder dairy production is dominated by women; they actually hire men for labour. It is also the women who decide how and where to market their animals and how the money will be used. They may share the profits with men but do not have to. This pattern changes in the more commercialized urban dairy units. Moreover, in the rural areas, and depending on the ethnic group, men have more power in dairy cattle production and decision-making. Even in these communities, women usually have an important role in feeding, watering, milking and disposing of the milk. This is not the case for the butcher trade which is dominated by men. The Safe Food, Fair Food project surveys on beef safety in peri-urban Kenya (Chapters 21 and 22) found only two female butchers; all of the other value chain actors were men.

FIGURE 68 A woman milks a goat in central Mali.

Source: Valentin Bognan Koné

Different roles imply different benefits and risks

These different roles of men and women naturally lead to different benefits and risks. In West Africa, men are more at risk from occupational zoonoses associated with direct contact with cattle during milking, while in Kenya farms where women are milking the situation is reversed.

It was found in Mali that cows are only slaughtered and eaten when diseased or when they die of exhaustion. In such cases, the men who slaughter the cows may be exposed to occupational diseases such as brucellosis or anthrax. However, since the meat is subsequently thoroughly cooked, the risk to consumers – who are both men and women – is low. During traditional ceremonies, the meat is grilled by men who do not wash their hands prior to food preparation as they assume hazardous bacteria will be killed when the meat is roasted. The rest of the edible carcass is then cooked by the women of the community and shared among everyone during the feast.

Gender segregation, and hence segregation of risks and benefits, was also seen with artisanal coastal fishing in West Africa. Men are responsible for the fishing but women are in charge of the on-shore processing (smoking) and marketing. In our survey in Côte d'Ivoire, the smoking process was found to be a high-risk practice for the women who are exposed to carcinogens such as PAHs (Chapter 33). Almost 90% of the 423 respondents of the survey were women, 59% of them with no secondary education. Smoking and selling fish is an important source of livelihood and one that women dominate. Most of them considered the revenues from their business as satisfactory but complained about symptoms related to the smoking process (headaches and eyestrain). Fish is consumed by men and women alike, so nutritional benefits can be considered similar.

In our study in Ghana (Chapter 32), women also had the main role in drying and selling fish. In addition, more than 60% of the fish consumers were women. However, this study did not find higher risks because the food-borne hazards identified were eliminated by cooking. So in this case, women capture benefits from processing, sale and nutrition without having to bear much extra risk.

In some cases, consumption patterns also varied by gender or other social grouping. A related study in Nigeria, for example, found that women were more likely to eat offal and men to eat muscle meat (flesh). This has also been reported in Somalia. Offal can be more contaminated than flesh, especially in the case of intestines. However, some offal such as liver can be even more nutritious than flesh.

Are women at extra risk?

In some cases, women may bear more of the risk because of greater vulnerability to pathogens. The study in Ghana was actually motivated when the lead researcher put two interesting findings together: first, the discovery for the first time of an important zoonotic disease in sheep in Ghana which he knew could cause abortion in women and, second, a worryingly high rate of abortion among women in some parts of Ghana. This zoonotic disease, listeriosis, caused by the bacterium *Listeria monocytogenes*, is considered to be one of the most important causes of food-borne illness in Europe.

Our study found that milk consumption levels were similar between men and women in Ghana; in fact, women made up a slight majority of consumers (55%). Unfortunately, the survey also found that there was a risk that milk could be contaminated by bacteria at the point of consumption. This was largely driven by the practice of drinking milk that had not been boiled or pasteurized. However, although women had the same level of exposure to the bacteria as men did, their health risk could be much higher. This is because many pathogens, especially *Listeria monocytogenes* or *Brucella abortus*, present more risk to pregnant women and their unborn babies. In case of an outbreak of listeriosis, 20–30% of people falling sick are likely to die.

Mortality in babies, pregnant women, elderly people and immune-compromised is estimated to be as high as 80–99%. Sadly, almost half of the interrogated women in our survey in Ghana (Chapter 16) had experienced spontaneous abortions, about one-third of them more than once. Almost 86% had experienced at least one case of stillbirth. Most of these lost the baby during the third trimester of the pregnancy. In food safety, we often talk about YOPIs – that is, the young, the old, the pregnant and the immune-suppressed – as being at most risk, as these are the groups that are most likely to have serious illness from food-borne disease.

Will modernization force women out of traditional processing or cause other less visible problems?

There is often concern that supporting newer, larger and more industrial agri-food enterprises can actually be detrimental to women, because openings in these industries are more easily filled by men. One way of preventing this is to ensure that development interventions are targeted at women or at least help them to participate.

In one study in West Africa, we found that new dairy cooperatives that were intended to benefit women processors succeeded at this. However, the higher standards these cooperatives introduced had some unanticipated effects on health risks.

In Mali, the women who traditionally process the milk are mostly married to the dairy farmers. They are in charge of the storage, processing and sales of raw, fresh and sour milk to customers in the villages. When the small dairy farm PAFLACIN was set up in Cinzana, Mali (Box 20), the traditional marketing channels started changing. Many of the women who formerly processed the milk were trained by PAFLACIN and began working for the cooperative that supplied the dairy plant. They collect the milk from producers and pasteurize it before delivering it to the dairy where it is eventually sold. While milk for sale is normally pasteurized, raw milk is still consumed at home (Chapter 20). The cooperative buys the milk from the women if it complies with certain quality standards like freshness and freedom from adulteration with water. Milk that does not meet the quality standards is rejected and is mostly processed into *féné* for home consumption; this may pose a health risk to the women and their families.

In Abidjan, milk production and marketing in the local dairy sector is dominated by men because the milk producers are largely immigrants who are not married. Africa is urbanizing rapidly, but in many places young men predominate among the new migrants to cities. This can mean that women are inadvertently displaced from their traditional occupations.

It is not only women who are at risk from changing food markets. Previously, in West Africa, hired herders were paid in kind with milk for their work, but today they are often paid in cash. This is because nowadays, women in Mali and Mauritania have better access to markets and can generate cash from selling the milk: money which can then be used to cover for expenses other than labour, such as food items. However, the herder stands to lose an important nutritional benefit. Not only the herder; one of the popular foods purchased with the 'milk money' is milk powder which is later reconstituted and fed to the children.

Where women find new opportunities in informal markets

Other studies show that informal marketing can open new opportunities for women. In Mozambique, contrary to most of the other countries in sub-Saharan Africa, there are a number of women involved in cattle trade as agents and intermediaries, the goat value chain is dominated by men and the informal poultry chain (as is usual) is dominated by women. Other projects in Kenya have found that women's pastoralist groups can successfully manage the traditionally male-dominated trade of transporting and marketing goats.

The fact that a few women are found in traditionally male occupations such as butchering suggests there may be openings for greater participation of women in some value chain activities. In many cases, the formal sector may also discriminate against either men or women. For example, in Mozambique, as in many African countries, it is only men who are employed in the formal poultry slaughter-houses, whereas in many developed countries the majority of poultry slaughter-house employees are women. This suggests there are also opportunities for improving the efficiencies of the informal sector by expanding the employment base. In other cases, for example slaughter of cattle, participation of women is limited by the lack of labour-saving equipment as well as the challenging work environment.

Findings from our studies in South Africa show that the majority of informal vendors involved in the sale of ready-to-eat chicken and chicken by-products in Tshwane, Pretoria are women between 25 and 50 years old (Chapter 26). The majority of the informal outlets are run as private business and only very few young people and males are involved in the trade. The majority of the women have completed secondary education; some of them even tertiary. These women traders run their businesses in the streets rather than inside open market areas provided by the municipalities for a daily fee in order to exploit areas with numerous clients such as bus terminals, taxi ranks and industrial sites which are sometimes violent working environments (Chapter 26). The vendors work for about 10–12 (sometimes up to 15) hours a day without taking a break, sometimes starting as early as three in the morning when commuters leave for work. But because it is their own business, they are able to capture many of the benefits of their hard work. Moreover, the products they sell are nutritious, attractive to their target audience and largely safe.

Several of the studies considered possible interventions that would increase the ability of women and men to manage risks. For example, in the case of smoking fish in Abidjan, the use of certain types of wood reduces risk. Many of the risks around exposure to milk-borne pathogens are also linked to lack of knowledge and skills on safe processing.

Conclusions

Given the important role of women in informal markets and the wide variation between men's and women's roles, risks and opportunities, it is clear that taking into account gender is important for understanding and improving informal food markets.

Examples from the Safe Food, Fair Food project studies help show how gender awareness can ensure:

- Men's and women's differential exposure to agriculture-related risks are better understood, particularly as it relates to health outcomes.
- Women have increased capacity to manage risks and are more involved in the surveillance of risks.
- Women directly benefit from interventions designed to reduce agriculture-associated diseases, taking into account roles and responsibilities that may put them at increased risk of exposure.

PART 2

Twenty-five proof-of-concept studies from sub-Saharan Africa

10

INADEQUATE ACCESS TO SAFE WATER FOR LIVESTOCK AND PEOPLE IN RURAL ETHIOPIA

Kebede Amenu, Kristina Roesel, André Markemann, Regina Roessler, Marianna Siegmund-Schultze, Anne Valle Zárate and Delia Grace

Key messages

- Clean water is essential for the production of clean and safe food.
- In the study area, farmers and their livestock have inadequate access to safe water, posing a potential health risk to both.
- The health impact of water-related diseases in people was found to be higher in Siraro District than in Lume District, which may reflect less water availability in Siraro.
- Water scarcity was ranked as the first and second major constraint to livestock production in Siraro and Lume districts, respectively.
- Water samples from rivers, dugouts, cisterns, springs and hand-dug wells were found to be highly contaminated with *Escherichia coli*, indicating poor water quality.
- Water from boreholes was found to be free from *E. coli* but the fluoride content was beyond the maximum limits for drinking water, indicating potential risk to health.

Background

Water is an important resource for the well-being of an ever-growing population, for a wide range of uses in agricultural, industrial and domestic activities (drinking, sanitation, cooking, etc.). Worldwide, the increasing deterioration of the quality and safety of water associated with declining resources, mismanagement and environmental pollution is becoming a challenge for development. These problems are even more pronounced in developing countries where technical, socio-economic and political commitments in the utilization of natural resources such as water do not exist.

Clean water is essential for the production of clean and safe livestock products. Livestock require water for drinking and large amounts of water are used for cleaning animals and their environment, as well as for abattoir operations. Water is also required for cleaning and sometimes as an input in the transport, processing, retailing, storing and cooking of livestock products. Shortage of water is one of the major problems faced by livestock keepers in tropical areas such as Ethiopia and there is an intricate interrelationship between livestock and people often sharing the same water sources. In this respect, the objective of this study was to assess the sources, quality and accessibility of water for livestock and people as perceived by farmers.

Quantity versus quality

The study was carried out in two districts in the Ethiopian Rift Valley region – Siraro and Lume – representing different challenges related to the quality and quantity of water in Ethiopia. The production systems of both districts are characterized by mixed crop-livestock farming. Lume is located about 70km south of Addis Ababa in the midlands and has a sub-humid climate. Reportedly, seasonal feed and water shortages are the second most important constraints to livestock production in the area.[1] Although there is relatively more water available in Lume District than in Siraro, it is believed to be highly polluted with effluent from industrial activities such as tanneries and abattoirs. The Siraro District is located about 308km south of Addis Ababa and is characterized by flat topography and frequent droughts resulting in chronic water shortage for both humans and animals. This is an area especially vulnerable to climate change.

A total of 320 households in four villages of each district were randomly selected to participate in a household survey. Prior to the interviews with the households, the objectives of the survey were explained and consent was sought. The interviews followed a structured questionnaire which had been translated into Oromo, a commonly spoken language in the study area. The result of the questionnaire survey was supplemented by farmers' group discussions and key-informant interviews.

The interviews and discussions aimed at finding out how farmers perceived access to clean water, where they sourced it, whether availability was a seasonal challenge and how they used the existing resources. The farmers talked about historical events related to water problems and how these problems were tackled in the past. Likewise of interest were livestock management practices in terms of feeding, housing and breeding. Assessment of the level of knowledge and the attitude of farmers about water diseases was another important aspect of the study. Consumption and handling practices were described and various questions on environmental hygiene discussed.

Water scarcity was ranked as the first and second major constraints to livestock management in Siraro and Lume districts, respectively. A word of caution here: in discussions with farmers, they often place greater emphasis on issues they know the research team is interested in. Other studies on animal disease in Ethiopia show that farmers consider livestock disease to be the major constraint! Based on the preliminary findings, the farmers and their livestock have insufficient access to safe water; the majority of households in Lume (60%) and Siraro (97%) reported that water was scarce for livestock and people with a peak during the dry season from December to March. Based on this survey, only 31% and 2% of the households in Lume and Siraro districts, respectively, had access to improved water sources (household piped connections, public standpipes, boreholes, protected dug wells, protected springs or protected roof rainwater collection) within a 30-minute round trip from their homesteads.

People and livestock in Lume used various alternative water sources (for example, rivers, lakes, hand-dug wells, standpipe boreholes, springs and dugouts), whereas in Siraro District, the Bilate River was the only permanent source of surface water. The river marks the extreme southwestern border of the district and is very inaccessible for most communities (about 25km straight-line map distance). Here, motorized boreholes constituted the common improved water sources in all seasons. Due to high competition for the boreholes, dugouts and cisterns were used during the rainy season.

One-year outpatient case records were obtained from the health offices of the respective districts to assess the occurrence and health impacts of water-related diseases in humans from June 2009 to June 2010. Malaria, internal parasites and diarrhoea were the most commonly reported infections. Additionally, 4.4% of the respondents in Lume and 14.4% in Siraro reported having suffered from diarrhoea in the six months preceding the household interviews in July 2010.

Water-related livestock illness or death was reported by 12.5% and 16.9% of the respondents in Lume and Siraro, respectively, during 12 months preceding the survey. The supposed reasons for livestock illness or death included drinking polluted river water (a common complaint in the surveyed villages located downstream of Mojo River, Lume), drinking stagnant water, sudden access to water after long deprivation and infection with liver flukes after grazing in water-logged areas. It is not clear how these perceptions of water-related illness reflect actual causality.

Samples of drinking water for people were collected from the source and at the point of consumption. People in the study sites obtained their drinking water from rivers, wells and pipes and stored them in containers. However, at the time this chapter was written, the results of the physical, chemical and bacteriological analysis of the water samples were not yet available. Preliminary results, however, showed that water samples from rivers, dugouts, springs and hand-dug wells were highly contaminated with *E. coli* indicating faecal contamination. Water from boreholes was found to be free from *E. coli* but the fluoride content was above the maximum limit for drinking. In small quantities, fluoride is essential for healthy teeth and bone development. However, long-term exposure to high levels of fluoride in drinking water can lead to dental fluorosis (mottled teeth). In children and adults alike, high amounts of fluoride cause skeletal fluorosis. This chronic disease is characterized by less flexible, stiff bones and joints and may even affect the spine.

Recommendations

Better management of surface water through fencing of dugouts or provision of watering troughs for livestock can minimize contamination with livestock faeces. Existing indigenous methods of rainwater harvesting such as dugouts and cisterns, to mitigate water scarcity, should be promoted. Industrial pollution of Mojo River, which is the main source of water for livestock in Lume District, must be tackled by involving the various stakeholders, especially the owners of the abattoirs and tanneries that are reported to discharge their effluent into the river.

Kebede Amenu holds an undergraduate degree in veterinary medicine and a Master of Science in tropical animal health. From 2002 to 2009, he worked as a lecturer at Hawassa University. In June 2009, he started his PhD and completed it in February 2013.

Title and authors of the study

Assessment of water sources and quality for livestock and farmers in the Rift Valley area of Ethiopia: Implications for health and food safety.

Kebede Amenu,[1,2] *André Markemann,*[2] *Regina Roessler,*[2] *Marianna Siegmund-Schultze*[2] and *Anne Valle Zárate*[2]

[1]Hawassa University, Ethiopia; [2]University of Hohenheim, Germany

Contact details

Kebede Amenu
Institute of Animal Production in the Tropics and Subtropics (480a)
University of Hohenheim, Garbenstrasse 17, 70599 Stuttgart, Germany
Email: kamenu@gmail.com

Note

1. www.tropentag.de/2011/abstracts/links/Amenu_YklHSjnk.pdf (accessed 9 July 2014).

11

LOW QUALITY OF WATER AND MILK IN RURAL ETHIOPIA POSES RISKS TO HUMAN HEALTH

Marisa Spengler, Kristina Roesel, Kebede Amenu, Anne Valle Zárate, André Markemann and Delia Grace

Key messages

- Most of the water and milk in Lume and Siraro districts in Ethiopia is not suitable for direct consumption and poses risks to human health.
- Only about 5% of sampled water sources were safe for consumption.
- Bacterial contamination of water varied with the region (lower in Lume than in Siraro).
- Industrial effluent was highly contaminated and released directly into rivers.
- Processed milk products showed no reduction of the bacterial load.
- Milk spoilage was mainly due to contamination with bacteria, some of which caused disease.

Background

Water is vital for every living creature on earth. Humans and water are intricately related and people rely on water for both consumptive and productive reasons. Water contaminated by microbes or chemicals can adversely affect human health. WHO frequently issues guidelines for drinking-water quality.[1] However, water of acceptable standards is often not accessible in rural areas of developing countries such as Ethiopia. This implies that farmers might be obliged to use poor-quality water for drinking as well as for various livestock operations. Water used in milk production and processing should comply with quality standards equivalent to those for drinking water.

The quality of water and milk is not necessarily monitored, especially in rural parts of developing countries such as Ethiopia. It is not clear to what extent water and milk are contaminated and where contamination occurs. Therefore, this study was carried out to assess the quality of water (at source and point of consumption), raw milk and fermented milk products in Lume and Siraro districts in rural Ethiopia. The study took place between July and August 2011.

From stable to table: contamination of water and milk along the path

Lume and Siraro districts in Ethiopia represent two characteristic situations in developing countries with regard to the challenges of availability of water of adequate quantity and quality for domestic and livestock uses. In Lume, surface water is relatively more accessible than in Siraro where chronic shortages of water prevail. However, the water in Lume is exposed to pollution from industrial effluent from tanneries and abattoirs. Both water scarcity and pollution pose risks to human and animal health.

Mixed crop and livestock farming is predominant in both districts. Farmers in Lume mainly grow teff (*Eragrostis tef*), wheat, maize and barley, and keep poultry, cattle, goats, sheep, donkeys, mules, horses and bees. Siraro District is about the same size as Lume (600 square kilometres) and is home to about 168,000 people, as well as a considerable number of domestic animals similar to those kept by farmers in Lume. Farmers in Siraro grow mainly maize, haricot beans and potatoes. Additionally, raw milk and traditional dairy products are consumed in many of the homes of the estimated 300,000 people living in the two districts.

Most of the milk is consumed at home (by 67% of households in Lume and 91% in Siraro), either raw or processed into sour milk (*ergo*), cottage cheese (*ayib*), skim milk or yoghurt. Results of the questionnaire survey indicated that approximately only 39% and 5% of respondents in Lume and Siraro, respectively, boiled milk prior to consumption.[2] The raw milk was stored in containers smoked with branches from the African olive tree (*Olea europaea* ssp. *cuspidata*), locally referred to as *ejersa* in the Oromo language. The smoke is said to enhance the taste of the fermented product and is also thought to have antimicrobial properties.

For production of *ergo*, the raw milk is placed in a gourd and stored in a warm place to induce natural fermentation. After approximately 24 hours, the product is similar to sour milk. When *ergo* is further processed by churning, the fat is removed and the residue (buttermilk) is heated to 40–50°C until the curd and whey separate. The cheese generated from this process is called *ayib*. If there is any surplus of milk, it is mainly marketed through informal channels by either giving it to servants as wages in kind or selling it to neighbours or hotels (32% in Lume and 7% in Siraro). Only about 2% of milk in both districts was channelled to milk collection centres for further processing or sales.

Water samples were taken from the commonly used sources in Lume and Siraro, namely rivers, dugouts, cisterns, rainwater from roofs, hand-dug wells and public borehole pumps. The samples were analysed following the WHO guideline protocol to determine physical and chemical parameters, as well as the bacterial counts of *E. coli* and total coliforms which are indicators of faecal contamination. *E. coli* in particular is internationally accepted as a key indicator of faecal contamination and the WHO guidelines for drinking water quality indicate that *E. coli* should be absent.

The results showed that only about 5% of the sampled water sources could be regarded as safe for human consumption. *E. coli*, if present in water, would be more likely found in surface water than ground water. In this study, the organism was isolated from a sample of borehole water in Siraro. This could be a sign of very poor sanitation facilities resulting in excreta reaching the groundwater or defects in the pipe system of the pump.

While water from borehole pumps in Lume was the least contaminated of the sampled water sources, rivers in the district were found to be highly polluted with industrial discharge and untreated sewage. Results of the chemical analysis showed that manganese concentrations exceeded WHO threshold levels by about 30% in water from hand-dug wells in Lume and dugouts in Siraro. Water sampled from boreholes in Siraro exceeded these cut-off points by 60%. Long-term exposure to high levels of manganese can lead to neurological disorders. The levels of chromium, which is toxic and carcinogenic, were also high and fluoride levels exceeded the WHO threshold by 20% for water from hand-dug wells in Lume and by 100% for borehole water in Siraro. This observation has been further investigated as part of a separate study (Chapter 10). In general, the analysis shows that water in commonly used sources was more contaminated in Siraro District than in Lume District.

Raw milk samples for microbiological analysis were taken from storage containers in homes and at the milk collection centre and from containers used to transport milk to the collection centre. The analysis revealed that all samples had high levels of *E. coli*, total coliforms and total aerobic plate counts. *E. coli* was detected in the milk obtained from the udder, indicating an infection of the cow's udder. The rate of contamination increased slightly along the production chain, probably due to poor handling and storage, but the findings suggest that the problem of poor hygiene starts at farm level.

Similarly, samples of traditional sour milk (*ergo*), locally produced soft cheese (*ayib*), yoghurt and skim milk were analysed for microbial quality. *Ergo*, *ayib* and skim milk had consistently high levels of *E. coli* and total coliforms as well as several spoilage bacteria. Some of the samples were contaminated with pathogenic species such as *Staphylococcus*, *Streptococcus*, *Escherichia* and *Salmonella*.

Several practices were observed during and after milking that could account for the high counts of bacteria in the raw milk samples. Before milking, the farmers cleaned the udders of the cows with dry hands or with water that was not of potable quality. Furthermore, the first squirts of milk that contain the highest levels of bacteria were not discarded. After milking, the teats were not dipped in antiseptic to prevent udder infection and the farmers only cleaned their hands with cold water from the same contaminated water source. None of the farmers in the study sites cooled the raw milk.

Recommendations

There is a need for provision of improved water sources by the government, training in hygienic handling of water and milk, and monitoring of milk quality at collection centres. Further research should focus on the correlation between the quality of water and milk and prevalence of human illness.

Marisa Spengler was awarded her Bachelor's degree in agricultural biology from the University of Hohenheim, Germany in 2012.

Title and authors of the study

Assessment of water and milk quality in rural mixed crop-livestock farming systems: A case study of Lume and Siraro districts, Ethiopia.

Marisa Spengler,[1] *Kebede Amenu,*[1,2] *Anne Valle Zárate*[1] and *André Markemann*[1]

[1]University of Hohenheim, Germany; [2]Hawassa University, Ethiopia

Contact details

Marisa Spengler
Institute of Animal Production in the Tropics and Subtropics (480a)
University of Hohenheim, Garbenstrasse 17, 70599 Stuttgart, Germany

Notes

1. WHO. 2011. www.who.int/water_sanitation_health/publications/2011/dwq_guidelines/en/index.html (accessed 9 July 2014).
2. Amenu K. 2013. Assessment of water sources and quality for livestock and farmers in the Rift Valley area of Ethiopia: implications for health and food safety. PhD thesis. University of Hohenheim, Stuttgart-Hohenheim, Germany.

12

IS ETHIOPIAN RAW MILK SAFE FOR HUMAN CONSUMPTION?

Fanta Desissa, Kristina Roesel, Kohei Makita, Akafte Teklu, Girma Zewde and Delia Grace

Key messages

- Sale and consumption of raw milk are common in Debre Zeit, Ethiopia.
- *Staphylococcus aureus* was present in milk at increasing levels from farm to milk collection centres.
- Traditional processing of milk into local yoghurt and cheese plays a role in reducing the risk of staphylococcal food poisoning and protecting public health.

Background

Milk is a very good source of energy, protein, calcium and Vitamin C, especially for infants and children. Despite all the beneficial effects, milk can be a source of disease; the consumption of raw milk is particularly risky but still popular amongst numerous people in sub-Saharan Africa (Chapter 20). According to a report by UNICEF/WHO,[1] Ethiopia has the world's fifth highest number of annual child deaths due to diarrhoea. However, the cause remains mostly unknown.

Staphylococcus aureus is a major cause of food-borne intoxications and outbreaks throughout the world because it is widespread and able to persist and grow under various conditions (Chapter 13). Staphylococcal food poisoning is one of the most common food-borne diseases in the world; it is caused by ingestion of a toxin that is produced by certain strains of the bacterium in food. The toxin resists heating to 100°C for at least 30 minutes, rendering it indestructible by pasteurization. Nausea, vomiting, diarrhoea, sweating and abdominal cramps are symptoms of staphylococcal food poisoning. The symptoms last for one to three days, the severity usually depending on the amount of contaminated food eaten and the levels of toxin ingested as well as the general health of the patient.

Raw milk has been reported to be a known vehicle for disease-causing microorganisms for more than 100 years and disease outbreaks associated with the consumption of raw milk occur frequently. In Ethiopia, the consumption and informal marketing of raw milk are very common. As a result, the possibility of occurrence of staphylococcal food poisoning is highly likely. However, there is a lack of data on the occurrence and magnitude of *S. aureus* in cow milk at different points of the dairy value chain in the country.

Are there implications for public health?

A risk in the context of food safety is the combination of probability and consequences of adverse health effects following the ingestion of food that harbours foreign agents (see Chapter 4). The separation of risk into two components is useful since it may be managed by actions to reduce both the probability of food intake high enough to cause disease and the consequences for public health and the economy. Whether or not there are public health implications associated with *S. aureus* in raw milk in Ethiopia depends on whether the microorganism and its toxin are present in the milk in the first place. The frequency of consumption of the milk and the quantity of microorganism and toxin ingested needs to be evaluated, as well as the factors that might reduce or increase the risk of ingestion by the end consumer. This assessment would help the authorities to manage the problem as they would know what risk factors to address. They would also be able to communicate the risk to the public in a way that would not cause panic among consumers but would provide alternatives for maintaining health.

The dairy industry in Ethiopia is growing steadily and a shift towards a market economy is creating opportunities for private investments in urban and peri-urban dairying. Smallholder farmers also have the opportunity to benefit from the growing demand for dairy products through income and employment generation, resulting in poverty alleviation in the rural areas.

Debre Zeit is located about 45km south of Ethiopia's capital city, Addis Ababa. The local Ada'a-Liben District Dairy and the Dairy Product Producer and Marketing Cooperative Society procure 24,000 litres of milk daily. The study found that 80% of the milk is supplied by urban farmers and the rest by peri-urban farmers. More than half of this milk is delivered to local milk collection centres, with a 10-fold higher share from urban farmers. From the collection centres, the milk is sold to processing plants in Debre Zeit and Addis Ababa and thus enters the formal market. The remaining milk is used for home consumption or sold to neighbours and milk bars. At milk bars, it is boiled and served to customers or used for traditional processing of yoghurt.

During the survey, more than 200 milk samples were obtained from farms and milk collection centres to test for the presence of *S. aureus*. The results indicated a very high prevalence of the organism along the dairy chain, with increasing levels from farms (44%) to milk collection centres (72%) where raw and contaminated milk was sold to consumers. Moreover, one-third of consumers drank raw and home-made fermented milk. Milk in peri-urban areas was found to be more contaminated than that sampled in urban areas, supposedly due to cross-contamination with unhealthy herds and poor handling practices during transportation.

About one-third of the 170 people interviewed drank half a litre of raw milk daily. Referring to the contamination rates shown in the present study, about 0.7% of the milk that is produced in Debre Zeit per day is likely to contain *S. aureus* and thus 333 out of the 95,000 people in Debre Zeit could fall ill from staphylococcal food poisoning every day.

How did *Staphylococcus aureus* enter the milk?

Interviews with key informants along the marketing chain made it possible to identify numerous points where the milk might have become contaminated with the bacteria. Dairy cattle were probably the main source of contamination of raw milk with *S. aureus*, as cows with asymptomatic udder inflammation may shed large numbers of the organism into the milk. Out of 24 respondents, 22 (92%) said their cows had recently experienced inflammation of the udder. Contamination from human handling is also possible as about 25% of the world population carries one or two strains of *S. aureus* on their skin and hair or in the nose and throat.

Milking was done by hand early in the morning and in the evening, after which the raw milk was stored outside the house awaiting delivery to the collection centres. The milk was stored at a mean temperature of 20°C for about three hours in either metallic (70.6%) or plastic (29.4%) buckets. Because *S. aureus* doubles every 15–30 minutes, one cell can multiply into more than 2 million within seven hours, which is enough time to allow for the production of sufficient amounts of toxin to cause disease. There is normally a 12-hour time lag between milking and pasteurization at the processing plant.

At the collection centres, the milk is checked for adulteration with water and contamination with hair, hay or faeces, after which it is collected in metal cans cleaned with soap and piped water. Only milk from cooperative members is purchased and pooled into a 50-litre container. The cooperative sells about 10% of the milk to the local community, local hotels and restaurants and the remainder is procured by the cooperative's processing plant and eventually sold to wholesalers that supply milk to various outlets in Addis Ababa.

Boiling of milk is a common practice in hotels and restaurants as the owners are familiar with the risk of food poisoning associated with consuming raw milk. However, they had no information or awareness of the possibility of *S. aureus* being introduced to milk by unhygienic handling. Regular training or health check-ups were not reported.

The common practice of storing milk at room temperature and transporting it in plastic containers, coupled with a lack of knowledge on the public health risks associated with consumption of raw milk and unhygienic milk handling, increases the risk of staphylococcal food poisoning in urban and peri-urban Debre Zeit.

However, quantifying the likelihood of the risk would require an assessment of the prevalence of *S. aureus* in milk and the level of toxin produced. Unfortunately, this was not done due to resource constraints and represents a substantial knowledge gap requiring further investigation.

Traditional milk fermentation protects public health

Despite these alarming results, previous studies show that traditional fermentation of milk inhibits the growth of disease-causing microorganisms, including *Staphylococcus*, due to the action of lactic acid produced during fermentation. The present study found that about one-third of the sampled population, 95% in peri-urban areas and 13% in urban areas, did not boil milk before drinking it. However, 82% of them stored the milk at room temperature for at least one day.

The fermentation of raw milk into traditional sour milk (*ergo*) and cottage cheese (*ayib*) was popular in many homes. Production of *ergo* involves leaving raw milk in a clay pot for three to five days at room temperature during which time spontaneous fermentation takes place through the action of the naturally occurring milk microflora. *Ergo* may also be used as a raw material in the production of *ayib*, whereby the fermented milk is regularly stirred, and with increasing acidity, the fat is skimmed off and used as butter while the residue curd is made into cheese.

Stochastic modelling showed that traditional fermentation reduces the risk of staphylococcal food poisoning more than 15 times compared to the risk in raw milk. The risk of staphylococcal food poisoning is only 19.7 per 1000 people per year. Further analysis showed that initial bacteria counts and temperature affect risk the most. This means basic training on hygienic milk handling can significantly improve public health through reduced risk of staphylococcal food poisoning. However, there are other bacteria in raw milk likely to cause disease (Chapter 19), thus further investigation is required into how long milk needs to be fermented to render it safe from disease.

Recommendations

Traditional risk mitigation strategies should be promoted, as well as training on hygienic handling and storage of milk at all levels of production and marketing. There is a need to increase awareness of producers and consumers on the importance of boiling milk before drinking it. Quality assurance along the value chain should be institutionalized and enforced at collection centres prior to pooling the milk. Raw milk should be particularly monitored by public health inspectors and further research should be carried out on quantifying the levels of toxin production in milk by *S. aureus*.

Fanta Desissa was awarded his Master of Science degree in tropical public health from Addis Ababa University in 2010. He holds a veterinary degree and works as a lecturer in veterinary medicine at Wollega University, Nekemte, Ethiopia.

Title and authors of the study

Quantitative risk assessment of consuming milk contaminated with *Staphylococcus aureus* in Debre Zeit, Ethiopia.

Fanta Desissa,[1] *Kohei Makita*,[2,3] *Akafte Teklu*,[1] *Girma Zewde*[1] and *Delia Grace*[2]

[1]Faculty of Veterinary Medicine, Addis Ababa University, Ethiopia; [2]International Livestock Research Institute, Kenya; [3]Rakuno Gakuen University, Japan

Contact details

Fanta Desissa
D. Wollega University
P.O. Box 395, Nekemte, Ethiopia
Email: fntdesi@yahoo.com

Note

1. UNICEF/WHO. 2009. www.who.int/maternal_child_adolescent/documents/9789241598415/en (accessed 9 July 2014).

13

MILK QUALITY IN PERI-URBAN DAR ES SALAAM: CREAM ON TOP OR TIP OF THE ICEBERG?

Kaiza Kilango, Kristina Roesel, Kohei Makita, Lusato Kurwijila and Delia Grace

Key messages

- The quality of milk in the study area was poor.
- Every third customer at local kiosks bought milk contaminated with *Staphylococcus aureus*.
- Poor quality was due to unhygienic milking and handling practices of farmers and traders.
- Most consumers are well informed on milk-borne diseases.

Background

In Tanzania, about 95% of the produced milk is consumed at home and seasonal surplus is marketed in urban centres through informal marketing agents. In Temeke Municipality, an urban district of Dar es Salaam, milk is sold to neighbours, local restaurants and milk kiosks where unpacked milk is retailed. These shops have mushroomed to meet the growing demand of the growing urban population. At kiosks, the milk is boiled before sale and served hot. Sometimes part of the raw milk is fermented and sold as sour milk.

Previous studies in central Tanzania found that bacterial contamination of milk and dairy products with *Staphylococcus aureus* was common. *S. aureus* occurs frequently as part of the normal microflora on the skin and in the nasal passages of humans and other mammals. However, it can cause pimples, skin infections, abscesses, pneumonia and even blood poisoning. Of particular relevance to the food processing industry is the ability of some strains of *S. aureus* to produce toxins that cause staphylococcal food poisoning, which ranks as one of the most prevalent causes of gastroenteritis worldwide. Within one to six hours after consuming contaminated food, staphylococcal food poisoning can cause diarrhoea, vomiting and cramps. People who are otherwise healthy recover rather quickly, but in susceptible individuals it can be fatal.

Boiling eliminates the bacterium but not its poison

Boiling milk prior to consumption easily kills the bacterium but the toxins it produces are heat-stable and survive the boiling process. Therefore, it is important to avoid the bacteria from multiplying in the milk in the first place. Where does *S. aureus* start growing and producing toxins? There are various possibilities, for example the cow can suffer from an udder infection, which means the milk is contaminated right from the start (Chapter 12). In Tanzania, it is known that *S. aureus* is the chief cause of udder infections in dairy cattle. Raw milk contamination may also arise if the milker's hands are dirty or if the cow's udder is not washed before milking. Bulking of raw milk in unclean containers is another source of contamination with *S. aureus*. In addition, holding milk for long periods without cooling it leads to rapid growth and multiplication of the milk bacteria. In brief: because up to 50% of the population are healthy carriers of *S. aureus*, contamination of milk with the organism could occur anywhere from farm to consumer.

The study was carried out in Temeke Municipality which is one of three districts that form Dar es Salaam, the biggest city in Tanzania. An estimated 1.1 million people live in Temeke along with 5000 beef and 4000 dairy cattle. As data on milk quality in the area were unavailable, the main research questions were: Is milk really contaminated with *S. aureus*? If so, where does the contamination occur? Internationally approved protocols were used to assess microbial contamination, complemented by participatory methods at every step of the dairy chain from farm to consumer. More than 20 milk kiosks were randomly selected and their supplying farmers were traced back and consumers identified.

From farm to kiosk

Facilitated by local extension staff, 29 smallholder farmers who owned at least one cow were visited twice. During the first visit, questionnaires were used to obtain information on the animals, farmers' knowledge of udder infections, the process of milking, the handling of the milk, farmers' knowledge of health risks associated with milk consumption and perceived factors affecting milk quality. All of the cows were milked twice a day, in more than half of the cases by an employee or a member of the farmer's family. Practices were reasonably good, although there was room for improvement. All of the milkers washed the udders before they started milking and around 75% used warm water; fewer used one cloth per cow to dry the udder. Washing the udder with warm water removes dirt and bacteria, while keeping the skin of the udder dry reduces infection. Using one cloth for each cow to dry the udder prevents transfer of bacteria and dirt from one animal to another. In fact, using a shared cloth for several cows may be worse than using no cloth at all. Only 17% of the milkers washed their hands with water and soap; the rest used water only.

Almost 90% of the farmers had encountered udder infections in their animals. However, only 21% used post-milking teat disinfection which is known to be effective in preventing udder inflammation. During the second visit, milk samples were taken directly from the udder of the cows and tested for *S. aureus*. About 25% of the samples tested positive for the presence of *S. aureus* and it can be assumed that this represents the occurrence of udder infections in Temeke Municipality.

Seven vendors (who were also suppliers of participating milk kiosk owners) were identified and interviewed. Intermediary sellers are not common as most farmers sell their milk directly to neighbours or milk shops. More than 25% of the vendors did not use any form of quality control checks before buying milk; most assessed the quality of the milk by simply looking at its viscosity and colour. None of the vendors pooled milk from different farmers because most of them knew that bulking milk could result in low quality and an increased health risk due to cross-contamination. All of the vendors used plastic buckets for handling the milk, a practice that is not recommended as plastic containers are known to be vulnerable to bacterial contamination as they are difficult to sterilize. However, none of the samples of milk from vendors was found positive for *S. aureus*. This is likely due to the small sample size (only seven vendors); hence it is difficult to be sure of the real status of milk sold by vendors.

Health officers in the respective wards facilitated access to randomly selected milk kiosks where fresh unpacked milk is sold. Data were collected by questionnaires and group discussions. We found that 85% of surveyed kiosks obtained their milk directly from farmers and the rest were supplied by vendors. Only half of the milk was chilled upon arrival at the milk shop after being transported on foot, by bicycle or public transport. Almost half of the kiosk owners did not use any form of quality control when receiving the milk for further sale or processing. However, many kiosk owners knew about the clot-on-boiling test to test whether the milk is no longer fresh and has started souring. The acidity of sour milk causes it to clot if boiled. Just like the vendors, kiosk owners stored milk in plastic containers but unlike the vendors, kiosk operators pooled milk from different sources, especially when demand was high.

The survey also assessed personal hygiene of milk handlers and hygiene facilities of the sales premises. About 95.5% of sampled premises had toilet facilities accessible to staff and customers. However, only 32% had hand basins with running hot water. Soap was used by about 82% of the staff for washing hands and utensils. Those without basins but with running hot water cleaned the milk handling equipment in the same bowl used for washing hands. Only one milk shop had a hygienic hand dryer, suggesting that the milk handlers in the other shops dried their hands either with cloths or nothing at all. Cloths get dirty after a while and can be another source of contamination of hands that were clean after washing.

All sampled milk kiosks stored the milk in refrigerators. However, electricity supply is often erratic with frequent interruptions and there is no monitoring of the storage temperatures. Only one kiosk owner out of the 22 surveyed had received formal training on food hygiene and only 59% of the staff working at milk kiosks wore clothes that were visibly clean. Following the interviews, discussions and observations, two samples were taken from each milk kiosk: one of raw milk just received from the farm and the other of boiled milk to be served hot to customers. The results showed that both the raw and boiled milk samples were contaminated with *S. aureus* to the same extent. This suggests that *S. aureus* in the raw milk received from the farm was eliminated through boiling but re-introduced into the boiled milk through contamination at the milk kiosk. Likely sources of contamination include poorly cleaned storage containers, contaminated equipment, or poor personal hygiene of those handling the boiled milk.

Almost all of the milk kiosks served their boiled milk hot because they believed that it was free from microbial contamination. This was also what the consumers preferred. We interviewed 120 consumers at the sampled milk kiosks about their perceptions on the quality and safety of milk. Consumers considered five different attributes to determine the quality of milk: viscosity, colour, taste, smell and cream at the top. During the focus group discussion, the majority of respondents said they normally drank milk from a kiosk which had a dust-free environment and where the workers were generally clean. Unexpectedly, almost 72% of the consumers were aware of health risks associated with the consumption of raw milk. This was surprising as former surveys suggested that only 21% of consumers were aware of milk-borne hazards. The most familiar health problems were stomach aches, diarrhoea and tuberculosis. This high level of awareness of milk-borne health risks could be one reason for the preference of buying boiled milk served hot. The consumers proactively suggested that health officials should train kiosk owners and farmers on milk hygiene. Furthermore, they suggested that milk collection centres should be registered and the milk inspected by health officials.

The milk kiosks also sold chilled milk which was not sourced from informal market channels but formally processed (homogenized and pasteurized) and packaged in pouches. Four samples of processed, packaged milk were purchased in each ward and tested to compare their contamination status with the milk that was marketed informally at the same milk kiosks. All of the samples of pasteurized, packaged milk were free of *S. aureus* but surprisingly all of them contained *Bacillus* species, another potential milk-borne pathogen (Chapter 18). Among other species of bacteria that were isolated from most of the milk samples in informal shops in Temeke was *E. coli* which is associated with udder infections in cows and gastroenteritis in humans.

How many people are at risk?

The results of the microbiological tests showed that 23% of the milk sampled at sale in milk kiosks was contaminated with *S. aureus*. From the interviews, it was found that the milk kiosks sold an average of 1792 litres of milk daily and consumers reported drinking about a quarter a litre of milk each per day. These data were used for statistical modelling which revealed that every day, 953 people purchase milk from milk kiosks in Temeke Municipality and therefore an estimated 217 consumers are likely to buy contaminated milk.

The East African standard for microbiological quality of milk establishes the maximum acceptable levels of bacterial load in milk depending on whether it will be further processed or sold as raw reconstituted milk. In this present study, 27% of the milk served hot at milk kiosks exceeded these cut-off points with increasing levels from farm to milk kiosk. The bacterial load was reduced significantly after boiling, indicating the effectiveness of the combination of time and temperature in killing bacteria. Unfortunately, boiling of milk does not always eliminate the risk of food poisoning as in the case of *S. aureus*. Its numbers might have increased during transportation of milk from the farm to the kiosk such that by the time the milk was boiled, it would already contain a high level of heat-stable toxins produced by *S. aureus*.

Recommendations

Dairy farmers and milk sellers should be given simple and practical training courses on hygienic milk handling. These training courses should be planned and prepared by researchers and implemented by extension workers. It is important that all milk handlers in the value chain be made aware of their important role and responsibility in protecting food from contamination or deterioration.

Kaiza Kilango is a food analysis officer at the Tanzania Food and Drug Authority and previously worked as a nutritionist at the Tanzania Red Cross Society. In 2011, he was awarded his Master of Science degree in human nutrition from the Sokoine University of Agriculture in Morogoro, Tanzania.

Title and authors of the study

Food safety in milk markets of smallholder farmers in Tanzania: A case study of peri-urban wards in Temeke.

Kaiza Kilango,[1] *Kohei Makita*,[2,3] *Lusato Kurwijila*[4] and *Delia Grace*[2]

[1]Tanzania Food and Drug Authority; [2]International Livestock Research Institute, Kenya; [3]Rakuno Gakuen University, Japan; [4]Sokoine University of Agriculture, Tanzania

Contact details

Kaiza Kilango
Directorate of Food Safety
Tanzania Food and Drug Authority
P.O. Box 77150, Dar es Salaam, Tanzania

14

EQUAL PAY FOR EQUAL WORK IN KENYA

Kevin Kabui, Kristina Roesel, Samuel M. Arimi, Erastus Kang'ethe, Amos Omore and Delia Grace

Key messages

- Milk in central and northwestern Kenya was of good quality, with reference to national microbiological quality standards.
- Infrastructure for quality-based payment for milk is in place.
- Farmers are well educated in terms of hygiene but some aspects need training.
- The majority of farmers are in favour of introducing quality-based payment.

Background

The dairy subsector in Kenya is among the largest components of the agricultural sector, contributing 14% of the agricultural GDP which accounted for 24% of national GDP in 2009.[1] The subsector has grown steadily over the years, with annual milk production rising from an estimated 2.8 billion litres in 2003 to more than 4 billion litres in 2009.[2] The monetary value of exports of milk and milk products (mainly long-life milk and powder milk) has also been rising steadily over the years from an estimated 100 million Kenya shillings (KSh) to more than KSh1 billion in 2008. Unlike many West African countries, Kenya imports only 2% of processed milk and milk products mainly for certain tastes and preferences and to cater for the tourist and expatriate communities. Farm gate price, animal productivity, herd size, access to support services and rainfall patterns have been identified as determinants for the domestic milk supply.[3]

Smallholder dairy farmers contribute more than 75% of the country's annual milk production. However, most of the milk is marketed informally to neighbours or at local markets and its quality is frequently questioned. Continuous upgrading of the dairy value chain is crucial for Kenya to maintain its market leadership. Inefficiencies must be eliminated to make the milk fit for regional and international export markets.

An earlier study conducted by Makokha and Fadiga (2010; see Note 3) in randomly selected households in Nairobi and Eldoret found that consumers were willing to pay more for improved milk quality, based on the price, smell and hygiene. This led us to consider whether a feasible system of payment based on milk quality standards could be introduced. On the domestic level, this would result in higher payment for all dairy farmers who meet the desired quality standards and, at the international level, it would help increase exports and subsequently create more jobs in Kenya.

We conducted a study to determine the quality of milk in an area representing the dairy industry of Kenya and the opportunities for farmers to exploit a quality-based payment scheme. Milk samples were collected to compare bacteriological and compositional quality with existing national standards for raw milk and to find out about farmers' perceptions of milk quality attributes and practices associated with variations in milk quality. We hypothesized that if farmers understood the benefits of a quality-based payment system and supported it, it would be easier to implement such a system.

The study was carried out in Limuru and Eldoret. Limuru is located on the eastern edge of the Great Rift Valley, some 40 kilometres northwest of Nairobi. Its residents rely mostly on farming and a shoe factory for employment. Eldoret is located in western Kenya and is currently the fastest growing and fifth largest town in Kenya. In Limuru, the study was conducted in zones that supply the Limuru Dairy Cooperative Society with milk. In Eldoret, the study was conducted in Metkei and Kipsaos dairy cooperatives.

Milk samples were collected at collection centres that were selected based on accessibility and the number of farmers supplying them with milk. The milk samples were collected from every third farmer who brought milk to the collection centres and analysed for microbiological and compositional quality. In Kenya, the microbiological quality standards for raw milk are set by the Kenya Bureau of Standards (KEBS), which are somewhat lower than European standards.

The compositional analysis of the milk was done using a *Lactoscan*, a machine that can easily analyse the contents of the milk such as fat and proteins. Using these data, the nutritional value of the milk sample can be determined. The more nutritious the milk, the more money the farmer should be paid. Conversely, milk that does not meet the quality standards should not receive the same price as milk that meets or exceeds them. Moreover, farmers who adulterate milk by adding water to sell more volume should be penalized. Not only is adulteration of milk illegal, but adding water from dirty sources presents a health risk to the consumer. Preliminary findings suggested that milk was adulterated with added water in Limuru and, to some extent, in Eldoret.

Milk is rich in vitamins that are vital for good eyesight (Vitamin A), healthy growth of bones (Vitamin D), protecting body tissue from radicals (Vitamin E) and blood clotting in wound healing (Vitamin K). As these vitamins are soluble in fat, the fat content of milk indirectly represents the content of fat-soluble vitamins. The average fat content of milk in Eldoret was higher than that of the milk in

Limuru but in both towns, the average milk fat content exceeded the KEBS specification of 3.25%. Protein content in the milk from Limuru was below the KEBS specification; this could be as a result of dilution through added water or poor animal feeding.

Results of the microbiological analysis found that 75% of the milk samples were of good quality, according to the KEBS specifications for total bacteria count and the remainder graded as unacceptable. Farmers whose milk was sampled were asked to fill in a questionnaire on their husbandry and milking practice. The questions and subsequent discussions aimed to find out about the farmers' knowledge of aspects of milk hygiene and their knowledge, perceptions and attitudes on quality-based milk payment schemes.

In both study areas, the majority of farmers washed their hands before milking and used water and soap. In addition, almost all washed the cow udders before milking. Unfortunately, most of them did not dry their hands or the udders, increasing the risk of contamination from dirty water running into the milk. The majority of farmers were located within 1 kilometre of a milk collection centre. In Limuru, all the farmers delivered their milk to the cooperative in aluminium cans while in Eldoret, the use of plastic containers for milk was still prevalent. As plastic containers are difficult to sterilize, their use is not recommended.

More than 75% of farmers had access to potable water although some used more than one water source including community pumps, rivers and streams. The use of dirty water for cleaning milk containers increases the risk of bacterial contamination. Most of the farmers knew about the proper use of antibiotics to treat dairy cows and the importance of adhering to the withdrawal period for milk from cows undergoing treatment. Most of the respondents from the two study sites said they would be in favour of a quality-based system of payment for milk if given appropriate incentives such as credit and animal feeds.

Recommendations

Some aspects of animal husbandry such as feeding, as well as milking hygiene, need to be improved. The milk testing structures that are in place need to be strengthened to enforce existing regulations.

Kevin Kabui holds a Bachelor's degree in veterinary medicine from the University of Nairobi. He has worked for the project *Heshimu Punda* (respect the donkey) in Mwea and at the Dagoretti slaughterhouses in Nairobi as a veterinary officer in charge of hygiene. He is involved in training animal health assistants at the Animal Health and Industry Training Institute (AHITI) – Ndomba. This study was undertaken as part of his specialist degree in veterinary public health at the University of Nairobi.

Title and authors of the study

Milk quality control by bacteriological and compositional quality-based payment system in smallholder farms in Limuru and Eldoret, Kenya.

Kevin Kabui,[1] *Samuel M. Arimi,*[1] *Erastus K. Kang'ethe,*[1] *Amos Omore*[2] and *Delia Grace*[2]

[1]University of Nairobi, Kenya; [2]International Livestock Research Institute, Kenya

Contact details

Kevin Kabui
P.O. Box 1525, 10100 Nyeri, Kenya
Email: kinyuakabui@gmail.com

Notes

1. Government of Kenya. 2010. *Kenya National Dairy Master Plan.* Ministry of Livestock Development, Nairobi.
2. Kenya Dairy Board. 2011. www.kdb.co.ke (accessed 9 July 2014); FAOSTAT. 2011. http://faostat.fao.org/default.aspx
3. Makokha S and Fadiga M. 2010. Exploiting markets for dairy and meat products' quality and safety: a Kenyan case study. In Jabbar MA, Baker D and Fadiga ML (eds), *Demand for livestock products in developing countries with a focus on quality and safety attributes: Evidence from Asia and Africa.* ILRI Research Report 24. ILRI (International Livestock Research Institute), Nairobi, pp. 72–92.

15

KENYA'S ECONOMIC GAIN LEADING TO HEALTH PAIN?

Flavien Ndongo, Kristina Roesel, Kohei Makita, Marianna Siegmund-Schulze, Hans-Peter Piepho, Delia Grace, Erastus Kang'ethe and Anne Valle Zárate

Key messages

- *Brucella* was not present in the sampled milk in Kasarani, peri-urban Nairobi.
- Exotic cattle breeds do not seem more susceptible to brucellosis than local breeds.
- Farmers, traders and retailers have risky practices that increase the risk of brucellosis and other milk-borne diseases such as tuberculosis, or diarrhoea caused by faecal contamination of milk.
- Marketing of milk through cooperatives proved to be safest and should be promoted.

Background

Dairy production in Kenya started before independence with the establishment of large-scale commercial systems in the central highlands in the 1950s. The indigenous zebu cattle were upgraded with European dairy breeds imported from South Africa to build up foundation stocks. When many colonial farmers left after independence in 1963, the large-scale production systems shifted to small-scale farming accompanied by an increase in the population of high-grade dairy cattle such as the Holstein-Friesian known for their high milk yields. Today, 80% of Kenya's dairy sector is supplied by small-scale farmers. The recent migration from rural to urban hubs resulted in a relocation of the dairy industry into and around the cities. In 1994, about 17% of urban households in Kenya kept cattle, a phenomenon also found in other East African capital cities where more than 50% of the households rely on livestock production as their secondary source of income. With the limited size of farmland, the breed preferences of farmers are strongly influenced by the milk production potential. Therefore, Friesian and

Ayrshire are the most preferred exotic breeds for high milk yield, with Ayrshire providing a high fat content.

Cities have become crowded and the lack of space can compromise hygiene. Moreover, the population is growing at a pace much faster than infrastructure for sanitation or sewage can grow. Though good for the producers, the rising demand for animal-source food will further enhance these problems. With crowding of people and animals, the occurrence of diseases that humans can contract from animals becomes more likely and requires action from local health authorities. Some of these diseases threatening the dairy sector are salmonellosis, listeriosis, tuberculosis and brucellosis. A recent study identified brucellosis in cattle, a disease that has often been reported in Kenya, as a major priority for prevention and control on account of its impact on animal and human health.[1]

Brucellosis is a bacterial disease which humans (and other mammals) acquire through direct contact with infected animals, by eating or drinking contaminated animal products such as unpasteurized milk or cheese, or by inhaling the airborne bacteria. In humans, the disease causes flu-like symptoms, including fever, weakness, weight loss and malaise.[2] These flu-like symptoms can also be mistaken for malaria (Chapter 19) and have been regularly reported in Kenyan clinics, with several cases diagnosed as brucellosis.

The crowding of animals and people in cities, coupled with a rising demand for dairy products in urban areas, puts pressure on dairy farmers to increase their supply. However, even though exotic breeds are known for higher production yields, they are also more susceptible to certain diseases. The present study therefore investigated the prevalence of brucellosis in peri-urban Nairobi as well as practices along the local milk marketing chain that might increase or decrease the likelihood of *Brucella* – the microorganism that causes brucellosis – ending up in the consumer's milk.

Kasarani Constituency in Kenya's capital city, Nairobi, is home to more than 300,000 people. Many cattle are kept in Kasarani but the occurrence of brucellosis had not been investigated prior to the present study. The survey was facilitated by the local extension officer. Samples of raw milk were collected from 100 farms and 20 milk shops and tested for the presence of *Brucella*. In addition, focus group discussions were facilitated to learn more about animal husbandry and milk processing practices to assess whether they increased or reduced the risk of brucellosis.

Brucellosis is more visible in pregnant cows where it causes abortion or premature calving, and can lead to temporary sterility, death from blood poisoning and decreased milk production. Other cows and bulls get infected if they ingest materials that were contaminated with afterbirth materials, the aborted foetus or raw milk. The disease can also be contracted during natural mating by blood or vaginal discharges. Cattle are normally not treated if infected. In areas with low occurrence of the disease, the animals identified are mostly culled, whereas vaccination may be carried out in areas with high occurrence. Otherwise, preventive measures and hygienic practices, such as wearing protective clothing when handling abortions or calves as well as boiling raw milk, are effective.

Interviews and discussions with 100 farmers showed that they owned herds ranging from as few as one to three, to as many as fifteen cows. Most of them kept exotic breeds such as Friesian and Ayrshire or crossbreds and used artificial insemination as a breeding technique. A small share kept local breeds such as zebu and borrowed the neighbour's bull for mating for reproduction. While exotic breeds are said to be more susceptible to disease, artificial insemination reduces the risk of transmission as semen purchased from good sources is usually free from disease.

Eighty-five per cent of the farmers kept their cattle in zero-grazing units. Because they do not own land on which to plant fodder crops, they spend a lot of money to buy fodder. On the other hand, they also reported high milk production and easier management and prevention of animal diseases such as liver flukes. They did not know about the possibility of bacteria contaminating the Napier grass which they sourced from peri-urban areas. The remaining 15% of farmers grazed their cattle as they believed grazing 'makes the animals stronger and healthier'. However, grazing increases the risk of infection with brucellosis. More than half of the milk from grazing cattle was consumed at home or fed to calves and the surplus sold to intermediaries, milk shops or directly to consumers.

Factors increasing and reducing the risk of infection

Only 1% of the respondents used a machine for milking, implying that the rest of the farmers are at high risk of infection if the cow carries the bacterium. If cows abort, the foetus is handled with bare hands and always buried. If properly done, this is as safe as burning of contagious material as practised by farmers in West Africa (Chapter 19). Despite most of the farmers in Kasarani having at least ten years of experience in dairy farming, their level of knowledge on brucellosis was low. Similarly, low levels of knowledge on brucellosis were observed at the marketing level. Of twenty retailers, only one knew about brucellosis as a disease that can be transmitted through raw milk. In general, retailers were aware that milk can transmit diseases but were not able to name specific diseases. Therefore, they boiled the milk sold at their shops but not the milk which they took home. They were convinced that 'it is the duty of consumers to boil it themselves'. They either collected milk from the farmers or were supplied through intermediary sellers. Most of the milk came from outside Kasarani and was pooled with that collected from the area, increasing the likelihood of mixing good and bad milk.

Short milk marketing chains minimize the extent of milk handling, thus limiting the likelihood of milk contamination. Most of the milk in Kasarani was sold directly to consumers, thus minimizing the chance of introducing bacteria during long transportation routes with multiple handlers. Milk collected at cooperatives was usually pasteurized before sale, effectively killing any milk-borne pathogens and significantly reducing the risk of brucellosis. Moreover, the milk was normally boiled before consumption which is a very effective risk-mitigation strategy. However, the retailers should not leave it to the consumer to boil the milk as a few of them use raw milk for fermentation.

All of the milk sellers produced *maziwa lala* (sour milk) – similar to *féné* in West Africa (Chapter 20) or *ergo* in Ethiopia (Chapter 12) – which is produced by spontaneous fermentation of raw milk. Even though lactic fermentation inhibits the growth of milk-borne pathogens, its effect on *Brucella* is not yet fully estimated. Higher-income consumers preferred to buy pasteurized milk as they viewed pasteurization as a guarantee of quality and longer shelf-life, and appreciated the convenience of packaged milk for transport and storage.

The present study found that none of the milk samples contained *Brucella*, which is good news. However, this finding cannot be generalized to the milk chain in Nairobi or the entire country. Since the sample size was not large enough to detect a low prevalence of brucellosis, further investigation should be carried out, making sure to avoid sampling bias in the selection of participating farmers. In the present study, it was the extension officer who chose the participating farmers and they might have represented best practice examples only.

Recommendations

Knowledge of the prevalence of brucellosis in various districts could help local extension workers to provide advice to farmers not to purchase animals or fodder from infected areas. Additionally, it would be easier to identify infected animals and isolate them to break the cycle of transmission. However, if farmers, traders, retailers and consumers were better educated on the disease, they would be better able to intervene and reduce the risk of transmission of brucellosis and other milk-borne diseases. Farmers should use protective clothing when handling raw milk and when attending to cows experiencing difficult calving, and should send for the veterinarian or extension officer if a cow aborts.

Farmers and milk sellers should be trained on milk hygiene and good manufacturing practice. The marketing channel from farmers to consumers via cooperatives has proved to be very safe and should be promoted and developed (Chapter 8). Future epidemiological investigations on the presence of *Brucella* in milk in peri-urban Nairobi should be carried out.

Flavien Ndongo holds a Master's degree from the University of Hohenheim in Germany and is pursuing postgraduate studies at the Faculty of Veterinary Medicine, University of Montreal.

Title and authors of the study

Choice of breeds and husbandry practices influencing the safety of milk and milk products in smallholder dairy farms in peri-urban Nairobi, Kenya, focusing on brucellosis.

Flavien Ndongo,[1] *Kohei Makita,*[2,3] *Marianna Siegmund-Schultze,*[1] *Hans-Peter Piepho,*[1] *Delia Grace,*[2] *Erastus Kang'ethe*[4] and *Anne Valle Zárate*[1]

[1]University of Hohenheim, Germany; [2]International Livestock Research Institute, Kenya; [3]Rakuno Gakuen University, Japan; [4]University of Nairobi, Kenya

Contact details

Flavien Ndongo
The *Escherichia coli* Laboratory (EcL)
Faculty of Veterinary Medicine
University of Montreal, 3200 Sicotte Street, Saint-Hyacinthe (Quebec), J2S 2M2, Canada
Email: ndongof@yahoo.fr

Notes

1. Smits H and Cutler SJ. 2004. Contributions of biotechnology to the control and prevention of brucellosis in Africa. *African Journal of Biotechnology* 3: 631-636.
2. www.who.int/topics/brucellosis/en (accessed 9 July 2014).

16

EMERGING DISEASES THREATEN GHANA'S EMERGING MILK MARKET

Joy Appiah, Kristina Roesel, Kwaku Tano-Debrah, Betty Bediako Amoa, Mohammed M. Alpha, Kohei Makita and Delia Grace

Key messages

- This study is the first ever assessment of *Listeria monocytogenes* in milk sold in Ghana.
- Detection of *Listeria* in sheep led to investigations of the disease in food which is a common source of human infection with the microorganism.
- There is a high risk of acquiring listeriosis from milk sold in informal markets in Ghana.
- The risk is especially high for fermented milk products because they are highly contaminated and consumed in relatively large quantities on a daily basis.
- The risk of listeriosis from raw milk is low because milk is often boiled before consumption.
- Boiling milk reduces the risk of listeriosis.

Background

In 2002, the Ghana Health Service spent approximately US$11 million in the health care sector. A significant part of this expenditure was for the treatment of diarrhoeal diseases, which also accounted for the loss of 3.4 million working days and associated productivity losses. Experts consider microbial hazards in food to be one the most frequent causes of diarrhoeal disease. More than 60% of all human infectious diseases are shared with animals and, like other animal products, milk is a common source of food-borne infections. Milk consumption in Ghana is low compared to the average per capita consumption in sub-Saharan Africa. However, it has been increasing over the past years and Ghanaian consumers now tend to prefer fresh local dairy products over imported milk powder. With more than half of the population living in urban areas, the convenience offered by long-life dairy products has become more important.

Generally, dairy production in Ghana is mostly pastoral and agro-pastoral with traditional cattle breeds predominating and little complementary feeding practised. This results in very low milk productivity which cannot meet consumer demand. Poor distribution policies, inadequate milk collection systems and unattractive prices offered for locally produced fresh milk led Ghana to rely on imported butter and skim milk powder to meet the demands of the formal market. Milk powder is reconstituted into liquid milk and may be further processed into yoghurt. But as well as low productivity, there is also concern about the safety and quality of locally marketed milk. If the burgeoning demand for milk and milk products is to promote the local dairy industry and offer a pathway out of poverty for farmers, then the milk sold must be safe for consumers.

Some milk-borne diseases such as tuberculosis and brucellosis are well understood, while others are new and many have never been properly assessed in developing countries. These emerging and less well-known food-borne diseases are often of high concern to the public and policymakers alike. Listeriosis is an example of a food-borne disease of high scare potential, as witnessed by the so-called '*Listeria* hysteria' which struck Europe when French cheeses were linked to illness in people. Listeriosis has all the characteristics of a disease that could seriously threaten Ghana's nascent market for home-produced milk: a new disease, capable of serious and unpleasant illness, very difficult to eliminate and impossible to identify by sight or taste.

Listeriosis is usually caused by eating food contaminated with the bacterium *Listeria monocytogenes* which is globally known to occur in 37 mammal species and 17 bird species as well as in shellfish, fish species and people. How does the microbe get into food? It is normally found in soil and water; animals can carry it, sometimes even without appearing ill, then contaminate food such as meat and dairy products. The bacterium is hardy and can even survive in a refrigerator. It has been found in a variety of raw foods, such as uncooked meat, vegetables and fruit,[1] as well as in products that were contaminated after cooking and processing, such as soft cheeses, sausages and smoked seafood (Chapter 17). Raw milk and products made from it are particularly likely to contain the microbe. Healthy children and adults occasionally get infected but they rarely fall ill; the disease primarily affects YOPIs. Often preceded by diarrhoea, these people usually experience symptoms such as fever, muscle pain, stiff neck, headache, confusion, loss of balance and convulsions. Pregnant women are about 20 times more susceptible to listeriosis than other healthy adults. They typically experience a mild flu-like illness. However, infections during pregnancy can lead to miscarriage, stillbirth, premature delivery or life-threatening infections of the newborn. If babies are infected during labour, it may lead to death or infections in the brain (meningoencephalitis) that cause life-long disability. People with clinical AIDS have a weak immune system and are 300 times more likely to develop listeriosis than healthy people.[2]

In the event of an outbreak of listeriosis, 20–30% of people falling sick are likely to die; the rates of death in infants, pregnant women and elderly and immunocompromised people are estimated to be as high as 80–99%. Therefore, many countries have a zero-tolerance policy to the presence of *L. monocytogenes* in food, as scientists are still not sure about how many *Listeria* cells are enough to cause disease in people. Incidentally, in Ghana, detection and surveillance of *L. monocytogenes* is not routinely done and thus there is no policy for it. However, recent years have seen increasing reports of human illness compatible with listeriosis. Additionally, raw, unpasteurized milk is regularly consumed in some communities in Ghana, especially among the Fulani ethnic group (Chapter 20).

Like many emerging food-borne diseases, listeriosis has not been properly assessed in many developing countries. In Ghana, scientists first found evidence of *Listeria* in sheep. This stimulated research into the occurrence of *Listeria* in food products, as food is a common transmission pathway of disease from animals and the environment to people. This example of One Health in action shows the importance of good communication between veterinarians and doctors.

The study described here took place in Ashaiman Municipality, located in the Greater Accra region some 4km from Tema and 30km east of Accra. The region has the highest urban growth rate in Ghana (4.6%) and diarrhoea ranks fourth among the top ten diseases. In 2009, meningitis accounted for a large proportion of notifiable diseases in the district, with many cases having occurred in Ashaiman. At Tema General Hospital, 513 cases of spontaneous abortions were recorded in 2008. A study in Ghana showed that raw milk from informal markets in the country is highly contaminated with several pathogens. Some retailers try to eliminate the germs and decrease spoilage by heating the milk in pots without any temperature control. The present study was conducted to investigate the risk of consuming raw milk and its products that may be contaminated with *L. monocytogenes*. It is the first study on the risk of exposure to listeriosis from raw milk in Ghana. The survey aimed to assess the level of *L. monocytogenes* in informally marketed milk and, therefore, investigated milk samples taken along the food marketing chain from farm to retail outlets and consumers. Potential sources of contamination were identified and the habits of sellers and consumers of raw milk products were assessed to identify their level of risk of exposure to listeriosis.

The power of participatory research

Participatory research takes into account all stakeholders involved in the marketing chain. By using tools such as diagrams, maps, analytical games, story-telling and group discussions, it is possible to identify hazards and habits that either increase or decrease risks to public health. At farms, seasonal calendars were drawn to assess disease periods and symptoms (Chapter 5). They showed that most cattle fell sick at the onset of the rains; farmers attributed this to the abundance of fresh grass. Farmers were able to describe symptoms in their cattle that suggested the occurrence of certain diseases. Deep dry chronic cough accompanied by weight loss, for example, indicated tuberculosis and was frequently reported. Udder inflammation (mastitis) did not occur very often but was very important to the farmers as milk is the most important animal-source food for the Fulani. When the udder is inflamed, milk loses its natural colour and smell and starts clotting. The calves eventually refuse to suckle and milk production stops. Animals turning in circles (a symptom of listeriosis in cattle and sheep) was reported to occur, yet it was not regarded as a disease but a bad habit and treated unconventionally by blows to the back of the animal.

Milk production varied depending on the season and herd production ranged from 0.75 litres daily in the late dry season to 135 litres daily in the rainy season. Retailers often complained about insufficient supply of milk from farmers during the dry season. As a result, some farmers adulterated the milk with water or sold reconstituted milk by mixing milk powder and water. On the other hand, in the rainy season, retailers received too much milk and often complained about a lack of adequate storage facilities for the milk. Based on reports from the retailers, who were exclusively women, raw milk was the least popular product. None of the retailers sold more than seven litres of raw milk per day. The demand for boiled milk was slightly higher but still much lower than that of fermented milk. The retailers sold at least 100 to 150 litres per day and one even reported selling more than 500 litres! Whereas raw or boiled milk was not refrigerated, the fermented milk was kept chilled with big ice blocks inside the storage container. The ice blocks are purchased from vendors who make them by filling polythene pouches with tap water and packing the pouches in a freezer. Hygiene is generally poor and quality control non-existent. For example, before adding the ice blocks to the milk, the blocks may be crushed with an unclean object on an unclean hard surface.

The consumer survey revealed that decisions on where to buy milk were based on attributes such as taste, availability and affordability of the product. Many of them consumed fermented milk on a daily basis, either at the milk shop or at home. During fermentation, milk sugar (lactose) is broken down by bacteria into lactic acid. Because many Africans are intolerant to lactose, fermentation is a good strategy for increasing the digestibility of milk. Other forms of milk were consumed less frequently; boiled milk was consumed twice a week and raw milk only once a week. Raw milk was mostly taken home and half of the respondents said they boiled the milk before drinking it.

Consumers were also asked about the occurrence of diseases and their symptoms. Four out of five reported symptoms could be attributed to listeriosis. However, the symptoms could also be due to other diseases such as malaria or the flu, which are probably more common. Most said they never experienced mental changes or convulsions after the initial symptoms (sometimes a sign of listeriosis), but the study found that people were often reluctant to report these signs as there is social stigma attached to mental illness. Sadly, almost half of the women surveyed had experienced spontaneous abortions and about one-third of them more than once. Almost 86% had experienced at least one case of stillbirth, with most of these losing the pregnancy during the third trimester.

To find out if milk was contaminated with *L. monocytogenes*, milk samples were taken at the farm and at the retail shop before and after boiling. Samples of fermented milk were also examined. Microbial analysis showed that the milk samples were contaminated with *L. monocytogenes* at all levels of the marketing chain, but contamination levels increased as the milk moved from the farm to the retailer. Boiling of milk resulted in a significant decrease in the numbers of *L. monocytogenes*, whereas levels in fermented milk were found to be as high as in the milk before it was boiled at the retail shop. Overall, fermented milk had the highest probability to cause illness because consumers drank it most often and in high quantities. Boiled milk also had a high probability for causing listeriosis for the same reason, although it had the least probability per serving. Raw milk at the farm was least likely to cause illness because milk was rarely consumed raw.

The surveyed consumers reported that they had experienced symptoms indicative of listeriosis, for instance the high occurrence of spontaneous abortion, meningitis and diarrhoea. The handling of milk by many different people can contribute to the increased risk of microbial infection, including listeriosis. Other practices that may increase the risk of disease include hand milking of several animals in dirty surroundings without hand cleaning in between cows and bulking of raw milk collected from several farmers without separating milk that is contaminated. In addition, the raw milk was collected in unapproved containers, which are difficult to sterilize, and transported over long distances without being cooled, thus allowing for spoilage bacteria to multiply quickly. This was compounded by the fact that retailers did not refrigerate the milk. On the positive side, however, both retailers and consumers reportedly boiled milk before drinking it, significantly reducing the level of contamination and thus exposure to *Listeria*. However, most consumers preferred fermented milk which was found to be highly contaminated with the microorganism.

Recommendations

An improved, standard way of processing fermented milk products would reduce the risk of listeriosis deriving from fermented milk products. As *Listeria* is known to survive in acidic media, a certain level of acidity needs to be achieved for a certain period of time to eliminate the microbe. However, people do not like fermented milk that is too sour. Another control option would be to ensure that milk is boiled prior to fermentation. It is also important to avoid cross-contamination of boiled or fermented milk with unclean utensils or those used to store or handle fresh milk.

Joy Appiah holds a Master of Food Science degree from the University of Ghana, Legon and presented this study at the 15th World Congress on Food Science and Technology in South Africa.

Title and authors of the study

Assessment of the risk of consuming milk/milk products from informal markets contaminated with *Listeria monocytogenes.*

Joy Appiah,[1] *Kwaku Tano-Debrah,*[1] *Betty Bediako Amoa,*[1] *Mohammed M. Alpha,*[2] *Kohei Makita*[3,4] and *Delia Grace*[3]

[1]Department of Nutrition and Food Science, University of Ghana; [2]Food and Drugs Board, Ghana; [3]International Livestock Research Institute, Kenya; [4]Rakuno Gakuen University, Japan.

Contact details

Joy Appiah
c/o Department of Nutrition and Food Science
University of Ghana
P. O. Box LG 134, Legon, Accra, Ghana
Email: jaga007joy@yahoo.com

Notes

1. http://yourlife.usatoday.com/fitness-food/safety/story/2011-09-28/Experts-fear-listeria-may-be-moving-into-produce/50589766/1
2. www.cdc.gov/listeria/index.html (accessed 9 July 2014).

17

HAND-WASHING IS LIKELY TO TURN IVORIAN MILK INTO A SAFE AND COMPETITIVE PRODUCT

Sylvie Mireille Kouamé-Sina, Kristina Roesel, Antoine Bassa Yobouet, Solenne Costard, Adjehi Dadié, Kohei Makita, Delia Grace, Koffi Marcellin Djè and Bassirou Bonfoh

Key messages

- Milk in the study site was highly contaminated with bacteria originating from faeces or the skin and hair of humans and animals.
- A small proportion of producers were responsible for a high proportion of risk to human health.
- Personal hygiene during milking, handling and selling was poor.
- The udders of cows and hands of milkers were identified as primary sources of milk contamination.
- Boiling the milk prior to consumption was not a common practice.
- Seventy per cent of consumers were at risk of illness from buying and consuming contaminated milk.
- If international quality standards were applied,[1] the majority of the milk would have to be discarded, causing significant economic losses to dairy farmers.

Background

Food-borne diseases include a wide spectrum of illnesses and are a growing public health problem worldwide. While most food-borne diseases are sporadic and not reported, outbreaks may take on massive proportions. In 1997 in Abidjan, 200 people fell ill from an infection with *Salmonella enteritidis* following the consumption of hamburgers in a modern fast-food restaurant. The majority of them had to be hospitalized.[2] The occurrence of *Salmonella typhi* in Abidjan has significantly increased from 3% in 2006 to 22% in 2008 and the microorganism was responsible for the deaths of thirteen people following the consumption of contaminated maize porridge in Bangouanou. In the same year, nine people fell ill in Alépé after eating manioc contaminated with three types of dangerous microbes at once: *Salmonella*, *Staphylococcus* and *Clostridium perfringens*.[3]

Salmonella species, *Staphylococcus* and *Clostridium* are all examples of bacteria that cause zoonoses, that is, diseases that are present in animal hosts and can be naturally transmitted from animals to people. Many of the studies reported in this book focus on zoonoses as these are among the most common food-borne diseases. However, food safety experts also have to worry about diseases that are not zoonotic. This study draws attention to the role of milkers as possible sources of contamination.

The most common clinical presentation of food-borne disease takes the form of gastrointestinal symptoms that range from mild to severe diarrhoea and vomiting followed by dehydration, which may require medical treatment or even hospitalization. In developing countries, many people lack access to affordable medical care so would rather work while suffering from mild food poisoning or take a few days off work and return when the diarrhoea stops. However, even if diarrhoea is mild, the patient is likely to be shedding a food-borne microorganism and many of the food-borne diseases are communicable.

In Africa, HIV/AIDS, lower respiratory infections and diarrhoeal disease are the leading contributors to the overall burden of disease.[4] Being sick for whatever reason means reduced productivity, less income and reduced quality of life, especially in the informal market where people do not have health insurance and only earn their wages if they show up for work. Not only are poor people more likely to fall sick, but falling sick keeps people poor.

Food-borne disease is an important public health and economic problem, but in Côte d'Ivoire it is difficult to obtain accurate estimates of its occurrence (WHO 2002).[5] Milk and dairy products have been found to contain *Listeria monocytogenes*, *Escherichia coli*, *Salmonella* spp. and *Staphylococcus aureus* (Chapters 12 and 13), all recognized to have the potential to cause disease in humans. The informal sector accounts for up to 80% of the local dairy production in Abidjan and supply largely depends on subsistence farmers who face a weak production infrastructure and hardly make enough profit for reinvestments. Furthermore, large parts of the population do not boil their milk prior to consumption.

However, even though all these aspects are obvious, it is not clear to what extent producers, vendors and the consumers themselves contribute to the dissemination and multiplication of microorganisms that could cause disease. Small informal dairy farms have been established in urban and peri-urban Abidjan to meet the growing demand for milk by the urban population. The present study aimed to better understand the structure, status, management and performance of the informal dairy chain in Abidjan to identify risky practices and to safeguard consumer health.

Producing, handling and consuming practices were examined through questionnaires and focus group discussions and helped shed light on production systems, milking practices and risk factors related to milk handling (Figure 22). The farmers were all male and 94.1% were of Fulani ethnicity (the Fulani are pastoralists by tradition). The farmers originated from Mali, Burkina Faso and Guinea and practised traditional animal breeding (Chapter 20). They did not physically separate animals of different species (cows, weaned calves, poultry, goats and sheep) at the farms. In addition, udder inflammation (mastitis) was reported in 6.7% of the farms in the two months preceding the survey. However, milk from infected cows was still sold. On average, eight cows were kept per farm. Milk production was very low, with each cow producing about 1.3 litres per milking. Milk production had decreased by 20% in the year preceding the survey and farmers attributed this to inappropriate treatment (especially of udder inflammations) by the farmers themselves as well as a lack of fodder.

Poor hygiene is pervasive

Prior to milking, 87% of the milkers did not wash their hands, and not a single cow's udder was washed; also in 87% of the cases milking utensils were not properly cleaned (that is, they were rinsed with cold water only). At selling points, part of the milk was stored in bottles and left to ferment before being collected at night by customers who had placed orders for fermented milk. Leftover unsold milk at the end of the day was either stored in a refrigerator for sale the following day or taken home for consumption or production of fermented milk or liquid butter. However, around 6% of farmers sold leftover milk that had been stored for up to three days at ambient temperatures of around 30°C. Although a relatively low proportion of farmers sold such milk, its consumption could result in many cases of illness. In food safety surveys, we often find that a small proportion of producers or sellers are responsible for many cases of food-borne illness.

To assess the level of milk contamination along the production chain, samples of milk were collected from the farm to the point of sale and analysed for the presence of disease-causing microorganisms that are normally not found in milk but in faeces or on the skin, hair and in the nose and mouth of humans and animals. The presence of these pathogens in milk indicates contamination as a result of unhygienic milk handling.

The results showed that 76.5% of the milk was contaminated with several species of pathogenic bacteria. Of the raw milk samples taken from the udders of cows, 81.5% were of good microbiological quality compared to 35.3% at the point of sale. The udders of cows and hands of milkers were identified as the primary sources of milk contamination. The equipment of farmers and vendors as well as the surroundings at the farm were identified as secondary sources of contamination. In addition, 24.7% of the milk samples contained antibiotics and 50% of the raw milk on sale was adulterated with water.

Poor hygiene is risky

The investigation of local raw milk consumption patterns showed that 51.6% of the respondents did not boil their milk before drinking it and 12.8% of consumers reported illness after drinking raw milk, citing symptoms such as diarrhoea, vomiting, fever and stomach cramps.

Based on the results of the microbiological analysis of marketed milk and data on the frequency of milk purchase, simulations were carried out to determine the probability of consuming contaminated milk. About 74% of the marketed raw milk was likely to be contaminated and there was a 30% chance of consumers getting infected with milk-borne pathogens through consumption of raw milk. This suggests that every day, 614 consumers in Abidjan risk getting sick as a result of drinking contaminated milk. Another simulation showed that more than 60% of the approximately 1000 litres of raw milk produced in the study area would have to be discarded every day if quality control according to EU standards were applied, resulting in daily losses of up to €600.

The problem as part of the solution

Apart from the disease-causing microbial species among faecal contaminants, there are also microorganisms that do not cause disease in humans. One example is *Bifidobacterium* species. Part of the study determined the biodiversity of *Bifidobacterium* species in informally marketed milk in Abidjan and evaluated their potential antibacterial activity against milk-borne pathogens.

Five different species of *Bifidobacterium* were present in 9% of milk samples, with most isolated from the hands of milkers and the cows' udders. The identified *Bifidobacterium* species produced organic acids that were found to inhibit the growth of certain pathogenic microorganisms in milk including *Listeria monocytogenes*, *Salmonella* spp., *Staphylococcus aureus* and *E. coli*.

Recommendations

Efforts towards risk mitigation should focus on reducing the contamination through pasteurization and good hygiene practices along the production chain. Although *Bifidobacterium* reduced the load of pathogens in milk through production of organic acids, it is no substitute for pasteurization and good hygiene practices. Standardization of management practices and monitoring should be considered by decision-makers.

Sylvie Mireille Kouamé-Sina is a microbiologist at the Centre Suisse de Recherches Scientifiques, Côte d'Ivoire. She is undertaking her PhD at the Université Nanguy Abrogoua in Côte d'Ivoire.

Title and authors of the study

Bacterial risk assessment in informally produced milk consumed in Côte d'Ivoire.

Sylvie Mireille Kouamé-Sina,[1,2] *Antoine Bassa Yobouet*,[1,2] *Solenne Costard*,[3,4,5] *Adjehi Dadié*,[2] *Kohei Makita*,[3,6] *Delia Grace*,[3] *Koffi Marcellin Djè*[2] and *Bassirou Bonfoh*[1]

[1]Centre Suisse de Recherches Scientifiques en Côte d'Ivoire; [2]Université Nanguy Abrogoua, Côte d'Ivoire; [3]International Livestock Research Institute, Kenya; [4]Royal Veterinary College, United Kingdom; [5]EpiX Analytics, USA; [6]Rakuno Gakuen University, Japan

Contact details

Sylvie Mireille Kouamé-Sina
Université Nanguy Abrogoua
Faculty of Food Sciences and Technology
Laboratory of Biotechnology and Food Microbiology, 02 B.P. 801 Abidjan 02, Côte d'Ivoire
Email: kouamesylviemireille@yahoo.fr or mireille.kouame@csrs.ci

Notes

1. European Commission Regulation No. 2073/2005 on microbiological criteria for foodstuffs. http://eur-lex.europa.eu/LexUriServ/LexUriServ.do?uri=OJ:L:2005:338:0001:0026:EN:PDF
2. Dosso M, Coulibaly M and Kadio A. 1998. Place des diarrhées bactériennes dans les pays en développement. *Bulletin of the Exotic Pathology Society* 5: 402–405.
3. Plan d'Action National de Sécurité Sanitaire des Aliments, République de Côte d'Ivoire, August 2010, page 48.
4. WHO. 2004. The global burden of disease: 2004 update. www.who.int/healthinfo/global_burden_disease/2004_report_update/en (accessed 9 July 2014).
5. WHO. 2002. WHO global strategy for food safety: safer food for better health. www.who.int/foodsafety/publications/general/global_strategy/en/ (accessed 31 July 2014).

18

WHEN CLEAN MILK PRODUCTION CANNOT BE ASSURED, BOILING BEFORE CONSUMPTION IS NON-NEGOTIABLE

Antoine Bassa Yobouet, Kristina Roesel, Sylvie Mireille Kouamé-Sina, Adjehi Dadié, Kohei Makita, Delia Grace, Leo Meile, Koffi Marcellin Djè and Bassirou Bonfoh

Key messages

- Informally marketed milk in Côte d'Ivoire is heavily contaminated with *Bacillus cereus*, a potential cause of food poisoning.
- The study team isolated strains which had the ability to produce toxins and were resistant to several antibiotics.
- Contamination tended to increase along the value chain; raw milk at farm level was less contaminated than milk at retailer shops.
- The presence of *Bacillus cereus* in milk was highly related to its presence in the environment, milking practices and the maintenance of the cold chain.
- In most cases, milk was consumed raw, thereby increasing the risk of contracting food-borne infection associated with *Bacillus cereus*.

Background

Milk has been called the 'ideal food' and plays an important role in human nutrition. While in the past it was mostly consumed by people in the rural areas, it is now also popular in urban and peri-urban areas. In Côte d'Ivoire, national milk production covers barely 10–18% of the demand for milk and dairy products. Most of this milk (92%) is supplied by small-scale farmers who raise their cattle in the traditional way and practise transhumance (the moving of cattle from place to place to make best use of seasonally available feed). These milk production activities are important in West Africa and generate one-third of the total income in rural households. However, the government has introduced a policy to promote dairy farming in peri-urban areas. Currently, the unregulated informal sector accounts for 80% of the country's milk production, distribution and marketing.

The complex milk production chain is an important source of livelihood, but is prone to contamination at every level. As a result, the nutritious attributes of milk can be negated by hazards to the health of consumers (Chapter 17). There is a variety of infections that escape the public health sector surveillance system. Contamination of milk with bacteria of faecal origin is a common cause of food-borne illness. However, another microbial cause of disease – which is also an indicator of environmental contamination – is *Bacillus cereus*.

Bacillus spp. are large bacteria which normally live in water and soil. They produce spores that are exceptionally resistant to unfavourable conditions like heat or drought. Although most species of *Bacillus* are harmless, some can cause disease in humans and animals. The most infamous is probably *Bacillus anthracis* which causes anthrax in humans and animals.

Bacillus cereus causes food poisoning similar to that caused by *Clostridium perfringens* and *Staphylococcus aureus* (Chapters 12 and 13). In the case of *Bacillus cereus*, some strains produce a toxin in food which cannot be destroyed by cooking and gives rise to vomiting within 1–5 hours of ingestion. Other strains produce a toxin in the human body once the bacterium enters the bowel; this toxin causes diarrhoea within 8–16 hours following ingestion.

The present study examined fifteen farms in peri-urban Abidjan to investigate whether *Bacillus cereus* was among the microbial contaminants in informally marketed milk in Côte d'Ivoire. The sources of contamination and potential health risk to consumers were also investigated.

Easy going for *Bacillus cereus*

In all of the fifteen farms examined, milking was done by hand. Our observations indicated likely contamination of the milk with *Bacillus cereus* from water and soil. The cowsheds were unsanitary, with cows lying in their own dung. Prior to milking, most milkers washed neither their hands nor the udders of the cows. While milking, they often dipped their fingers into the milk to use it as a lubricant to help them milk faster. Only one out of fifteen farmers reported cleaning his utensils after milking and only one-third of the respondents filtered their milk.

Traders and retailers reported that the milk they received from the farms was not cooled and, upon receipt, was bulked in a single storage tank. Thus, if the milk from one supplier was contaminated, then there is a higher chance that the entire batch in the tank will be spoiled. Adulteration of milk by adding water was relatively widespread among retailers, with 47.1% of them reportedly adding water to the milk before selling it. Not only is adulteration of milk illegal, but it also presents a health risk to consumers if the added water is dirty.

Most of the milk retailers opened for business at 0530 hours and worked for long hours along roadsides under plastic-covered sheds or parasols, causing the milk to be exposed to the sun, dust and vehicle exhaust fumes. At around 1030 hours, they would heat up the milk for about thirty minutes to reduce spoilage. However, in the case of *Bacillus cereus*, this practice is risky as the heat causes any bacterial spores present to germinate into cells which can double every twenty minutes and spoil the milk. Leftover unsold milk at the end of the day (about a quarter of the milk stock) was refrigerated overnight and sold early the following morning before the next delivery around 0900 hours.

A total of 150 milk samples from fifteen farms were collected for laboratory analysis. The milk was sampled from the udders and the milking containers. In addition, swabs were taken from the skin of the udders and the hands of the farmers as well as from the close environment of the animals. Samples of milk were also collected from fifteen milk shops. Water samples for analysis were taken from the sources used by the farmers (for cleaning of equipment) and by retailers (as they added water to the milk prior to selling it to their customers). Half of the respondents obtained their water from a public water supply while the other half used water from ponds.

Bacillus cereus was found in about 27% of the milk samples at farm level and 41% of the samples taken from pooled milk of the vendors. If the milk were to be assessed according to the EU standards for food safety[1] then all of the samples of the vendors' pooled milk would be judged as contaminated beyond acceptable limits with either poor (57.1%) or unacceptable (42.9%) microbiological quality.

Consumer interviews revealed that about 13% of those consuming raw milk had experienced diarrhoea, fever, bloating, vomiting or nausea – with varying degrees of severity – within 20–36 hours of drinking the milk. It is interesting to note, however, that some people who routinely boiled their milk before drinking it also reported similar symptoms. It is therefore crucial to undertake a proper diagnosis following a microbiological protocol prior to medical treatment with antibiotics or de-worming pills because there are numerous causes of diarrhoea.

Action from public health authorities overdue

The presence of *Bacillus cereus* in food does not necessarily imply a health risk to humans because not all strains are pathogenic. Whether a strain makes one sick depends on its ability to produce toxins that cause vomiting or diarrhoea and the number of bacteria ingested. In total, ninety-four strains of *Bacillus cereus* were detected, most of which were diarrhoea-causing strains and none of which was able to produce toxins that cause vomiting. The toxins that cause vomiting are produced by the microorganism as it grows in the milk, cannot be destroyed by pasteurization and are harder to detect. Thus, the absence of this strain of *Bacillus cereus* was good news.

Given the high levels of contamination in milk sold in informal markets and poor hygienic practices along the chain from farm to retail shops, boiling of milk before consumption would help to reduce public health risks from milk-borne pathogens. However, interviews of 188 consumers revealed that 54% of them consumed their milk without first boiling it, almost all drank raw milk at least once a week and one-third drank raw milk daily. This finding is in sharp contrast to findings of studies in the informal milk markets of East Africa where nearly 100% of urban consumers boil milk before drinking it. This is not done always with food safety in mind, but because they prefer to consume milk in tea or porridge which are prepared by boiling. Once again, we see the importance of cultural practices in affecting risk.

Not just bacteria but resistance to antibiotics too

In Côte d'Ivoire, food poisoning is commonly treated with broad-spectrum antibiotics like tetracyclines. Therefore, part of the study determined whether this group of antibiotics was still effective against the strains of *Bacillus cereus* which had been identified. The shocking result was that 92% of the strains showed resistance to tetracyclines. The survey found that 60% of the farmers used oxytetracycline to treat mastitis and residues of this antibiotic were found in several milk samples throughout the study sites. This suggests widespread non-adherence to the stipulated withdrawal period for milk from cows undergoing antibiotic treatment, a practice which can lead to the emergence of strains of bacteria that are resistant to several types of antibiotics. Ciprofloxacin, a broad-spectrum antibiotic, was found to be ineffective against 72% of the *Bacillus cereus* strains.

Recommendations

There is need to raise awareness among farmers, traders and consumers that they should boil their milk prior to consumption and to cool it quickly before storing it at low temperatures. In addition, there is need for education on the proper use of antibiotics and the public health implications of the misuse of antibiotics.

Antoine Bassa Yobouet works as a researcher at the Centre Suisse de Recherches Scientifiques, Côte d'Ivoire. From 2010 to 2011, he spent fourteen months at ETH University in Zurich, Switzerland to conduct his laboratory work, and is currently analysing the data to complete his PhD thesis.

Title and authors of the study

Bacillus cereus risk assessment in raw milk produced in traditional dairy farms and consumed in the informal dairy sector in Abidjan, Côte d'Ivoire.

Antoine Bassa Yobouet,[1,2] *Sylvie Mireille Kouamé-Sina,*[1,2] *Adjehi Dadié,*[1] *Kohei Makita,*[3,4] *Delia Grace,*[4] *Leo Meile,*[5] *Koffi Marcellin Djè*[1] and *Bassirou Bonfoh*[2]

[1]Université Nanguy Abrogoua, Côte d'Ivoire; [2]Centre Suisse de Recherches Scientifiques en Côte d'Ivoire; [3]Rakuno Gakuen University, Japan; [4]International Livestock Research Institute, Kenya; [5]Swiss Federal Institute of Technology Zurich, Switzerland

Contact details

Antoine Bassa Yobouet
Université Nanguy Abrogoua
Faculty of Food Sciences and Technology
Laboratory of Biotechnology and Food Microbiology, 02 B.P. 801 Abidjan 02, Côte d'Ivoire
Email: antoine.yobouet@csrs.ci or bassaantoine2007@yahoo.fr

Notes

1. Regulation (EC) No 1441/2007: http://eur-lex.europa.eu/LexUriServ/LexUriServ.do?uri=OJ:L:2007:322:0012:0029:EN:PDF (accessed 9 July 2014); Laboratoire National de Santé – Contrôle des denrées alimentaires, 2011. Critères microbiologiques des denrées alimentaires, lignes directrices pour l'interprétation. www.securite-alimentaire.public.lu (accessed 9 July 2014).

19

ARE MALARIAL SYMPTOMS MISTAKEN FOR BRUCELLOSIS IN MALI?

Ibrahim Sow, Kristina Roesel, Kohei Makita, Delia Grace, Solenne Costard and Bassirou Bonfoh

Key messages

- The prevalence of brucellosis in Mali is generally lower in rural areas than in urban areas.
- The inhabitants of Cinzana in rural Mali have habits that increase the likelihood of infection with brucellosis, in particular consuming raw milk and handling aborted material.
- Our study did not find the disease present in sheep or goats.
- Symptoms of brucellosis can be mistaken for malaria which is treated differently.

Background

Approximately 15 million people inhabit Mali, with the majority living in the southern regions of this vast country covering more than 1.2 million square kilometres. The Sahel is the horizontal transition to the north of Mali whose borders reach deep into the sparsely populated Sahara desert. Following cotton and gold, livestock farming is the third most important contributor to the country's GDP, of which one-quarter is from farmers in the rural areas. Mali's goat population exceeds its human population by 1 million and the country is home to 11 million sheep and 9 million cattle providing 300,000 tons of milk per year. However, supply of milk and dairy products is still not sufficient and the country relies heavily on annual imports of milk powder worth more than €30 billion to cover the demand. The Malian government has therefore started to implement dairy development projects to cover the supply for an ever-growing urban and peri-urban population. These dairies aim to optimize collection of milk from small-scale farmers for processing (pasteurization and packaging) and sale through wholesalers to the formal markets in urban and peri-urban areas.

Small-scale farmers are organized in cooperatives, which are business organizations owned and operated by groups of individuals for their mutual benefit.[1] The cooperative's committee appoints members who are in charge of collecting the milk and selling it to the dairy farm. The dairy farm trains these collectors in good hygiene practices and processes the milk prior to procurement. However, once a dairy farm is well established and business runs smoothly, expansion and intensification are the natural consequences.

Microbiological hazards are the main food safety concern in the dairy sector. They originate from animals that carry disease, the environment, milk handling equipment and milk handlers. Brucellosis is one of the major zoonotic diseases and is endemic to sub-Saharan Africa. It is present in Mali, affecting 30% of cattle in urban areas and 4% in rural areas.

Brucellosis is a disease of mainly cattle, swine, goats, sheep and dogs. Humans contract the disease from animals through direct contact with infected materials like afterbirth or indirectly by eating animal products or inhaling germs from the air. Consumption of raw milk and cheese made from raw milk is the major source of infection in people. It is considered to be an occupational disease for people who work in the livestock sector but human-to-human transmission is very rare.[2] In humans, brucellosis can cause a range of symptoms that are similar to the flu and may include fever, sweats, headaches, back pains and physical weakness. Severe infections of the central nervous system or lining of the heart may occur.[3] In women it may lead to miscarriage, while men may suffer from a painful inflammation of the testes. Brucellosis can also cause chronic symptoms that include recurrent fever, joint pain and fatigue.

The flu-like symptoms of brucellosis, in particular the recurrent fever, mean it is often confused with malaria and therefore misdiagnosis can occur and the wrong treatment be prescribed. While malaria is caused by a blood parasite, brucellosis is caused by the bacterium *Brucella* against which the standard malaria treatment is not effective. Treatment with antibiotics is possible for brucellosis but can be difficult as several antibiotics need to be combined. Depending on the timing of treatment and severity of the illness, recovery may take a few weeks to several months and largely depends on access to drugs and their regular intake over a long period. The entire population of Mali is at risk of malaria and over 80% live in high-transmission areas. In 2009, only 32% of febrile children received any anti-malaria medicine.[4]

Brucellosis is likely to have a significant socio-economic impact in rural areas where people largely depend on the trade of dairy products. Hence, a survey was carried out in central Mali in the region of Ségou. According to the 2010 WHO World Malaria Report, this region is the only one of Mali's eight regions with no data available on the occurrence of malaria. The site was selected because it is easily accessible, has large numbers of cattle and goats for dairy production and has a local dairy plant installed. The municipality of rural Cinzana comprises 72 villages and is home to about 37,000 people. It is located in central Mali just south of Ségou, about 240 kilometres east of Bamako. The household survey covered twelve villages, including three that were attached to several cooperatives supplying the *Projet d'Appui à la Filière Lait de Cinzana* (PAFLACIN) dairy. The dairy was opened in 2008 with the aim of benefiting five different groups: livestock owners, wives of dairy farmers, herders, unemployed youth and consumers. The project has installed six cooperatives to promote the collection and processing of milk, to supply wholesalers, retailers and end consumers with pasteurized and fermented milk (for *féné*, see Chapter 20) and to render technical and social services like loans to producers (Chapter 8).

Using participatory methods such as questionnaires and focus group discussions, the local milk marketing chain was mapped. Complementary information on livestock management practices and milk consumption habits was obtained to describe attitudes and practices that might lead to risky behaviour. Livestock husbandry in rural Cinzana still follows rather traditional ways, such as extensive grazing and feeding on leftovers from the previous harvest. Before farmers run short of fodder, they take their cattle on transhumance to the south in the region of Sikasso. Cattle, sheep and goats are the most popular animals in the region and are kept for multiple purposes including savings, production of natural manure for the crops and, most importantly, production of milk.

Normally, cattle belong to the entire community but the owners get the milk of their own cows. However, there are exceptions depending on the ethnic group of the farmers. Whereas the Bambara (traditionally farmers) keep cattle for prestige and insurance, the Fulani and their cousins the Djawambé have always been cattle herders and define themselves by their animals and sincerely revere them. The sale of a cow or a bull indicates there is a major problem in a family or there is an urgent need for a lot of money; the sale is normally decided by the male head of the house. The sale of a goat, on the other hand, can be decided by other males in the family or the elder women. While the male head of family decides which animal is sold or killed for sacrifice, the women are in charge of the milk. Depending on the ethnic affiliation, the milking is done by (hired) Fulani herders (Chapter 20), male children or both. The man as the head of the family hardly ever does the milking; the women must not do it at all.

In the villages that deliver milk to the project dairy for processing, the family first takes its share for home consumption. The rest of the milk is collected by members of the cooperative every morning and delivered to the dairy by motorcycle. In the rainy season when there is plenty of milk, it is delivered in separate containers, whereas in the dry season the small amounts of milk are pooled for transport. The herds of the families delivering to the plant are mainly managed by the heads of the families in order to keep track of the revenues. The other villages appoint somebody to collect the milk and deliver it to the Cinzana dairy in Ségou or they sell it individually in nearby towns on market days. The milk is normally pooled and transported on foot, by waggon or vehicle.

During the household survey, all the respondents stated they consumed cow's milk without boiling it first. Goat milk was consumed raw by 98% of the farmers. Colostrum (the first milk) was not consumed for reasons of taste and was used for feeding the calves and kids.

During sampling of blood from humans and animals, information on the female animals was obtained. About 12% of farmers reported their cows had aborted once, approximately 2% twice, while 27% reported their female goats had aborted once, 4% twice and 1% three times. Abortion often occurs in the dry season when food and fodder are scarce. Almost 75% of respondents reported they handled the aborted material of their goats; for instance, they would handle the foetus with bare hands and later burn it. Whereas the latter reduces risk of transmission of brucellosis, touching the aborted material with bare hands makes transmission very likely.

However, to assess whether brucellosis was present among humans, cattle and goats in the area, blood and milk were sampled. Almost 6% of the cattle and slightly over 1% of the goats tested positive for brucellosis. The test applied is very fast and suitable for mass screening in the field but reacts to some other microbes as well. Therefore, confirmatory laboratory tests were carried out on the initial positive samples. From the confirmatory tests, it turned out that none of the animals in Cinzana tested positive for brucellosis. Amongst the 213 people who were tested, only one was found to be infected with brucellosis, a 44-year-old woman of the Djawambé ethnic group who normally consumed milk raw. During the interview, she reported experiencing fever, fatigue, joint pain and having handled aborted material. She came from a village where cattle are managed individually rather than by the group.

Recommendations

It is important to confirm the presence of zoonoses with tests of high accuracy as field screening tests may be unreliable. Even though the prevalence of brucellosis appears low, infected animals in the herds must be detected and systematically eliminated. In areas with intensified livestock production, such as cities, vaccination schemes should be introduced. Producers should be trained on brucellosis and safe handling of milk and aborted materials. The training could be facilitated by PAFLACIN. Milk must be boiled or pasteurized prior to consumption. The cultural perception of raw milk must be taken into consideration when setting up awareness programmes (Chapter 20).

Ibrahim Sow holds a veterinary degree and a Master's degree of applied microbiology from the University of Bamako in Mali.

Title and authors of the study

Investigation on the risk of brucellosis linked to the production and consumption of milk in rural Cinzana, Mali.

Ibrahim Sow,[1] *Kohei Makita,*[2,3] *Delia Grace,*[2] *Solenne Costard*[4,5] and *Bassirou Bonfoh.*[6]

[1]Central Veterinary Laboratory, Bamako, Mali; [2]International Livestock Research Institute, Kenya; [3]Rakuno Gakuen University, Japan; [4]Royal Veterinary College, UK; [5]EpiX Analytics, USA; [6]Centre Suisse de Recherches Scientifiques en Côte d'Ivoire

Contact details

Ibrahim Sow
Laboratoire Central Vétérinaire
B.P. 2295, Bamako, Mali
Email: sowbreh@yahoo.fr

Notes

1. O'Sullivan A and Sheffrin SM. 2003. *Economics: Principles in action.* Prentice Hall, Upper Saddle River, New Jersey.
2. WHO. 2011. www.who.int/zoonoses/diseases/brucellosis/en (accessed 9 July 2014).
3. Centers for Disease Control and Prevention. www.cdc.gov/nczved/divisions/dfbmd/diseases/brucellosis (accessed 9 July 2014).
4. WHO. 2010. World Malaria Report. www.who.int/malaria/publications/country-profiles/profile_mli_en.pdf (accessed 9 July 2014).

20

BOILING MILK DISRUPTS THE SOCIAL ORDER OF COMMUNITIES IN MALI

Valentin Bognan Koné, Kristina Roesel, Gilbert Fokou, Kohei Makita, Delia Grace, Gnabeli Y. Roch and Bassirou Bonfoh

Key messages

- In our study, milk and meat were ranked the most important food products.
- Different perceptions of quality of milk for home consumption and milk for sale led to bias in behaviour; at home, milk was almost always consumed raw whereas milk for sale was boiled.
- People believed raw milk was best and could never make people sick. Boiling of milk was considered a disruption of the social order.
- Meat was mostly consumed from sick animals or from those that died of disease, but was thoroughly cooked.
- Milk that did not meet quality standards was not always thrown away or processed to make it safe. In some cases, it was consumed with minimal processing.
- The trade of milk and meat in the informal market was mainly based on trust in the producer rather than price or hygiene of the setting.
- One source of milk or meat fed many people.

Background

The rapid urban growth in African cities is accompanied by an increase in demand for meat, milk and fish products. This growing urban demand for animal-source foods is sometimes difficult to cover through domestic production. In Mali, however, the government and development partners have initiated strategies to tackle this issue on a local level to avoid increasing dependency on imports. The population of cattle in Mali is approximately 8 million and the country has millions more sheep and goats; this should be adequate to meet the domestic demand for milk. However, dairy production and productivity are still low. Thus, dairy farms and cooperatives were established to upgrade the local dairy sector through formal milk processing whereby raw milk is tested before procurement and pasteurization and staff are trained in basic hygiene.

In semi-arid areas of West Africa (such as much of Mali), livestock keeping is one of the main livelihood strategies of millions of rural populations. Since dairies are accessible to rural farmers, they are now able to gain access to markets formerly out of reach for them. Despite all these efforts, risks of food-borne diseases are believed to be increasing. What are possible reasons for this? Is it because people are ignorant about food hygiene or because they simply set different priorities? Is it that we are becoming more aware of problems that were always there?

According to social scientists, people's knowledge and perception of reality becomes embedded in the institutional fabric of society. Reality is therefore said to be socially constructed. Definitions of terms such as health, disease, quality, risk or hazard are therefore interpreted subjectively.

When defining quality, microbiological and other standards have been extensively studied but may exclude one key factor: the consumer (who could simultaneously be a producer, transporter and intermediary). Consumers make strategic decisions and follow their own interests but technical experts may consider their behaviour as irrational. Marketing experts, for example, know that quality responds to consumer expectations which are constantly changing. Consumers' decisions depend on several factors such as level of education, economic background, social environment, ethnic affiliation, and so on. For this reason the perception of what is hygienic varies greatly between, say, Africa and the United States of America.

Thus, the safety of food products of animal origin needs to be addressed by additional sociological and anthropological approaches. To understand why people are more or less exposed to objective risks, one must understand their subjective perception and examine how they produce, process and consume products of animal origin. Consumption habits are largely influenced by status within the value chain (producer, intermediary, processor, seller or consumer). Habits, beliefs and the social status of a population determine their perception of the quality and safety of food and the consideration of exogenous (quality standards set by government) and endogenous (religious views) factors are helpful instruments for mitigating risks in animal-source food.

The data in the study were obtained through questionnaires, individual interviews, focus group discussions and observations. Unlike most food safety studies, it involved anthropologists. It focused mainly on the producers of milk and meat because they are also consumers and know most about the local methods of production, collection, marketing and consumption. The participants in the study represented all the ethnic groups residing in the study area. In African countries, many ethnic groups share the same resources and are intricately related in production chains. Therefore, ethnicity can be an important determinant of one's health.

The Bambara are the largest of Mali's approximately thirty ethnic groups. They are mostly farmers who grow millet, sorghum and groundnuts among other food crops. Another significant proportion of the population consists of the nomadic Fulani (also known as Peul or Fulbe). Though they depend on livestock for their livelihoods, the Fulani consider their animals to be of much more value than merely economic; livestock are the pillar of social and cultural life and are associated with many social, therapeutic and economic functions. Somewhat similar beliefs of the central position of cattle exist among the pastoralists of East Africa.

The study area of Cinzana covers about 1100 square kilometres and is located in the centre of Mali in the Sahel zone where most of the people have been semi-nomads, farming and raising livestock in a system of transhumance. Approximately 40,000 people live here and are mostly Bambara and Fulani. Other groups are the Sarakolé (traders), Bobo (cotton farmers), Bozo (fishermen), Somono (fishermen), Mianka (farmers), Djawambé (livestock keepers, cousins of the Fulani) and Mossi (craftsmen). They all live together in harmony, their common tie being Islam except for one Christian village in the study area. Social life is mostly marked by Bambara culture, for instance social hierarchy and respect for the elders.

Direct observations revealed that distances between the seventy-two villages in rural Cinzana were quite substantial (7–29km), limiting the influence of media to run sensitization campaigns. It was also observed that traditions had a strong influence on husbandry practices, and rules of basic hygiene were sometimes neglected in favour of traditions. Moreover, solidarity between the people was also found to be very common within communities, especially when animals were sick or about to die. Sick animals were slaughtered and every member of the community bought a piece of meat from the owner at a small fee. This money was supposed to support the farmer who had experienced the loss of an animal.

The question of the perception of quality, consumption habits and risk management was tackled in face-to-face interviews in 207 households in the twelve villages. The study sought answers on social and economic factors, risk mitigation strategies for milk and meat, risk management strategies and suggestions for improving food safety. These interviews were facilitated by a mediator and took place in a local restaurant with the head of each household or his deputy. It was remarkable that each household head sometimes fed more than fifty people, mostly his sons and their families or his younger siblings if he was the first-born.

Prior to the interviews, the village chiefs were asked for permission to undertake research into their respective territories. With respect to the traditional hierarchy and religion, the Imam or the priest needed to be involved too as they are usually involved in local decision-making or problem-solving. The field-based research was done during the rainy season when farmers are normally busy planting, selling or grazing their animals. As a result, it was sometimes a challenge to interview the farmers as scheduled. Travel was difficult during the rains as many roads were rendered impassable by flooding or muddy sections. Some villagers found it hard to accept researchers at their homes. They initially thought the researchers were on a development aid mission and were not very pleased, having received many others in the past who failed to leave a positive impact.

Milk is a life essence

Milk is the most important food of animal origin in rural Cinzana. The Fulani are traditionally herders and therefore milk is always accessible to them. The Bambara, who used to be farmers, have diversified their activities due to seasonal shortages of rain. Manure from goats is commonly used for fertilizing their fields, and cows are kept as a financial backup for hard times. Thus, they have also increased their milk consumption. On average, over 90% of people consumed milk without any prior heat treatment (Chapter 19). For the Fulani, it is unacceptable to boil milk as it is considered a life essence because of its highly nutritional value and thus vital for physical well-being, health and strength. During transhumance, raw milk is the only food that keeps the herders alive. Boiling of milk is thought to result in loss of its beneficial attributes, leaving it as a simple 'white liquid'. It is even believed that boiling milk leads to burns of the teats or mastitis in the animal whose milk is heated. The Bambara, who have just recently discovered livestock keeping, rely on and trust in the knowledge of the Fulani who they consider the true herders.

There are similar beliefs about special properties of camel milk among some camel keepers in East Africa; camel milk is often consumed as a nutraceutical (a food with health-giving properties). It is interesting that similar beliefs around the special properties of raw milk are held by some people in the United States of America; some buy shares in a cow because the only way it is legal to drink raw milk is if you own the animal.

Milk also serves several religious purposes like sacrifices. It has been observed that especially on Fridays (holy day in Islam), raw milk is consumed in the company of the entire community. Homemade sun-dried dumplings accompanied by raw milk are frequently given out to children, neighbours or people in need. During wedding ceremonies, raw milk is served as an appetizer during the reception of all the invitees. Therefore, milk is a common tie of the social structure in rural Cinzana. However, a few people boil milk prior to consumption but these are mostly those who have lived away from their rural homes, for example young people who have migrated to the cities in search of employment.

If milk is not consumed raw or boiled, it can be eaten as *féné* (partially fermented milk). Traditionally, *féné* is made from raw milk. The dairy in Cinzana, however, made *féné* from pasteurized milk. *Féné* is popular in remote villages without regular access to fresh milk, such as Bobo village in the study. Although fermentation can be effective at inhibiting some milk-borne pathogens, partial fermentation of milk will probably not result in the production of enough lactic acid to inhibit pathogenic bacteria and thus should be considered a risky practice. However, the health risks of *féné* have not been widely studied, thus little is known about them.

If milk must be bought, the most important attribute is trust in the person who sells it. Good milk is considered to be cow milk that is not mixed with that from other species or milk powder. Other criteria are the yellowish colour of the milk, viscosity, clotting and homogeneity. Camel milk, for instance, is considered 'too liquid' and therefore not popular.

Meat is consumed infrequently. Healthy cows are not slaughtered for meat as it is preferred to keep them alive for milking. Most people also cannot afford to buy meat on a regular basis. If meat is bought, it is normally from an animal that died of disease or exhaustion. The meat is bought from the local butcher at a reduced price, cooked thoroughly and served in a sauce. However, meat is a crucial part of the meals eaten during feasts at religious ceremonies, weddings and baptisms. The community members contribute towards the purchase of an animal which is then slaughtered and part of the meat roasted by men and the rest cooked by the women of the community and shared among everyone during the feast.

In the streets of bigger towns, local butcheries with a rotisserie attached are common. These butcheries are called *dibitéries* and are comparable to the *nyama choma* pubs in East Africa. The owners are mostly livestock keepers and animals are either brought to their facility or collected from farms in case a sick or dying animal is too weak to walk to the abattoir. At the butcheries, there is no inspection of the meat by state or private veterinarians. The interviewed households named three attributes that were most important to judge whether the meat was suitable for consumption: the meat must be of red colour, still covered with some fresh blood and fat must be clearly visible. However, these physical attributes are not very useful in determining microbial contamination. Meat was only bought from trusted people (friends, neighbours or relatives) and the cleanliness of the butchery was an important aspect that customers considered during purchase. Once the meat was cooked, there was no need to worry about risks to health.

Soap kills taste

The livestock in rural areas in Mali is mainly in the hands of male Fulani, Djawambé and Bambara. Milking of cows and goats is done twice a day. The morning milk is for sale whereas the evening milk is reserved for feeding the family. In the dry season, only surplus milk is sold once the family is fed. Milking is usually done after the morning and afternoon prayers. Before prayers, the hands are normally washed with water and are still considered to be clean once milking starts. During the milking, it was observed that fingers were habitually dipped in the milk. The farmers considered it necessary to grease the teats with milk and they were not aware that this practice presented a risk of milk contamination. The milk is collected in calabashes that are later cleaned with water after the morning milking is complete and left to dry in the midday sun. Soap is normally not used to clean the calabashes as the inner surfaces are not smooth and thus harbour soap residues that taint the taste of the milk. Instead, leaves from commonly found bushes are used to scrub the containers and calabashes.

Traditionally, processing of milk was done by the wives of the dairy farmers who were in charge of storage, processing and sale of raw, fresh and sour milk to customers in the villages. When the PAFLACIN dairy was set up in Cinzana, the traditional marketing channels changed. Many of the women who formerly processed milk started working for the cooperative that supplied the dairy. They collected the milk from producers and pasteurized it before delivering it to the dairy where it was eventually sold. While milk for sale is normally pasteurized, raw milk is still consumed at home.

Although dairy plants are not operating in every village of Cinzana, the producers have started selling their milk to the cooperatives or directly to the dairy. The raw milk is tested for freshness and adulteration. Milk that passes the test is pasteurized (if not already done at cooperative level), processed into *féné*, then sold to private individuals or wholesalers, the latter providing access to markets previously not available before the establishment of PAFLACIN (Chapter 8). Milk that does not pass the quality test is rejected and is mostly processed by the women into *féné*, which may present a health risk. This study suggests that in poor countries, valuable livestock products are not likely to be discarded even if they fail to meet defined quality standards.

Recommendations

Risk mitigation should focus on educating consumers, especially the farmers' families who prefer to sell milk that meets dairy industry standards but drink that of lower quality. However, education and raising awareness are not enough when practices are the result of deeply held cultural beliefs. It is important to understand risks and try and mitigate them in culturally appropriate ways. Project officers and promoters of public health must raise awareness among consumers but these efforts should not be focused on the farmers only but on all players in the complex process of production, processing, distribution and consumption.

Valentin Bognan Koné holds a Master's degree in sociology from the Université Félix Houphouët-Boigny, Côte d'Ivoire. He was the only social scientist in the first phase of the Safe Food, Fair Food project.

Title and authors of the study

Social representation and perception of the quality of animal-source food in Cinzana, Mali.

Valentin Bognan Koné,[1,2] *Gilbert Fokou*,[1] *Kohei Makita*,[3,4] *Delia Grace*,[3] *Gnabeli Y. Roch*[2] and *Bassirou Bonfoh*[1]

[1]Centre Suisse de Recherches Scientifiques en Côte d'Ivoire; [2]Université Félix Houphouët-Boigny, Côte d'Ivoire; [3]International Livestock Research Institute, Kenya; [4]Rakuno Gakuen University, Japan

Contact details

Valentin Bognan Koné
Centre Suisse de Recherches Scientifiques en Côte d'Ivoire
01 B.P. 1303 Abidjan 01, Côte d'Ivoire
Email: Konebognan1@yahoo.fr or kbognan@csrs.ci

21

BEEF IN EXPORT ABATTOIRS NOT SAFER THAN THAT IN LOCAL ABATTOIRS

Cameline Mwai, Kristina Roesel, Kohei Makita, Samuel M. Arimi, Erastus Kang'ethe and Delia Grace

Key messages

- *Escherichia coli* O157:H7 is present on carcasses leaving slaughterhouses in Nairobi, Kenya.
- The same risk of contamination exists in all categories of slaughterhouses in Nairobi (local, local improved and export).
- Abattoir workers significantly contribute to carcass contamination.
- Improving food safety through training of staff and improving terms of employment is crucial.

Background

In 2011, Central Europe was ravaged by an outbreak caused by the bacterium *Escherichia coli* that was found in contaminated sprouts from one producer. Within five weeks, over 4000 people in Germany fell sick and forty-nine people died, including one in Sweden. Unusually, it had mostly affected people who were healthy, female and over 20 years of age. Cases occurred in fifteen countries outside Germany, mostly in people with travel links to Germany.[1]

E. coli is commonly found in the gut of humans and warm-blooded animals. While most strains are harmless, some can cause severe food-borne disease. The infection is usually transmitted through consumption of contaminated water or food, such as undercooked meat products and raw milk. Symptoms of disease include abdominal cramps and diarrhoea, which may be bloody. Fever and vomiting may also occur. Most patients recover within ten days, although in a few cases the disease may become life threatening.[2] The bloody diarrhoea can sometimes develop into haemolytic uraemic syndrome which has the potential to cause kidney failure and death. It is a severe complication as some of the strains produce a toxin. This group is called verotoxin-producing *E. coli*.

Long before the outbreak in Germany, another strain of *E. coli* called O157 capable of producing the same symptoms had been found in faeces and raw milk from urban dairy cattle herds in Nairobi. The same culprit was identified in 1992 in a 2-year-old boy suffering from bloody diarrhoea in Malindi Hospital on the Kenyan coast. The government thought the country was safe as only one case was reported. It is commonly known that diarrhoea is ranked very high on the list of diseases in sub-Saharan Africa. Many cases of diarrhoea have been reported at Kenyatta National Hospital but the causes are unknown. It is also not known how many cases of kidney failure can be attributed to *E. coli* but were not diagnosed as such. Officially, amoebiosis is the most common diarrhoeal disease diagnosed by microscopy. Amoebiosis results from an infection with amoeba and is characterized by watery to bloody diarrhoea, though it is not as dangerous as *E. coli* infection. However, tests are rarely done to determine if bloody diarrhoea is due to *E. coli* or amoeba infection.

Since *E. coli* is part of a family of bacteria that has previously been identified in beef carcasses in Nairobi, the present study was designed to assess the likelihood of meat being contaminated during slaughter. This can happen when carcasses get in contact with faeces from the slaughtered animals during flaying and dressing.

Three slaughterhouses with different levels of hygiene control – classified as local, local improved and export – were selected for the study which was carried out in 2009. A total of 300 animals were tracked along the slaughtering process to sample faeces and carcass swabs. Faecal samples from the rectum were taken from each animal after stunning to trace how many animals were responsible for contamination of the meat. Two carcass sites – flank and brisket – were swabbed after flaying, evisceration and cleaning. In total, seven samples were taken from each carcass.

Out of 2100 samples, 280 (13.3%) were positive for *E. coli*. Further tests were done to find out whether the strain O157 which causes bloody diarrhoea was among them. Indeed, 4.3% were positive for *E. coli* O157 and some were found to be toxigenic.

The probability of a carcass being contaminated with *E. coli* O157 was 4.8% in the local improved abattoir, 3.8% in the local abattoir and 2.9% in the export abattoir. However, these differences are not statistically significant, thus the risk of contamination is the same irrespective of the type of abattoir.

Recommendations

More research on handling, transportation and slaughter processes must be done since some of the slaughterhouses have adopted more standard sanitary operating procedures. The government levy of US$1–3 per carcass that is charged in local and export slaughterhouses should be allocated for inspectors as enforcement of existing laws is crucial.

Nairobi City Council regulations state that contaminated meat must be confiscated. Routine sampling of carcasses and workers should be done as part of the HACCP plan for monitoring and intervention. Staff should be hired on an employment basis and training provided regularly.

Cameline Mwai holds a Master's degree in veterinary public health from the University of Nairobi. She is a government veterinary officer for food safety and hygiene and previously volunteered in an animal welfare project at the Kenya Network for Development of Agricultural Technologies.

Title and authors of the study

Risk of contamination of beef carcasses with *Escherichia coli* O157:H7 from slaughterhouses in Nairobi, Kenya.

Cameline Mwai,[1] *Kohei Makita,*[2,3] *Samuel M. Arimi,*[1] *Erastus Kang'ethe*[1] and *Delia Grace*[2]

[1]University of Nairobi, Kenya; [2]International Livestock Research Institute, Kenya; [3]Rakuno Gakuen University, Japan

Contact details

Cameline Mwai
P.O. Box 2940, 00100 Nairobi, Kenya
Email: camelinemwai@gmail.com

Notes

1. www.euro.who.int/en/what-we-do/health-topics/emergencies/international-health-regulations/outbreaks-of-e.-coli-o104h4-infection/questions-and-answers-q-and-a-on-the-outbreaks-in-germany-and-france (accessed 9 July 2014).
2. www.who.int/topics/escherichia_coli_infections/en (accessed 9 July 2014).

22

A SINGLE SLIP MAY CAUSE LASTING INJURY: BEEF IN KENYA CONTAMINATED FROM THE START

John Kago, Kristina Roesel, Erastus Kang'ethe, John Wangoh, Kohei Makita and Delia Grace

Key messages

- Only a few strains of *E. coli* are capable of causing disease.
- *E. coli* was detected in meat at the slaughterhouse and contamination levels increased along the value chain.
- Personnel involved in handling, transporting and selling meat are poorly trained and are a significant source of contamination.
- The risk of purchasing tainted meat from butcheries is high due to multiple malpractices.

Background

According to the Export Processing Zones Authority in Kenya, exports of beef in 2005 earned the country KSh34.4 billion (about €400 million). The country's beef sector is supplied mainly by small-scale traders and is therefore largely informal. Data from Kenya's Ministry of Agriculture indicate that the humid weather in 2010 helped raise the annual red meat production to 430,000 tons against domestic consumption of 330,000 tons. Nonetheless, Kenya's livestock export remains restricted by the EU and some countries in the Middle East due to the failure to meet safety standards.[1] Good farming practices, good hygiene practices and HACCP have been identified as helpful measures of meat safety control[2] but the informal meat industry with its numerous players is very hard to monitor.

Escherichia coli O157:H7 was found in the guts of ruminants and on the surface of meat in abattoirs in Nairobi (Chapter 21). Sporadic outbreaks have shown that improperly cooked meat, raw fruits and vegetables contaminated with the bacteria can cause diarrhoea and sometimes even kidney failure and death. *E. coli* is not hazardous by nature and only some strains cause disease. While the regular strains lead to diarrhoea if large amounts are ingested, only 10 to 100 individual microbes of the dangerous strains like O157:H7 can cause disease. Therefore, the presence of *E. coli* is generally used to indicate faecal contamination of food. If contamination is high, chances increase that some of the contaminants include *E. coli* O157:H7.

The study suggests that good hygiene at the slaughterhouse and during transportation can eliminate contamination and cross-contamination of meat with *E. coli* O157:H7. Following the confirmation that meat is contaminated at slaughterhouse level (Chapter 21), investigation focused on determining the level of bacterial contamination between loading of meat at the abattoirs and offloading at retail shops. Handling practices were surveyed by interviewing and observing chain actors.

The largest slaughterhouses in terms of throughput and supplying local butcheries in Nairobi, Limuru and Eldoret were selected. They are either privately owned or under the control of the local authorities. Meat transporters using vehicles mounted with veterinary-approved boxes and supplying two or more butcheries were involved. These butcheries were included in the survey too.

Surface swabs of carcasses were taken for laboratory analysis as the carcasses were loaded into the vehicles at the slaughterhouses and offloaded at the butchery. The temperature and humidity inside the transportation boxes were measured as these two factors influence the rate of bacterial growth and spoilage. At the butchery, working surfaces were sampled to determine contamination levels. By observing the process and interviewing the workers, practices that might compromise meat safety were identified. Preliminary findings show that *E. coli* O157:H7 was found at every level from loading to offloading with the highest occurrence on working surfaces and equipment at the butcheries.

A white coat alone does not do it

Transporters seem to lack formal training on meat hygiene which became apparent when almost all of them reported that they did not wash their hands frequently. The loaders used white coats for protective clothing which were either privately owned or hired from people near the slaughterhouses. However, the coats were not changed in between loading sessions. Loading was done by carrying the carcasses on the shoulders, resulting in the coat becoming bloodstained. Working surfaces were not properly cleaned and transportation boxes lacked cooling facilities.

One cell of *E. coli* doubles every 20 minutes. Therefore, high levels of contamination at the slaughterhouse will result in multiplication of the organism during transport (one hour or more) to levels high enough to cause disease. *E. coli* O157:H7 is quite hardy. It can survive for extended periods in water and soil, under frozen and refrigeration temperatures and in dry conditions. It also can adapt to acidic conditions. The organism is destroyed by thorough cooking or pasteurization.[3]

Most of the workers at the butchery were aware of the importance of frequent hand washing and knew that spoiled meat can cause disease and that intestines should be stored separately from meat. On average, two out of every 100 carcasses during loading at the slaughterhouses were contaminated with *E. coli* O157:H7, as were four out of every 100 carcasses during offloading at the butcheries. A follow-up visit the following day revealed that three carcasses at the slaughterhouses were contaminated with *E. coli* O157:H7.

At the butcheries, cloths were used to wipe the benches, knives, weighing scales and wooden chopping board after contact with intestines and before handling the meat. There was no use of hot water to sterilize the implements and surfaces. Most of the butcheries used wooden cutting boards which are easy to chip and hard to clean. To avoid this, the boards are scratched off with the knives and fat from the meat is applied in the morning before starting work. The board is then used the whole day and only wiped clean the following morning.

Many of the butcheries did not have a working refrigeration system and stored the meat for up to three days, thus encouraging the growth of *E. coli* in the meat. In some butcheries, leftover meat was reportedly stored in deep freezers though power blackouts were sometimes experienced. Most butchers prepared ready-to-eat food in their premises; cooking is likely to eliminate *E. coli*. However, cross-contamination of the cooked meat can occur if it is cut on the chopping board used for raw meat.

Butchery owners and their staff regularly received complaints from customers about the meat being tough or foul smelling. The preliminary conclusion is that most of the transporters and butchers were poorly educated on good hygiene practices. They had not received any formal training on hygienic meat handling but had acquired skills on the job by observation. Data on the level of spoilage will indicate the likelihood of infection after consuming meat from local butcheries.

Recommendations

The personnel along the meat value chain must be properly trained in hygienic aspects and good hygiene practices and compliance with the cold chain must be promoted. Innovative ways are needed for improving practices along the value chain as currently many actors are not observing good practices. Legal Notice 110 of 2010 allows for classification of slaughterhouses based on throughput and facilities. It lists a requirement for personnel working in slaughterhouses/meat transportation to have obtained certain qualifications. However, they should also maintain their knowledge through a certain number of training courses in a year.

John Kago holds a Bachelor of Science degree in food science and technology from the University of Nairobi. He carried out this study towards his Master's degree from the University of Nairobi. He was previously a tutor at the Kenya

Polytechnic University College, sales executive at Lasap Limited and supervisor at Frigoken Limited.

Title and authors of the study

Assessment of the risk of beef contamination with *Escherichia coli* O157:H7 along the transportation value chain.

John Kago,[1] *Erastus Kang'ethe,*[1] *John Wangoh,*[1] *Kohei Makita*[2,3] and *Delia Grace*[2]

[1]University of Nairobi, Kenya; [2]International Livestock Research Institute, Kenya; [3]Rakuno Gakuen University, Japan

Contact details

John Kago
Department of Food Science, Technology and Nutrition
University of Nairobi
P.O. Box 29053-00625, Nairobi, Kenya
Email: jkago73@yahoo.com or jkago73@gmail.com

Notes

1. CNC News. 2011. www.cncworld.tv/news/v_show/11923_Kenya_s_meat_export.shtml (accessed 9 July 2014).
2. Buchanan RL and Doyle MP. 1997. Foodborne disease significance of *Escherichia coli* O157:H7 and other enterohemorrhagic *E. coli*. *Food Technology* 51:69–76.
3. www.ext.colostate.edu/pubs/foodnut/09369.html (accessed 9 July 2014).

23

RISKY ROAST BEEF IN TANZANIA

Edgar Mahundi, Kristina Roesel, E.D. Karimuribo, Kohei Makita, H.E. Ngowi, Delia Grace and Lusato Kurwijila

Key messages

- Beef in Arusha is highly contaminated with thermophilic *Campylobacter*.
- Raw meat is least contaminated while skewer beef is most contaminated.
- The contamination rate is higher in poor areas.
- There are several good practices by all actors but further improvement is needed along the supply chain to reduce risk of disease.

Background

Campylobacteriosis is a widespread infection caused by the bacterium *Campylobacter*. Livestock and poultry are the main source of *Campylobacter* as they can carry the bacteria in their intestines without being ill. The organism is transmitted by eating raw meat or drinking raw milk contaminated with faeces. Water that has been polluted with *Campylobacter* is another source of infection in humans.

The most common symptoms of *Campylobacter* infection include diarrhoea, abdominal pain, fever, headache, nausea and vomiting. Symptoms usually start 2–5 days after infection and last for 3–6 days. Specific treatment is not usually necessary, except to replace electrolytes and water lost through diarrhoea, but antimicrobials may be needed to treat severe cases and the carrier state.[1]

A very low number of *Campylobacter* organisms (fewer than 500) can cause illness in humans. Only one drop of juice from raw chicken meat can infect a person. In some cases, the infection may lead to chronic health problems like damage in joints or nerves, and in people with compromised immune systems, *Campylobacter* occasionally spreads to the bloodstream and causes a serious life-threatening infection.[2] A special feature of some types of *Campylobacter* is that they grow best at temperatures above 45°C; they are referred to as thermophilic (heat loving).

In Tanzania, the occurrence of campylobacteriosis is not well studied, especially in the informal markets where 80% of local inhabitants buy their food. The municipality of Arusha in central Tanzania is home to about 300,000 people[3] and about five times as many cattle. By regulation, slaughter of all animals is carried out at a modern abattoir owned by the Arusha Meat Company.[4] The meat is then sold to private butcheries. Several bar owners buy meat from the private butcheries and prepare it for sale to customers as roast meat.

Popular ready-to-eat meat products in Arusha are roast beef (*nyama choma*) and skewer beef (*mishikaki*), which are normally served with *ugali*, a stiff porridge made from maize flour. Bananas and vegetable stew (*sukuma wiki*) as well as semi-cooked or raw cabbage mixed with chopped tomatoes and onions are often eaten as an accompaniment.

The aim of the present study was to investigate whether thermophilic *Campylobacter* was present in raw and roast beef in Arusha and to assess possible public health risks associated with ready-to-eat roast meat products.

Arusha Municipality is divided into a northern and a southern part, the latter characterized by a higher population density and fewer sanitary facilities available. Samples of raw meat were collected from butcheries while samples of roast and skewer beef were collected from local beer bars (pubs).

Thermophilic *Campylobacter* was found in one-quarter of all sampled beef products in the municipality. Its occurrence was five times higher in beef sold in the poorer southern part of the municipality than in the northern part. Bacteria were detected in raw meat but contamination levels were significantly higher in meat served at the beer bars. Possible sources of contamination can be identified by using a fault tree to trace the steps from the live cattle to the customer's plate (Chapter 5). If the animal was not infected prior to being slaughtered, the meat can subsequently be tainted at the abattoir, during transport to the local butchery and at the butchery itself. In the present survey, the sampling of meat only started at the butcheries where it was found to contain thermophilic *Campylobacter*. Further investigation on the source of initial contamination is therefore necessary.

Thermophilic *Campylobacter* was detected in over 20% of samples of roast beef served to customers. Again, the occurrence of microbial contamination was higher in the southern part of the municipality. However, more investigations along the supply chain are needed to identify the sources of contamination so that appropriate preventive measures can be put in place. Skewer beef was generally more contaminated than roast beef; this might be due to the larger surface area providing an even greater breeding ground for bacteria.

Discussions with consumers and pub owners revealed that *nyama choma* and *mishikaki* are very popular in Tanzania. Beef was the favourite meat of more than 75% of the respondents. Most private households surveyed reportedly ate beef about three times a week. The pub owners sold about 3500kg of roast meat and 165kg of skewer meat a day.

When purchasing raw beef, customers and pub owners usually judged the quality of the meat by its fresh red colour and fat content and bought the meat before noon. More than 50% served or ate it within 30 minutes of cooking. Almost 75% of the respondents considered good personal hygiene practices such as washing hands as very important. However, 75% of pub owners had never received training on food hygiene. Therefore, it was not surprising that none of the respondents knew about campylobacteriosis. When asked what disease is commonly associated with food, people mostly mentioned gout which they thought was caused by eating too much meat. They also mentioned Rift Valley fever, a disease that can result from direct contact with the blood of infected cattle during slaughtering. In 2007, Kenya, Somalia and Tanzania suffered from an outbreak of the viral disease which killed hundreds of people and, seemingly, many locals recalled this vividly.[5]

Taking into account the handling and consumption practices of the consumers and that 500 *Campylobacter* organisms can make a person fall ill, it was calculated whether the level of *Campylobacter* detected on samples of ready-to-eat beef in Arusha posed a public health risk. It was found that 13% of the healthy population are at risk of infection, with immunocompromised people at higher risk. Every day, about 1800 people are exposed to the risk of campylobacteriosis from 16% of servings of roast beef and 35% of skewer beef.

Recommendations

Additional studies on the concentration of *Campylobacter* at different stages of the value chain are needed to identify the sources of contamination and quantify the risk to consumers. Public health programmes, consumer awareness and training of food handlers should be promoted. Budgetary allocation should be made towards regular inspection of food outlets by health officers as well as laboratory testing of food samples.

Edgar Mahundi holds a Master's degree in veterinary science. After several years in private practice, he worked as veterinary officer at the Ministry of Livestock Development and Fisheries in Tanzania until he took up his current position as drug inspector at the Tanzania Food and Drugs Authority in the Ministry of Health and Social Welfare in Dar es Salaam.

Title and authors of the study

Food safety risk assessment of thermophilic *Campylobacter* and marketing channels of beef in Arusha Municipality, Tanzania.

Edgar Mahundi,[1] *E.D. Karimuribo*,[2] *Kohei Makita*,[3,4] *H.E. Ngowi*,[2] *Delia Grace*[3] and *Lusato Kurwijila*[2]

[1]Tanzania Food and Drugs Authority; [2]Sokoine University of Agriculture, Tanzania; [3]International Livestock Research Institute, Kenya; [4]Rakuno Gakuen University, Japan

Contact details

Edgar Mahundi
Tanzania Food and Drugs Authority
P.O. Box 77150, Dar es Salaam, Tanzania
Email: mahundiabc@yahoo.com

Notes

1. WHO. 2011. www.who.int/topics/campylobacter/en (accessed 9 July 2014).
2. National Center for Emerging and Zoonotic Infectious Diseases. Centers for Disease Control and Prevention. www.cdc.gov/nczved/divisions/dfbmd/diseases/campylobacter/#what (accessed 9 July 2014).
3. United Republic of Tanzania. 2002. Population and housing census. www.tanzania.go.tz/2002census.PDF (accessed 9 July 2014).
4. Letara J, MacGregor J and Hesse C. 2006. Estimating the economic significance of pastoralism: The example of the *nyama choma* sector in Tanzania. http://pubs.iied.org/pdfs/G00242.pdf (accessed 9 July 2014).
5. WHO. 2007. www.who.int/csr/don/2007_05_09/en/index.html (accessed 9 July 2014).

24

RISKY ROAST BEEF IN TANZANIA? NOT YET CONFIRMED!

Haruya Toyomaki, Kristina Roesel, K. Ishikara, P. Sanka, Lusato Kurwijila, Delia Grace and Kohei Makita

Key messages

- None of the raw beef samples contained thermophilic *Campylobacter*.
- While *Campylobacter* was not detected in raw meat, it was found in 1.4% of roast chicken samples.
- The bacterial load of *Campylobacter* was generally low.
- In spite of training, poor handling practices were observed.

Background

Nyama choma (roast beef) and *kuku choma* (roast chicken) are popular ready-to-eat foods in Tanzania. A separate study revealed that beef in Arusha is contaminated with a bacterium – *Campylobacter* – likely to cause severe diarrhoea in people (Chapter 23). The same study estimated that every day, approximately six new cases occur per 1000 people in Arusha. People with a feeble immune system are probably even more at risk. The author recommended determining the concentration of *Campylobacter* at the various steps along the supply chain. People can only fall sick if they ingest enough bacteria. His calculations were based on contamination levels published in medical literature which assessed the average load of bacteria in other study areas. These figures do not necessarily have to apply to the situation present in Arusha.

In Tanzania, people suffering from diarrhoea do not always seek medical attention depending on their budget and distance from the health care centre. Therefore, diarrhoea is most likely to be underreported. If people seek medical care, the cause of diarrhoea is hardly investigated because of the costs involved. Campylobacteriosis is not a notifiable disease, thus health care centres are not likely to provide information on whether it is a problem in the area.

The common routes of transmission for *Campylobacter* are faecal-oral and the ingestion of contaminated food such as raw meat, milk or water. What could be the route of transmission in Arusha? Eating undercooked chicken and beef could be a possibility. For this reason, the present study sought to assess the level of thermophilic *Campylobacter* in raw beef and roast meat sold in beer bars. The study found that there was no risk of contracting campylobacteriosis by eating roast beef or chicken at local restaurants in Arusha. Only one out of 70 samples (1.4%) of roast chicken was found to contain *Campylobacter*.

In addition to microbiological assessment, the study also interviewed butchers and bar owners who sold the roast meat to identify other possible routes of *Campylobacter* transmission related to meat handling practices and the personal hygiene of the meat handlers. They were asked about how they handled the meat and the facilities they used to store, prepare, cook and serve the product.

It was found that less than a quarter of the 30 butchers and 40 bar owners interviewed had a refrigerator. However, all the respondents used tap water during their operations. Half of the respondents said they had been trained in basic hygiene practices. Therefore, it was surprising to observe that most bar owners did not use separate knives and cutting boards for the raw and roast meat, a practice that greatly increases the chances of cross-contamination of cooked meat. Cross-contamination is also possible if utensils used to cut raw meat are used to prepare the vegetables that are served along with the *nyama choma* or *kuku choma*.

Are these practices due to ineffective training of pub owners on food hygiene? Do the local health authorities regularly update pub owners on food-borne hazards, or is it just not cost-effective to buy separate knives, cutting boards and plates for raw and roast food? These questions need to be investigated in future through participatory techniques.

Recommendations

The separation of raw and roast products – including the utensils for preparation such as knives and cutting boards – should be promoted. Meat handlers should be trained in personal and processing hygiene. Health authorities should assess the compliance of trained food handlers and consider the implementation of incentives. The government could support budgetary allocation to investigate the level of contamination of thermophilic *Campylobacter* in chicken.

Haruya Toyomaki undertook this research during his final year of studies towards a Bachelor's degree in veterinary medicine at Rakuno Gakuen University in Japan.

Title and authors of the study

An estimation of thermophilic *Campylobacter* population in ready-to-eat roast beef and chicken sold and hygiene practices of sellers in beer bars in Arusha Municipality, Tanzania.

H. Toyomaki,[1] *K. Ishikara,*[1] *P. Sanka,*[2] *L.R. Kurwijila,*[3] *D. Grace*[4] and *K. Makita*[1,4]

[1]Rakuno Gakuen University, Japan; [2]Veterinary Investigation Centre Arusha, Tanzania; [3]Sokoine University of Agriculture, Tanzania; [4]International Livestock Research Institute, Kenya

Contact details

Haruya Toyomaki
Faculty of Veterinary Medicine
Rakuno Gakuen University, 582 Bunkyodaimidori-machi Ebetsu-shi, 069-8501 Hokkaido, Japan
Email: yahahuhru@gmail.com

25

INFORMAL MARKETS IN MOZAMBIQUE RISKY FOR LOCAL CHICKEN

Ana Bela Cambaza dos Muchangos, Kristina Roesel, Cheryl McCrindle, Helena Matusse, Saskia Hendrickx, Kohei Makita and Delia Grace

Key messages

- Investigating food safety in the informal sector can be challenging; it is much easier for regulators to engage with agri-business than with independent small-scale operators!
- Poultry meat is contaminated at all levels of the market chain from farm to sale, with highest contamination in live bird markets.
- Lack of food safety prerequisites and low levels of awareness on hygienic practices were identified as the main reasons for contamination.

Background

Since independence from Portugal in 1975, Mozambique has been battered by civil war, economic problems, natural disasters and hunger. Gifted with rich and extensive natural resources – including water and recently discovered gas, coal and mineral sources – Mozambique's present-day economy is considered one of huge potential as its assets have remained largely untapped.

On arrival in Inhambane, the fifteenth-century Portuguese explorer Vasco da Gama was reportedly so charmed by the locals that he gave the area the name *terra da boa gente* (land of the good people)[1] and since peace has arrived in Mozambique at last, tourists are pouring into the country that is stretched out between the Indian Ocean, South Africa, Lake Malawi and Tanzania with its enticing magical islands, sandy beaches and laid-back hospitality.

Some of the best cuisine of the region, blending African, Indian and Portuguese influences, is found here and always served with a dab of *piri piri* (hot chili pepper) alongside. Among seafood and freshwater fish, *inteiro com piripiri* (whole chicken in chili pepper sauce) is particularly popular.

The Mozambicans themselves enjoy their local backyard chicken, also known as 'hard chicken'. Most of them do not trust in chicken 'that is fully grown within five weeks' and are reluctant to buy meat imported from Brazil or Australia. Fortunately for local producers and consumers who like local products, the amount of imported chicken has decreased significantly over the past years thanks to a fast-expanding national poultry sector.

However, the risk to human health of consuming poultry meat obtained from both the formal and informal market is unknown in Mozambique. According to the Ministry of Health, diarrhoeal diseases remain an important cause of illness but it is unknown whether and to what extent poultry meat consumption contributes to this. In other countries, including many in Europe, poultry has been shown to be a major source of food-borne disease and diarrhoeal illness, which may be a reason to view poultry in Mozambique with caution. Since poultry is a major component of the diet and a valuable and affordable source of protein for all levels of society, the present study aimed to investigate poultry to identify potential hazards and their likelihood of occurrence. The study considered the entire marketing chain in a 'farm-to-fork' approach, as this is considered the best way to understand how and where food safety problems occur.

At farm level, food safety begins with the suppliers of agricultural inputs to farmers and those involved in food production, since materials such as pesticides and veterinary drugs pose different risks and therefore require specific attention. Special attention is also needed when animals are slaughtered at abattoirs as this is a common point for contamination with health hazards. Food retailing involves the sale of foods in supermarkets and shops and in the informal sector, such as street-food vendors and market stalls. Practices and conditions regarding storage, transport and distribution of foods can have an influence on product safety. Food safety does not end at the point of sale. Improper handling and preparation by consumers often negate the food safety measures introduced by other sectors in the earlier stages of the food chain.[2]

HACCP was first developed to ensure food was safe for astronauts in space voyages, as illnesses in these circumstances would be intolerable. Since then, it has become the universally recognized and accepted method for food safety assurance. Hazards and their points of entry into the food chain can be identified and feasible measures taken to reduce the risk of consumers ingesting food that can cause disease.

This study investigated and described the value chains for poultry production in Maputo, the capital city of Mozambique. The study applied prerequisite tools for HACCP in small-scale poultry production in Maputo. In this way, it was possible to identify the stages of the value chain that could compromise or increase the safety and quality of the end product.

Mapping a value chain involves a lot of logistics. At first, the livestock service and the central laboratory in Maputo were approached to establish contact with the head of the provincial livestock services, who in turn contacted the national poultry farmer association. In cooperation with TechnoServe, a United States-based non-profit organization, the study team held a workshop with farmers and processors from abattoirs and government-accredited meat inspectors, municipal members, researchers and academics. Before visits to production and marketing sites were facilitated, a lot of letters needed to be exchanged in order to link up inspectors with abattoir managers, poultry associations with farmers, and consumer associations with the study in general. The preliminary results were taken back to be presented during a second workshop.

During visits to informal markets, first-hand information from vendors was obtained to complete the map of the marketing chain for street-vended chicken. This mission proved to be a challenge! A lot of explaining was necessary to make the concept of participation clear to all participants. In a country with sixteen major ethnic groups where not everyone speaks Portuguese, misunderstandings were on the daily agenda. The most striking example was somebody mistaking the researcher for a health officer who had come to fine the vendors or close down the food stands; the researcher's camera was snatched and thrown in a water tank! Thankfully, another butcher voluntarily joined the survey to learn from the findings of the research.

Petrifilm dishes as a fast, reliable and convenient tool at each step of the food chain

A total of 330 samples of poultry meat from freshly slaughtered and frozen fowls were randomly collected from formal abattoirs, live bird markets and farms. Contamination rates were assessed by using 3M™ Petrifilm plates. This all-in-one plating system is a very handy method to quickly detect and quantify various microorganisms. It is designed to be as accurate as conventional methods used in the laboratory, with the special benefit of being handy in the field. Therefore, it is often used for testing foodstuffs throughout the world.

The results showed a significantly higher microbial load in live bird markets (63%) than at farms (40%) and formal abattoirs (39%). The detected microorganisms are good indicators of the level of contamination. Good hygiene practices and good manufacturing practices are easy to assess. The results suggested that poultry meat from live bird markets was more risky than poultry purchased from the formal sector or directly from the farm. However, the comparison was not entirely fair because samples from markets were at point of sale and samples from abattoirs were at point of slaughter. As contamination increases with time, we would normally expect birds at point of sale to be more contaminated than those freshly slaughtered. Other studies in Vietnam and the Gambia focusing on point of sale only found that meat sold in the formal sector (supermarkets) was actually more heavily contaminated with microbes than meat sold in traditional (wet) markets.

However, all meat samples from the three market channels in Maputo province were contaminated with microorganisms of faecal origin and could therefore have the potential to cause diarrhoeal disease if not washed, cooked and stored properly.

These objective results correspond with the observations made at all stages of the marketing chain. The cold chain was not maintained during transportation from the formal abattoir to retail shops, and chicken meat sellers used the same water through the poultry processing in an open environment under high ambient temperatures. Weather patterns in Maputo are characterized by a rainy season (22–31°C) from November to March and a dry season (13–24°C) from April to October.[3]

Recommendations

Following these preliminary results, a hygiene assessment system is proposed for all market channels, with focus on the critical points that were identified during the study and that can be easily controlled and monitored. For the hygiene plan to be effective, a strong foundation of safety-related prerequisites is essential. Regular training in hygiene practices is crucial at every level of the food chain. Raising consumer awareness might be an incentive, as demand for quality products influences supply. Audit checklists based on the HACCP plan resulting from this study can be used by inspectors to maintain suitable standards. Moreover, it could be the basis for developing a set of standards for a code of practice for poultry producers and processors (good agricultural practices, good hygiene practices and good manufacturing practices). The role of the inspection services and collaboration of inspection authorities with the poultry industry association should be reinforced to improve the quality of final products.

Ana Bela Cambaza dos Muchangos holds a Master's degree in veterinary science and obtained her specialist degree in veterinary public health at the University of Pretoria in 2012. After working as livestock programme manager for World Vision and the UK Department for International Development, she coordinated the Southern Africa Newcastle Disease Control Project in Mozambique (Australian Government Overseas Aid Program) and now holds the position of veterinary public health officer at the Ministry of Agriculture in Mozambique.

Title and authors of the study

Prerequisites for HACCP in small-scale poultry production and processing in Maputo, Mozambique.

Ana Bela Cambaza dos Muchangos,[1] *Cheryl McCrindle,*[1] *Helena Matusse,*[2] *Saskia Hendrickx,*[3] *Kohei Makita*[3,4] and *Delia Grace*[3]

[1]Faculty of Veterinary Science, University of Pretoria, South Africa; [2]Directorate of Animal Science, Mozambique; [3]International Livestock Research Institute, Kenya; [4]Rakuno Gakuen University, Japan

Contact details

Ana Bela Cambaza dos Muchangos
Ministry of Agriculture and Rural Development
Praça dos Heróis Moçambicanos, Caixa Postal 1406, Maputo, Mozambique
Email: controlodo@yahoo.com.br

Notes

1. Murphy A, Ham A, Morgan K, Corne L, Waters R, Fitzpatrick M, Holden T, Grosberg M and Armstrong K. 2005. *Lonely Planet Southern Africa travel guide*. Lonely Planet.
2. WHO. 2011. www.who.int/foodsafety/fs_management/en (accessed 9 July 2014).
3. BBC Weather. 2011. www.bbc.co.uk/weather/1040652 (accessed 9 July 2014).

26

ARRIVE ALIVE IN SOUTH AFRICA: CHICKEN MEAT THE LEAST TO WORRY ABOUT

James Oguttu, Kristina Roesel, Cheryl McCrindle, Saskia Hendrickx, Kohei Makita and Delia Grace

Key messages

- Street food is very popular in South Africa. While previous studies have focused on pathogens in street food, this is the first study to assess the risk associated with contaminated food.
- Street vendors source the chicken meat mostly from formal retailers such as supermarkets or commercial farms (suppliers with means to produce safe chicken). As a result the market chain is very short.
- Traders are aware of risks associated with food of animal origin and have developed risk mitigation strategies.
- The working environment proved to be an important source of contamination of street-vended food.
- Unavailability of potable water and lack of proper infrastructure for the production of safe food have led to the quality of street-vended ready-to-eat chicken being compromised by faecal and environmental contaminants and pathogenic organisms like *Staphylococcus aureus*.

Background

The multibillion-rand minibus taxi industry carries over 65% of South Africa's commuters[1] and is expected to be even more important in the future in light of the country's growing urban population. The taxi industry consists of minibuses, dominating 90% of the market, and metered taxis active in the remaining 10% of the market. The turnover of the sector comprising 20,000 owners and 200,000 employees is estimated to be more than 16.5 billion South African rand per year (approximately €2.1 billion).[2] Unfortunately, the highly competitive taxi industry has been heavily embroiled in aggressive conflicts that have claimed thousands of lives.[3]

Violence is not the only threat to commuters at taxi ranks in South Africa. In September 2011, about 40 people, including several children, collapsed at a taxi rank in Rustenburg, North West, in a suspected poisoning incident. The victims told medics they had fallen ill after eating food at a nearby restaurant.[4]

An estimated 2.5 million people live in Tshwane metropolitan area,[5] which is among the biggest metropolitan municipalities in South Africa. It forms the local government of northern Gauteng Province including the city of Pretoria. Pretoria is just 50km from Johannesburg and is expected to form part of a megalopolis of 20 million people within the next 10 to 15 years.

In many African cities, informal markets are an integral part of the food supply network and are particularly important to the urban and peri-urban poor as sources of affordable ready-to-eat foods. In South Africa, taxi ranks are the most popular food-vending posts due to the high frequency of a broad clientele. Informal food vending is a major contributor to South Africa's economy, with about 44.7 million rand spent on street food outlets in Gauteng in 1994 alone. In other parts of Africa where there have been extensive studies on informal food markets, income is usually three to 10 times higher than the prevailing minimum wage. Studies show that informal food vending is particularly important to women, the first victims of increasing unemployment and subsequent poverty.

With chicken consumption growing along with the informal market, the question as to whether street-vended chicken and its by-products are safe for human consumption is the logical consequence. By proving that informal markets are well established and provide the poor in urban areas with affordable and wholesome food, evidence generated could enhance growth of the sector, leading to increased job creation while securing the income of the vendors and ensuring that consumers have access to wholesome and nutritious food.

Preliminary findings of this study show that the majority of informal vendors involved in the sale of ready-to-eat chicken and chicken by-products in Tshwane are women aged between 25 and 50 years. The majority of the vending outlets are run as private businesses. Very few young people and males are involved in the trade. The majority of the vendors have attained secondary education, with a few holding a tertiary qualification.

Using a structured questionnaire and focus group discussions with informal traders, the marketing chain for street-vended chicken was established. Observations using checklists for hygiene audits were also applied to identify risky behaviours during food preparation. This was complemented by microbiological sampling of ready-to-eat chicken prepared in various ways.

Three sources of chicken for informal traders were identified, all of which are linked to the formal market. Street vendors, who cook and sell broiler meat, buy the chicken from butchers and supermarkets which are usually supplied by accredited wholesalers (formal sector). Vendors who sell off-layers (spent hens) source them directly from commercial farmers and slaughter them at their homes. In some instances, informal intermediary sellers collect and slaughter the chicken before delivering them to the vendors. According to the South African Meat

Safety Act of 2000, slaughter of animals outside designated abattoirs is prohibited if the meat is for sale and not for home consumption. Therefore, the slaughter of birds either by the vendors themselves or the intermediary sellers is deemed illegal.

We found that most vendors did not hold a certificate of acceptance, a permit issued by the department of health authorizing them to operate as food vendors. Despite this, the informal vendors generally followed good basic hygiene practices such as keeping short fingernails, wearing protective clothing, keeping food covered and over fire, and not picking up food with bare hands. The structures where meat was prepared and sold were very rudimentary: for example, operating under a tent on bare ground that was not cemented and in surroundings that do not meet basic requirements for siting a food-vending outlet. Many vendors work in open areas that are prone to flooding during the rainy season and exposed to dust during the dry season. Microbiological analysis of chicken showed evidence of contamination. The environment is a significant contributor to contamination of ready-to-eat chicken, given the number of samples that were positive for coliforms and not faecal contaminants.

Though the vendors studied adhered to some hygiene principles of preparing food that is safe, there is a problem when food has to bought and taken away to be consumed later. In such instances, the food is presented in various ways: wrapped in a newspaper or packed in plastic bags or polysterol foam boxes. Depending on where the packaging materials are stored and how they are handled and cleaned, this practice could increase the risk of contamination of food. However, when food is eaten directly at the vending site, it is served on plates that are washed between servings. Even then, previous studies showed that this practice too has potential to introduce germs into the food because some vendors will offer the dishwashing water to their customers for washing their hands. Water analysis returned samples that contained faecal contaminants (*E. coli*); this implies that the water used by some of the vendors is not potable.

Focus group discussions revealed that to most vendors, cleanliness of the working environment ranks first among the factors that compromise food safety. The respondents considered it the greatest constraint in producing safe food and gave examples such as rats infesting most of the stalls or operating in open areas where food is exposed to dust, among others.

The ready-to-eat chicken was tested for the presence of indicators of faecal contamination and some well-known pathogens associated with food. Just under half of the samples tested were positive for *Staphylococcus aureus* and the number of positive samples varied between markets, though not significantly. Risk analysis based on information obtained in this study and published data from other studies show that the likelihood of contracting staphylococcal food poisoning following consumption of chicken sold on the informal markets in Tshwane metropolitan area is low (0.73%).

On the contrary, fewer samples were positive for *E. coli* and coliforms (faecal and environmental contaminants, respectively). While the presence of *E. coli* indicates faecal contamination, occurrence of samples with exceedingly high coliform counts but negative for *E. coli* suggests that the environment is a contributor to food contamination. This finding was expected given the poor conditions under which the food is prepared.

Observations and interviews revealed that vendors have adopted strategies to mitigate microbial risks associated with their products. They have adopted measures which ensure that displayed food is not held for prolonged periods: for example, chicken for sale ready to eat is prepared in small amounts to allow for it to be finished before more chicken is bought or brought from home and prepared.

The focus group discussions further demonstrated the existence of systems by which vendors are able to tell if their food caused food poisoning. For example, customers return and complain to the vendors personally in case of illness after eating food from their stalls. Given the risk of losing clientele with repeated incidences of food poisoning, vendors are forced to ensure that the ready-to-eat chicken they sell is safe for human consumption.

The survey and interaction with the vendors during focus group interviews have already had a positive spin-off. Following the focus group discussion with one of the survey groups, the vendors from that market decided to explore the option of forming either an association or a cooperative to facilitate dealing with common issues such as rat infestation at the stalls. Before the survey, they had not realized the need for having a common voice (Chapter 5).

Recommendations

The demographic survey of the vendors shows that mostly adults of employable age are involved in the informal trade. This indicates that the sector contributes to job creation in the Tshwane metropolitan municipality. Given the economic benefit of informal food vending, the municipality needs to provide prerequisites for production of safe food such as well-constructed food stalls suitably located so that food is protected from environmental contamination and easily accessible to the customers. This will enhance both the viability and the sustainability of the sector.

According to the Meat Safety Act of 2000, the inspection of poultry is not mandatory. In view of this, it is advisable for the municipality to encourage the vendors to establish the equivalent of slaughter slabs in the red meat industry for slaughter of chicken by vendors and the intermediaries who supply chicken sourced from commercial farms. These could be established in homes or at farms where the chickens are sourced. This would help enhance the safety of the chicken sold by the informal vendors.

Much as the risk of contracting staphylococcal intoxication was low – which is good news for the sector – the high prevalence of contaminated products is a concern. In view of this, training is needed for the vendors on hygienic food production. Given that the majority of the vendors completed secondary education, provision of training on the principles of food hygiene seems feasible. Moreover, this should not be a problem since most run their businesses either on a personal or a family basis. Furthermore, inspection at informal markets should emphasize the working environment since it proved to be a significant contributor to contamination of the ready-to-eat chicken. Inspection should also be directed at the containers used to serve ready-to-eat food, given the widespread practice of wrapping food in paper of questionable quality in terms of food safety. The provision of potable water is an absolute necessity in markets where vendors buy water that is delivered to them in plastic containers. This will ensure that the water used by vendors to prepare food and wash utensils is potable.

Originating from Uganda, James Oguttu pursued his PhD at the University of Pretoria while teaching at the College of Agriculture and Environmental Sciences at the University of South Africa campus located at Florida in Johannesburg. Before his engagement at South Africa's largest distance education university in 2006, he taught for several years at the University of Lesotho.

Title and authors of the study

Participatory risk analysis of street-vended chicken bought at the informal market in Tshwane municipality in Gauteng, South Africa.

James Oguttu,[1] *Cheryl McCrindle,*[1] *Saskia Hendrickx,*[2] *Kohei Makita*[2,3] and *Delia Grace*[2]

[1]Faculty of Veterinary Science, University of Pretoria, South Africa; [2]International Livestock Research Institute, Kenya; [3]Rakuno Gakuen University, Japan

Contact details

James Oguttu
Department of Agriculture and Animal Health, College of Agriculture and Environmental Sciences
University of South Africa
Private Bag XII, 1710 Florida, South Africa
Email: joguttu@unisa.ac.za

Notes

1. Boudreaux KC. 2006. *Taxing alternatives: Poverty alleviation and the South African taxi/minibus industry.* Mercatus Policy Series Policy Comment No. 3/2006.
2. OANDA. 2004. www.oanda.com/currency/converter (accessed 9 July 2014).
3. Sekhonyane M and Dugard J. 2004. www.issafrica.org/pubs/CrimeQ/No.10/3Violent.pdf (accessed 9 July 2014).
4. *Independent* Online. 2011. www.pretorianews.co.za/poisoned-40-collapse-at-taxi-rank-1.1134953 (accessed 9 July 2014).
5. www.sacities.net/workwith/tshwane/news/618-city-to-become-largest-in-sa (accessed 9 July 2014).

27

INFORMAL SELLING OF MEAT IN SOUTH AFRICA

Alexander Heeb, Kristina Roesel, Cheryl McCrindle, Shashi Ramrajh, Kohei Makita and Delia Grace

Key messages

- Meat products marketed informally were found to be safe for human consumption.
- The quality of an initially safe product is compromised after processing due to inadequate prerequisites and handling practices.
- Training will be of little use unless adequate infrastructure is provided.
- Marketing channels to sell game meat products are in place but not communicated.
- Game meat sources perceived as safe must be reviewed critically.

Street vending: an important part of the economy with most products safe for human consumption

South Africa is characterized by a rich cultural diversity but also by strong disparities between developed and developing areas, resulting in large discrepancies between the rich and poor. Increasing rates of unemployment also resulted in an increase of self-employment, mostly in the informal sector. In 2007, about 25% of the population was unemployed and about 15% was active in the informal sector. The country's informal sector thus remains relatively small compared to those of other countries in sub-Saharan Africa. Street food vending has been considered to be the single largest employer in the informal sector and a major contributor to the country's economy.

The present study involved informal traders of seven towns in northern KwaZulu-Natal where 80% of the population lives below the poverty line. These traders, mostly women, run their businesses in the streets rather than in open market areas provided by the municipalities for a daily fee, in order to exploit areas with many customers such as bus terminals, taxi ranks and industrial sites. The vendors work 10–15 hours a day without taking a break, sometimes starting as early as 0300 hours when commuters leave for work.

Most of the traders sold their products from fixed premises and the sale of meat products was the primary source of income for almost all of them. Interviews showed that half sold only one product and beef was most preferred, followed by chicken. Additionally, one-third also sold less expensive products such as offal from impala (*Aepyceros melampus*). Almost all vendors sourced the raw meat from formal retail outlets such as butcheries or supermarkets. Therefore, the products can be assumed to have passed primary as well as secondary meat inspection and to be safe for human consumption, at least until they enter the informal market.

Price was the most important attribute that consumers considered when buying meat; less important were the type of meat and the relationship to the supplier. Most informal traders could afford to pay US$3.50–5 per kg of red meat at supermarkets or butcheries; cheaper cuts of beef and lamb could be purchased within this price range and special cuts were about twice as expensive. Prices at the abattoir were affordable but obtaining meat was hampered as the minimum sale quantity was 200kg. Lamb was generally more expensive than beef, and goat meat was not encountered in the formal retail shops (Chapter 31).

When the raw meat from the formal retailer was grilled and cooked for sale, it entered the informal market. Therefore, samples of raw meat and end products such as fried steaks, beef stews, chicken stews, gravies and salads were obtained to assess their overall level of contamination. Whereas three-quarters of the samples of cooked meat were of acceptable quality, all of the raw meat samples proved to be of unsatisfactory quality. It is unlikely, albeit not impossible, that raw meat sourced from a formal retailer was unsafe for human consumption (Chapter 3). Assuming that the bacterial load must have been reduced during the preparation of the meat prior to selling it, more interviews were carried out with the vendors who had been sampled before in order to identify the source of contamination.

Unfortunately, the second survey revealed that unsuitable prerequisites (infrastructure and utilities such as running water, sanitation, rubbish disposal and electricity) are the major constraints of the street vendors. These are likely to be the major source of contamination which resulted in 'only' satisfactory results in the laboratory. Almost all vendors stated they would build a shelter if they could improve something about their stand. Indeed, roofs, floors and walls proved to be inadequate.

Nearly every vendor lacked cooling facilities and half of them claimed that their biggest constraint was the lack of water. When observing the sites, it turned out that hardly anybody had running water available. They brought their own water from home and many times, the same bucket or bowl of water was used to wash hands, utensils and dishes. One respondent reported that he would have to 'steal' water from the nearby petrol station in order to avoid transporting water on a daily basis. Most of them lacked drainage facilities for dirty water and 16% lacked access to public toilets.

Electricity was also not available to most of the vendors; only one had access to a refrigerator. The stand of this particular vendor was a self-made shack, and at night he relied on the security guards employed by an adjacent supermarket to keep an eye on his premises. Another respondent used a gas refrigerator, which most of the other vendors could not afford. Hygiene practices were generally poor, most likely due to a lack of knowledge. All but one respondent handled food and other things such as money and cigarettes without washing hands in between.

Almost all of them reported that they grilled and cooked the meat products. Most of the food was sold right away, and storage times were generally short. Through these practices, they reduced the risk of contamination of the cooked food products which were sold to consumers. Some retailers bought the raw meat in the morning and prepared it at home before selling it in the streets. Others stored the meat in cooling boxes but most of them transported and stored the meat without cooling (one for even a week!) prior to cooking. At the end of the day, leftovers would be taken home to eat although some respondents tried to sell them the following day (Chapter 4). Even though these preconditions must be improved, the quality of meat products marketed informally is considered to be safe for human consumption.

Opportunity for sale of by-products of the game industry through informal vendors instead of throwing them away

In order to see if game could provide an untapped supply of nutritious and inexpensive offal for informal street vending, we conducted an additional survey among biltong hunters. Generally, they hunt for recreation rather than for meat. If they trade, they shoot 'on order', give away the meat for free or sell it to butcheries and supermarkets. Biltong hunters commonly use slaughter facilities provided by game ranches if no evisceration takes place in the field. Unlike commercial game harvesting, standards and regulations are almost non-existent for biltong hunters. Those trading the meat can directly sell it to licensed butcheries and supermarkets instead of delivering it to registered game abattoirs, as this is not yet required by South African law. Only 5% of biltong hunters had attended training courses to become professional hunters, and most courses attended focused on weapon safety and competency rather than food safety.

As the meat is not inspected at any point and a cold chain is not maintained, the quality of the meat was investigated (Chapter 29). The survey also investigated possible risk factors associated with this kind of meat production. Trophy hunting can be associated with negative effects on meat quality from the animal being stressed over a longer period (missed shots or being chased for a long time). In case of abdominal shots, the bowels might be damaged, resulting in faecal contamination of the meat. However, the interval between the killing of the animal and bleeding is one of the most important parameters for meat hygiene and food safety. If bleeding is delayed and blood remains in the vessels, this will result in poor quality and multiplication of bacteria in meat.

According to the biltong hunters, the greatest obstacle for further expansion of the game meat market was inadequate promotion and support, including the provision of a cold chain from farm to supermarket. The survey revealed that most of them had not considered selling the offal. However, the locals frequently asked them for the offal. While biltong hunters cannot guarantee consistent quantities and quality of game meat and its by-products, commercial game harvesters can (Chapter 28). While almost all the informal traders purchased their meat from formal sources such as supermarkets or butcheries, they had little access to meat from licensed game abattoirs. Why? Hunters and game harvesters do not see marketing potential for game meat and would rather throw it away in the bush to feed the vultures. This study and others (Chapter 28) prove that this is a waste of resources which could easily be a source of food and cash to those in need (Chapter 8).

The first part of the study showed that marketing channels do exist that could include game meat and edible by-products in the future, and the biltong hunter survey suggested there was potential supply. We also sought to find out whether consumers would purchase this kind of product. During the survey, traders were encouraged to cook the game meat for themselves and they found that they liked the taste of the game meat stew. The informal meat traders were happy to include game meat in their product range, given that it was made available cheap and legally. After proving that the demand was there, possible sources of supply were investigated. Marketing chains for game meat provided by occasional biltong hunters and commercial game harvesters were established to find out whether supply and demand could be linked.

Recommendations

If prerequisites such as running water, public toilets and electricity are provided by the municipalities, training in basic hygiene must be regularly carried out. Consequently, minimum requirements based on national hygiene regulations should be enforced by regular check-ups.

Game meat products can be traded informally, if meat inspection is assured at the harvesting level. Therefore, participatory risk assessment should involve biltong hunters as part of the informal market.

Alexander Heeb undertook this study on risk assessment of game meat products in South Africa towards a Master's degree at the University of Hohenheim. He works as a meat inspector at a formal abattoir in Germany.

Title and authors of the study

Participatory risk assessment of game products marketed through formal and informal chains: hazard identification and risk assessment.

Alexander Heeb,[1] *Cheryl McCrindle,*[2] *Shashi Ramrajh,*[2] *Kohei Makita*[3,4] and *Delia Grace*[3]

[1]Consultant, Germany; [2]Faculty of Veterinary Science, University of Pretoria, South Africa; [3]International Livestock Research Institute, Kenya; [4]Rakuno Gakuen University, Japan

Contact details

Alexander Heeb
Semmelweg 95, 32257 Bünde, Germany
Email: redheeb@web.de

28

HOW AN ANTELOPE COULD ALLEVIATE POVERTY IN SOUTH AFRICA

Shashi Ramrajh, Kristina Roesel, Cheryl McCrindle, Alexander Heeb, Kohei Makita and Delia Grace

Key messages

- Edible meat by-products that passed formal inspection are safe for human consumption but discarded for vultures.
- Demand for these products exists and marketing of edible meat by-products is feasible.
- It is a social responsibility to make this protein source legally accessible at affordable prices to those who are in need.

Background

The meat obtained from trophy hunting, culling and harvesting indigenous game animals has been used in the past by biltong hunters and local butchers and for export markets. The edible by-products, currently discarded, could be exploited as a potential niche meat product and used as a source of protein in low-income communities (Chapter 27). Such edible by-products are heads (including the brain which is known for its rich content of omega-3 fatty acids), feet and offal.

Offal refers to the internal organs and entrails of a butchered animal. There are two kinds of offal: the red offal or pluck (comprising the liver, spleen, kidney and lungs) and the green/rough offal or tripe consisting of the stomach and intestines. The word offal derives from late Middle English and probably suggested *afval* meaning 'fall off'[1] or 'waste' in Dutch. Therefore, it is sometimes perceived as food of inferior quality which is rather unjust! If served meticulously cleaned and thoroughly cooked, it is considered a specialty in many cultures. The French make sausages out of it. In the United States of America, it is a crucial part of the Philadelphia Pepper Pot. In the south of Germany, it is cooked with vinegar and wine into a delicious stew, while in Japan the stew is known as *motsu*. In Africa as well, green offal is popular in many cultures. The Yoruba of Nigeria call it *saki* and use it in various stews. In Eritrea, it is served stir-fried in butter with liver, ground beef, lamb or goat and spiced with *berbere* (chilies). The Kikuyu of Kenya love their *matumbo* and it is said that 'if Kenya's Luo people leave Nairobi to go home for the Christmas holidays, the local offal market in the capital city collapses' (Cameline Mwai). In South Africa, tripe are known as *mala mogodu* and eaten as a stew with hot pap.[2]

Why would anybody throw away food in a country where more than one-quarter of the population is living on less than US$1.25 per day and where the national income distribution is among the most unequal in the world?[3]

Healthy children learn better

Proper nutrition is a powerful good: people who are well nourished are more likely to be healthy, productive and able to learn. Good nutrition benefits families, their communities and the world as a whole. Malnutrition is, by the same logic, devastating. It blunts the intellect, saps the productivity of everyone it touches and perpetuates poverty.[4]

South Africa is rich in wildlife and the game meat market seems to be a multimillion-euro business. South African game animals are usually extensively ranched under natural conditions and the marketing of game meat as an organic product has great potential (Chapter 27). Constraints on the utilization of edible by-products of game meat include lack of recognized food value chains in informal markets, food safety concerns and limited market access. Therefore, a value chain for the 'harvest' of impala (*Aepyceros melampus*) was established with all stakeholders from shooting to secondary meat inspection. They included game harvesters at the beginning of the process, informal traders at the possible outlet and veterinarians along the way. The first-hand experience 'from farm to fork' proved to be very helpful in identifying needs and capacities.

Samples were submitted to an accredited laboratory for microbiological assessment in line with EU guidelines and veterinary procedural notices. Structured and informal interviews were held with stakeholders, including veterinarians, game harvesters and informal traders. Scenario planning and decision tree analysis were used to develop a feasible food marketing chain. Based on identified hazards along the marketing chain, critical control points were estimated, mostly time and temperature parameters as well as possible contamination from a dirty working environment.

Commercially hunted game destined for export originates mostly from privately owned land or government-owned natural reserves. The hunting normally takes place during the South African winter months when temperatures are low enough to keep meat spoilage at bay. If cooling facilities are readily available, hunting can be done all year round. The game ranches that produce for export are required to register with the local controlling authority and are issued with a licence which is renewed every year. Harvesting teams – comprising the driver/hunter, the spot-light operator and the field meat inspector – and game depots must be registered too. Before the start of a harvest, the vehicles and equipment need to be inspected in order to secure compliance with valid standards.

The hunting is mostly carried out at twilight by registered professional hunters. The animal is blinded by a spotlight and shot in the head; missed or inadequate shots are very rare. In many respects, this slaughter is much more humane than that experienced by cattle that are often transported over long distances to abattoirs, a process that is much more stressful than the precision killing of wild animals at night.

After an animal is shot, it is bled in the field with a sterile knife and given an identification number. It is then hung by the hind legs onto the side of the collecting vehicle. Normally, animals are hunted one by one and the collecting vehicle delivers the carcasses to the depot once sufficient numbers have been shot. If the carcasses are not eviscerated in the field, they must reach the game depot within two hours after the fatal shot, otherwise the intestines turn into a perfect breeding ground for spoilage microbes.

At the depot, the 'dirty team' removes hides, feet and heads: everything outside which might be dirty. Another team only deals with the 'clean' inner parts of the carcass and removes the internal organs, weighs the remaining meat and loads it onto the chiller truck. Prior to loading, everything needs to be inspected by an accredited health official and each carcass and its pluck is marked with identity tags. The red offal is sent to the export abattoir together with the corresponding carcass. They are tagged together and the red offal is put into a plastic bag and attached to the carcass it was taken from. All livers with flukes are condemned at primary inspection.

The carcasses must reach the export abattoir within 72 hours, and prior to off-loading, the seals are checked for integrity. The abattoir is approved by the EU, and the processing procedures must follow stringent regulations. The South African standards for the export of game meat consist of an intensive residue monitoring programme as well as health and hygiene requirements before export, and the meat is inspected again at its final destination.

The red offal undergoes secondary inspection at the export abattoir and is then sold as pet mince. The rough offal never reaches the game depot but is discarded to the 'vulture restaurant' at the game farm. During the survey, samples were taken to see whether offal from impala that had passed primary meat inspection was suitable for human consumption.

At the other end of the marketing chain, participatory risk analysis was used to investigate the feasibility of using edible offal as a source of protein to address food security issues in poor communities bordering game parks in South Africa. Existing marketing channels had been identified (Chapter 27) and focus group discussions indicated that vendors were willing to cook and sell game offal in informal food markets or at schools.

Recommendations

The marketing chain of edible by-products from game meat is feasible and the current practice of leaving the offal for vultures was reviewed. Training in environmental awareness, effluent and waste management, food handling, personal hygiene and food-borne diseases is needed in the future to ensure the safety of edible offal from game meat.

Shashi Ramrajh holds a Master's degree in veterinary science (hygiene) and has several years of practical field experience. In 2012, she obtained her specialist degree in veterinary public health from the University of Pretoria. She is the deputy manager of veterinary public health at the Department of Agriculture, Environmental Affairs and Rural Development in KwaZulu-Natal, South Africa where she successfully handled an outbreak of foot and mouth disease in 2011. Her research was featured in the November 2011 issue of the *New Agriculturist* online magazine.[5]

Title and authors of the study

Participatory risk analysis for the harvesting of impala (*Aepyceros melampus*) for the export abattoir and the provision of edible by-products to the communities in KwaZulu-Natal, South Africa.

Shashi Ramrajh,[1] *Cheryl McCrindle,*[1] *Alexander Heeb,*[2] *Kohei Makita*[3,4] and *Delia Grace*[3]

[1]Faculty of Veterinary Science, University of Pretoria, South Africa; [2]Consultant, Germany; [3]International Livestock Research Institute, Kenya; [4]Rakuno Gakuen University, Japan

Contact details

Shashi Ramrajh
Department of Agriculture, Environmental Affairs and Rural Development
Veterinary Services, Province of KwaZulu-Natal, Private Bag X1048, 3900 Richards Bay, South Africa
Email: shashi.ramrajh@kzndae.gov.za

Notes

1. http://oxforddictionaries.com/definition/offal (accessed 9 July 2014).
2. www.mycitycuisine.org/wiki/Mala_mogodu (accessed 9 July 2014).
3. UNICEF. 2010. *The state of the world's children special edition*. www.unicef.org/publications/index_51772.html (accessed 9 July 2014).
4. UNICEF. 2010. www.unicef.org/nutrition/index.html (accessed 9 July 2014).
5. www.new-ag.info/en/focus/focusItem.php?a=2303 (accessed 9 July 2014).

29

SUSTAINABLE LIVELIHOODS IN SOUTH AFRICA THROUGH MARKETING OF BILTONG

Erika Van Zyl, Kristina Roesel, Cheryl McCrindle, Kohei Makita and Delia Grace

Key messages

- The odds of buying contaminated biltong at informal retail outlets are twice as high as for biltong sourced from the formal market.
- Contamination mostly occurs after processing due to poor handling and packaging hygiene.
- Marketing of biltong could increase value added income for farmers and improve nutritional security for consumers.

Background

The traditional meat product known as biltong is now popular among many South Africans as well as foreigners. It is even being exported, as noted by the various companies that advertise biltong on the internet.[1] The word 'biltong' is derived from the Dutch *bil* (rump) and *tong* (tongue or strip). It can be produced from any species of animal, but preferably cattle and wild ungulates such as kudu antelope, springbok or ostrich. It is a raw, salted, dried meat product with different spices added according to the specific recipe and is consumed without cooking or rehydration. Some recipes are family secrets. Biltong was originally prepared by hunters who ventured inland from coastal areas and needed a source of protein that did not decay in the hot African sun. It was described as early as 1851, well before the Great Trek, an eastward migration away from British control in the Cape Colony during the 1830s and 1840s by the Boers (Dutch/Afrikaans for 'farmers').

Little research has been done on food safety aspects of biltong, even in South Africa. The last seminal research published on this product was over 40 years ago.[2] But since then, the making and marketing of biltong has evolved considerably, with customers now preferring a softer, moister product. Legal requirements are already in place to monitor the quality and safety of meat and meat products in South Africa. These are the Meat Safety Act No. 40 of 2000 and the Foodstuffs, Cosmetics and Disinfectants Act No. 54 of 1972. It is a legal requirement that all meat destined for export must be inspected, sampled and tested. However, the fact that biltong is a raw, dried, salted meat product often flavoured with spices makes the use of routine microbiological tests difficult.

Is it made of beef or bush meat?

It is rather difficult to distinguish normal beef biltong from other dried meat strips that could have originated from a poached animal. Bush meat is an escalating industry that is not easily monitored, thus it is possible that dried bush meat strips could enter the human food chain. Springbok biltong is highly regarded, but one may sometimes hear about biltong from 'sitbok', meaning 'the antelope that sits down' (that is, the baboon)!

Substitution of high-quality meat products with cheaper alternatives of inferior quality is a problem in the meat industry. It is also a problem for people who cannot eat certain types of meat because of culture or religion. For this reason, it has become important in the industry to identify the species of origin of fresh and processed meat. The identification of the species of origin of raw and cooked meat would help apply stricter monitoring and regulation of meat products such as biltong and protect consumers from fraud and potential health risks. This is an effective way to monitor meat from illegal abattoirs and informal bush meat outlets that is passed off and sold as beef.

Furthermore, it is very important that all meat comes from healthy animals and that strict hygienic practices are adhered to during slaughter and processing of the meat into biltong. Contamination of the raw meat could occur during the slaughter process and when cutting and handling the meat in the process of making biltong. Biltong is made from the prime meat cuts, usually the silverside, topside, rump and sirloin cuts. All the recipes require that the meat cuts be salted and marinated in vinegar. Depending on the recipe, different spices and chemicals are then added to give biltong its distinctive taste and texture. These substances should always comply with the Foodstuffs, Cosmetics and Disinfectants Act.

A value chain for biltong was mapped using information from direct observation and structured interviews with value chain actors at biltong kiosks, service stations, supermarkets and butcheries. Participatory methods have proved to be a good technique for investigating food value chains as they can be combined with quantitative methods such as laboratory tests. Random samples of labelled beef biltong produced and marketed by formal and informal channels were tested to verify that it was indeed beef and not any other type of meat labelled and passed off as beef.

The microbiological quality of beef biltong in informal and formal markets in the Tshwane municipal area of Gauteng was also assessed according to national standard tests. During mapping of the processing chain, handling and hygiene practices were assessed by a checklist for national hygiene audits. Possible risky practices were later modelled in validated statistical computer programmes to estimate the risk and distribution of pathogenic organisms that might be present in biltong.

The analysis showed that the odds of buying contaminated biltong were twice as high at informal biltong kiosks as at the formal market. The value chain assessment revealed an increased risk of consuming contaminated biltong as a result of packaging it in newspapers (rather than a plastic or vacuum bag), slicing of meat (rather than hanging) and handling of the meat by several traders. These factors can be addressed easily by regular quality checks.

One kilogram of cattle generates US$6 net profit for a small-scale farmer

Market research at local taxi ranks and group discussions with farmers showed that biltong could be a lucrative business for small-scale cattle farmers as there is high local demand for biltong. Processing biltong from beef of communal cattle slaughtered at a small-scale, registered abattoir could increase value added income for small-scale farmers and improve nutritional security for consumers as it is a protein-rich product and can be stored for a long time without refrigeration. After deducting all input costs – such as for transport, processing and the commission for the retailer (usually 10%) – the farmer's net profit is US$6 per kilogram of beef.

Recommendation

A communication and incentive strategy should be developed to alleviate microbiological food safety hazards, in particular those due to unhygienic processing and marketing.

Erika van Zyl is a veterinarian and holds a Master's degree from the University of Pretoria in South Africa where she works as a lecturer. She previously worked in a private veterinary practice in Pretoria.

Title and authors of the study

Hazard identification and characterization for quality control of biltong through application of appropriate microbiology and biotechnology methods.

Erika Van Zyl,[1] *Cheryl McCrindle,*[1] *Kohei Makita*[2,3] and *Delia Grace*[2]

[1]Faculty of Veterinary Science, University of Pretoria, South Africa; [2]International Livestock Research Institute, Kenya; [3]Rakuno Gakuen University, Japan

Contact details

Erika van Zyl
Faculty of Veterinary Science, Veterinary Public Health Section
University of Pretoria
Private Bag 04, 0110 Onderstepoort, South Africa

Notes

1. www.biltongusa.com (accessed 9 July 2014); www.biltongsuperstore.com (accessed 9 July 2014); www.biltong.de (accessed 9 July 2014).
2. Van der Riet WB. 1976. Water sorption isotherms of beef biltong and their use in predicting critical moisture contents for biltong storage. *South African Food Review* 3(6); Bokkenheuser V. 1963. Hygienic evaluation of biltong. *South African Medical Journal* 37: 619-621.

30

PARTICIPATION: (UN)MANAGEABLE TOOL FOR RISK ANALYSIS OF TRADITIONAL SLAUGHTER OF GOATS IN SOUTH AFRICA?

Nenene Qekwana, Kristina Roesel, Cheryl McCrindle, Saskia Hendrickx, Kohei Makita and Delia Grace

Key messages

- Ritual slaughtering of goats is a crucial part of social life in South African communities.
- An estimated 95.5% of goats are slaughtered without meat inspection prior to consumption.
- There is a lack of awareness of health risks associated with informally slaughtered goat meat.
- Participation allows identifying hazards and risky practices but complicates quantifying the risks.

Background

Traditions involving the use of animals at special occasions have been performed all over the world for thousands of years. From Christmas and Thanksgiving turkey, Tabaski rams and Easter eggs, to scapegoats and birds released in Southeast Asia, examples abound. Ritual slaughter means slaughtering livestock for meat following a prescribed method of killing an animal for food production. Animal sacrifices, by comparison, involve motives beyond mere food production. Traditional slaughter is the killing of animals by people without training or licence and without following any prescribed method of killing.

Dhabiha, for instance, is the method of slaughtering animals prescribed by Islamic law (Chapter 7), whereby the animal is killed by a deep incision to the front of the throat with a well-sharpened knife by an authorized person who utters a prayer before killing. Only if everything complies with Islamic law is the meat considered permissible to be eaten by Muslims (*halal*). Food that is in accordance with the Jewish dietary laws (*kashrut*) is called *kosher*, meaning fit or clean.

Slaughtering *(shechita)* follows principles that are similar to those in Islamic law, the common tie being humanity – avoiding unnecessary pain for the animals – and aversion to eating the flesh of a dead animal. However, there are concerns that animal suffering may be greater with this form of slaughter than methods which involve trauma to the brain stem.

In present-day Africa, traditional religions play an important role in cultural understanding and awareness of people within their communities.[1] For many of them, traditional rituals and ceremonies are performed to address personal problems, to show respect towards the ancestors and for celebrations such as weddings and childbirth but also for funerals.[2] The animals most often slaughtered in traditional African ritual ceremonies are goats, sheep, cattle and occasionally chickens. There are about 2 million goats in South Africa[3] but less than 0.5% of them are slaughtered at registered abattoirs.[4] Presumably, the remaining 99.5% are used for traditional or informal home slaughter.[2,4,5] An unknown proportion of this slaughter may fit the definition of ritual slaughter.

The consumption of uninspected meat can compromise the health of those eating it. In many ritual or traditional slaughter practices, meat is not inspected and very little research has been done on food safety issues. Most animals used for ceremonies are traded informally and there are no accurate figures available on South Africa's goat market. However, it is estimated that in KwaZulu-Natal, an average of 10,000 to 12,000 live goats are sold per month.

The study described here aimed to determine the risk associated with eating meat from ritually slaughtered goats by investigating cultural practices and informal food chains in South Africa. The different ritual slaughter procedures were first identified. Many practitioners were interviewed and they sometimes facilitated visits and even allowed their photographs to be taken. During these visits, hygiene practices were observed: for example, to what extent protective clothing was worn, whether carcasses were handled hygienically and whether animals were slaughtered in humane ways. The interviews helped to assess the procedures in detail and the hygienic precautions taken. The practitioners were interrogated on attributes that determined why particular animals were chosen and to what extent they were aware of diseases that derive from slaughtering practices and particular animal species.

Ritual slaughter practices are complex and there is no simple way to explain them as they involve a lot of steps and inputs. There are numerous hazards that have been identified and complex risk pathways that are intricately related. The interviews showed that, in general, the level of awareness of diseases was low and everyone involved in slaughtering and meat consumption is exposed to the risk of disease. For instance, one practitioner who was interviewed said that one of the reasons a person can fall ill following the consumption of meat is if 'the hand of the person that slaughtered the animal is not right'.

There are strict control measures in terms of access to these ceremonies which again complicated the collection of data. Preliminary results show that a lot remains unknown about these practices and there are several hazards associated with them, including occupational health risks and possible zoonotic and food-borne diseases. Cultural beliefs can also result in different groups being exposed to different health risks and nutritional benefits. For example, some people reported that kidneys were not fed to children 'to avoid them from suffering from kidney problems while still young'.

Quantifying the risks associated with these practices therefore proved to be very challenging as in many of the communities, the meat is not allowed to leave the ceremony. Taking samples for laboratory examination was hardly possible. However, despite the difficulty of quantitative risk assessment, participation as a technique for risk assessment proved to be an excellent tool to better understand the ritual slaughter of animals. Hazards were identified through observations and first-hand narration. By taking into account who was involved in the slaughtering, what part of the animal was used for what purpose and by whom, and whether raw or processed meat was used, it was possible to identify which groups of people were more exposed to risk than others. Participation also allows for the slaughter methods to be evaluated and culturally acceptable alternatives suggested, taking animal welfare into account.

Recommendations

Standardized African slaughter methods for goats are required in order to prevent and reduce food-borne and occupational hazards. Investigations need to be made into cultural beliefs as well as slaughter methods that are acceptable, safe and humane. Local veterinarians must work closely with the traditional practitioners.

Nenene Qekwana holds a Master of Medicine degree in veterinary science and is a lecturer in veterinary public health at the Faculty of Veterinary Science, University of Pretoria. He has authored a chapter in an Italian book on ritual slaughter: Cenci Goga B and Fermani AG. 2010. *La macellazione religiosa: Protezione degli animali e produzione igienica delle carni* (available at www.pointvet.it/web/index.php?com=ermes&option=index&id=648).

Title and authors of the study

Occupational health and food safety risks associated with traditional slaughter practices of goats in Gauteng, South Africa.

Nenene Qekwana,[1] *Cheryl McCrindle,*[1] *Saskia Hendrickx,*[2] *Kohei Makita*[2,3] and *Delia Grace*[2]

[1]Faculty of Veterinary Science, University of Pretoria, South Africa; [2]International Livestock Research Institute, Kenya; [3]Rakuno Gakuen University, Japan

Contact details

Nenene Qekwana
Faculty of Veterinary Science
Department of Paraclinical, Veterinary Public Health Section
University of Pretoria
Private Bag 04, 0110 Onderstepoort, South Africa
Email: nenene.qekwana@up.ac.za

Notes

1. Thorpe S. 1993. *African traditional religions.* 3rd edition. University of South Africa Sigma Press, Gauteng.
2. Michel AL, Meyer S, McCrindle CM and Veary CM. 2004. Community-based veterinary public health systems in South Africa: Current situation, future trends and recommendations. In: *Expert consultation on community-based veterinary public health systems.* FAO Animal Production and Health Proceedings. FAO, Rome, pp. 71–78.
3. Department of Agriculture, Forestry and Fisheries. 2012. *Abstract of agricultural statistics.* Department of Agriculture, Forestry and Fisheries, South Africa.
4. Department of Agriculture. 2006. Provincial livestock numbers 1995–2005. In: *Livestock statistics for 1995-2005.* National Department of Agriculture, Pretoria.
5. Simela L and Merkels R. 2008. The contribution of chevon from Africa to global meat production. *Meat Science* 80: 101–109.

31

A CRITICAL REVIEW OF FOOD SAFETY AND LAND POLICIES IN SOUTH AFRICA

Margaret Molefe, Kristina Roesel, Cheryl McCrindle, Christo Botha, Kohei Makita and Delia Grace

Key messages

- In South Africa as elsewhere in sub-Saharan Africa, overall demand for animal-source food products is increasing with growing urban populations, a phenomenon known as the Livestock Revolution.
- Cultural background, urbanization and media are among factors that influence individual consumption patterns.
- Fragmented government responsibilities complicate the implementation of policies for food safety.

Background

Animal health relies heavily on veterinary drugs for controlling diseases. Movement of animals and animal products is a potential method of transmitting diseases within and between countries, thus compromising regional and international trade. Human health is inextricably linked to animal health and livestock production through zoonotic and food-borne hazards. The study described here assessed the dietary intake of organic persistent pollutants, pesticides and veterinary drugs in food of animal origin sold at informal markets in South Africa. The actual dietary intake depends on the kind and quantity of animal products consumed as well as the presence and degree of contamination. Therefore, it was necessary first to assess the production and consumption patterns of livestock products and fish. Additionally, the legal and political framework with regard to subsistence and communal farmers was evaluated.

Livestock and fisheries production and consumption in South Africa

The livestock and fisheries sectors in South Africa are affected by various extraneous conditions such as weather patterns, disease occurrence and consumer preferences. However, growth and development are expected as national demand for animal-source food increases in line with overall population growth and urbanization. The South African population grew at a rate of almost 2% per year from 44 million in 2005 to 49 million in 2010. In addition to the increasing population, consumer dietary habits have changed and there is greater awareness of the pros and cons of eating foods rich in fatty acids and animal protein.

This study reports the results of surveys and a 'Strengths, Weaknesses, Opportunities and Threats' (SWOT) analysis conducted on livestock and fisheries farming and consumption of animal-source foods in South Africa. The findings provide information on the current state of affairs, highlighting the constraints and opportunities for the sector that will enhance competitiveness and improve both local and export performance.

The SWOT analysis was conducted by four multidisciplinary working groups of six to nine people including members of the Department of Agriculture, Forestry and Fisheries (DAFF), the Department of Health (DOH), the Department of Trade and Industry (DTI), the National Regulator for Compulsory Specifications (NRCS) and the South African Bureau of Standards (SABS) as well as the pharmaceutical and food processing industry, academic and research institutions, farmers and consumers. Topics addressed included livestock farming practices and current government policies, production inputs such as feeds, the role of agriculturists in food safety education, food processing and handling practices, food preparation practices of retailers, vendors and caterers at home and point-of-sale, markets, shelf life, storage, transport and preparation. Additional information was obtained through annual reports and newsletters from DAFF and the food industry.

Highly fragmented political responsibilities

South Africa has three capital cities: Cape Town, as the seat of Parliament, is the legislative capital; Pretoria, as the seat of the President and Cabinet, is the administrative capital; and Bloemfontein, as the seat of the Supreme Court of Appeal, is the judicial capital. Just as divided as the location of state authorities, responsibility for the safety of animal-source food is also very fragmented. This complicates the implementation of policies at national, provincial and local levels.

Different aspects fall under national government departments (DOH, DAFF, DTI, NRCS and SABS). There are also a number of non-governmental stakeholders and role players involved. At international level, these include the FAO, WHO, OIE, Codex Alimentarius and ISO. At national level they include the South African National Accreditation Service, SABS, ISO and the private sector standards used by producers and processors of animal-source food. At local level, there are provincial and municipal regulations in charge of the implementation of national directives as well as private standards of supermarkets, butcheries, dairies and other retailers of animal-source foods. As a result, lines of responsibility are not always well understood as they sometimes overlap or are inconsistently applied. In May 2009, a new cabinet was formed and set its focus on the livestock and fisheries sector as a strategy for developing the rural economy and improving productivity and livelihoods in rural areas.

South Africa occupies the southern tip of Africa, its long coastline stretching more than 2500 kilometres from the desert border with Namibia on the Atlantic coast, southwards around the tip of the Cape of Good Hope, following north to the border with subtropical Mozambique on the Indian Ocean. South Africa covers a land surface of more than 1.2 million square kilometres (world rank 25); 69% of this land is suitable for grazing and livestock farming. The 1994 elections ended the apartheid regime and resulted in a land reform policy, land redistribution and restitution determined by the Land Rights Act. This law aimed at the creation and maintenance of an equitable and sustainable land dispensation resulting in the social and economic development of all South Africans. Previously disadvantaged individuals and victims were supposed to obtain benefits. To reverse the damage caused by land mismanagement, the government set up the Comprehensive Agricultural Support Programme in 2004 to promote sustainable development and use of natural resources. Today, South Africa runs a dual agricultural sector with a well-developed farming sector on one hand and subsistence or communal farming on the other hand.

Rural farmers are left behind

The SWOT analysis found that there is a high demand for livestock products. The livestock sector is the largest agricultural sector and animal production has increased over the past six years with poultry and cattle dominating the market, followed by field crops and horticulture. The consumption of chicken has increased and already exceeds the total consumption of red meat. There is a lack of data on goat meat consumption due to cultural or religious taboos (Chapter 30). The fisheries sector is well established and produces 600,000 tons per year (including molluscs and crustaceans) but aquaculture is under-exploited.

The SWOT analysis also showed a substantial lack of data on the number of subsistence farmers and their produce, and post-land reform settlement seems to be ineffective. The farmers do not have adequate knowledge about the management of livestock and related finances. Moreover, the emerging rural communal farmers do not utilize the available natural resources to their full extent due to various reasons such as lack of investments in rural areas, budget constraints for production inputs and lack of skills. In general, they have been left behind and have only minimal influence on policies. They are mostly told what to do and do not question the underlying policy.

Consumption behaviour is considered to be another weakness. The South Africans call themselves the ‘Rainbow Nation’ as the population is very diverse.

About 79% of South Africans are of Black African ancestry, 9% Whites, 9% Coloured and 3% Indians/Asians. Up until 1991, the South African constitution divided its habitants into four groups: Blacks, Whites, Coloured and Asians. Even though this division does not exist in the constitution any more, many South Africans as well as government statistics maintain this classification.[1] The demographic, religious and cultural diversity results in different consumption patterns. Whereas some are influenced by the media in their eating habits of pork (risk of cardiovascular diseases) or poultry (unjustified fear of avian influenza), others like or dislike animal-source food for religious (Muslims do not eat pork) or cultural reasons (seafood phobia of Blacks).

Outlook

There is a need for DAFF to implement its integrated rural development policies with a particular focus on the sustainable utilization of natural resources. The land reform project ought to be resuscitated in order to redistribute the land and provide agricultural education and training as well as extension, advisory and veterinary services to subsistence farmers. One priority should be the retention of skills to encourage the transfer of skills from white farmers to black farmers and avoid production losses. On a communal level, data on farmers and their produce must be collected in order to analyse demand and supply. Optionally, seafood and fish consumption should be promoted and the security of farmers should be improved.

There are other factors affecting the development of the sector. Stock theft and even killing of farmers are serious problems that the government should address, in addition to poaching and over-fishing. Climate change and environmental issues might cause an increase in natural disasters such as floods and fire. Farmers need to have adequate access to land and water sources as well as finance models, in light of increasing input costs of fuel, equipment, animal health care and animal feed. There is a shortage of academic institutions devoted to teaching of applied regulatory toxicology and aquatic animal health. Furthermore, since one responsibility is shared by two authorities, the registration of veterinary medicines and stock remedies is regulated just as poorly as is the monitoring and surveillance of veterinary drugs for animals intended for human consumption. Africa needs a comprehensive veterinary legislation which covers animal disease control, registration and control of veterinary drugs (including insecticides manufactured for administration to animals), food safety including food protection, prevention and elimination of zoonoses, aspects of laboratory animal facilities and diagnostic laboratories as well as health care education and extension.

To estimate the chronic dietary intake of pesticides and veterinary drug residues, further research is necessary and currently under way. This involves evaluation of the patterns of consumption of eggs, dairy, fish, sea food, meat products, alternative indigenous protein sources and honey. Subsequently, the most widely consumed products of animal origin such as milk, chicken, liver, eggs and meat will be analysed to determine the content of residues of pesticides and veterinary drugs commonly used to treat livestock animals.

Margaret Molefe holds a Master of Science degree in agriculture with a specialization in animal science and nutrition and is undertaking PhD studies at the University of Pretoria. She is the deputy director of the Directorate of Food Control at the National Department of Health in South Africa and manages the sub-directorate of chemical safety of food.

Title and authors of the study

Situation analysis on South African animal medicines, animal health and veterinary drug residues in foodstuffs.

Margaret Molefe,[1,2] *Cheryl McCrindle*,[1] *Christo Botha*,[2] *Kohei Makita*[3,4] and *Delia Grace*[3]

[1]Faculty of Veterinary Science, University of Pretoria, South Africa; [2]National Department of Health, South Africa; [3]International Livestock Research Institute, Kenya; [4]Rakuno Gakuen University, Japan

Contact details

Margaret Molefe
National Department of Health, Directorate of Food Control
Private Bag X828, 0100 Pretoria, South Africa
Email: molefe.mabunda@gmail.com or molefs@health.gov.za

Notes

1. www.info.gov.za/otherdocs/2003/census01brief.pdf (accessed 9 July 2014).

32

IS GHANA THREATENED WITH DISEASE FROM ITS HEAVY FISH CONSUMPTION?

Kennedy Bomfeh, Kristina Roesel, Kwaku Tano-Debrah, Firibu K. Saalia, Betty Bediako-Amoa and Delia Grace

Key messages

- This study is the first ever assessment of *Listeria monocytogenes*, a serious and emerging pathogen, in fish in Ghana.
- *Listeria monocytogenes* was detected in all fish products purchased from informal markets in the study area.
- Contamination levels were low, hence the risk of ingestion and infection was generally low for otherwise healthy consumers.
- Poor post-process handling practices could be the main source of contamination.
- A control organism used to simulate a worst-case scenario survived domestic soup preparation.

Background

Listeriosis is an infection caused by the bacterium *Listeria monocytogenes*. In several countries which have good information on the health effects of different pathogens, it is considered the leading cause of death among food-borne bacteria. Listeriosis is fatal in 20–30% of cases and up to 75% in individuals with a compromised immune system. In pregnant women, infection can lead to miscarriage, stillbirth, premature delivery or infection of the new-born. Apparently healthy individuals infected with the organism show such symptoms as fever, muscle aches and, sometimes, nausea or diarrhoea. If infection spreads to the nervous system, headache, neck stiffness, confusion, loss of balance and seizures may occur.[1] Human listeriosis is not documented in Ghana. However, cases of the disease in sheep have been reported. *Listeria* has also been found in coleslaw from restaurants as well as in raw milk and dairy products from informal markets in the country and ready-to-eat meat and fish products.

Ghana is a heavy consumer of fish

Ghana's fishery sector accounts for 3% of the national GDP and employs about 10% of the population. While men are mostly responsible for fishing, women are in charge of on-shore processing and marketing. The marine sub-sector is the most important source of local fish production. It delivers more than 80% of the total supply and consists of three main categories: small-scale (artisanal on canoe), semi-industrial (or inshore) and industrial.[2] About 60–70% of the domestic marine fish supply comes from artisanal fishery.[3] The most important marine resources are small pelagic, especially the round sardinella, flat sardinella, anchovy and chub mackerel. These species account for about 70% of the total marine fish landing.[4]

While fish accounts for more than 50% of the country's earnings from non-traditional exports, the most important use of fish in Ghana is domestic consumption. The average annual per capita fish consumption in the country is estimated at 20–25kg, which is much higher than the world average of 13kg. Fish accounts for more than 25% of food expenditure in poor households and for up to 60% of animal protein in the Ghanaian diet. People along the coastal areas consume the majority of fresh catch and inland areas are more frequently supplied with processed fish, mainly smoked and salted.

Salting, drying and smoking have been used for many years to preserve fish. Drying slows down spoilage since bacteria, yeast and moulds generally cannot grow without enough water. Unfortunately, *Listeria* is an exception to this rule as it can grow in food that has high salt or low water contents. Furthermore, it can grow at very low temperatures (-1.5°C), so refrigeration alone is not enough to inhibit it.

In the absence of recorded cases of human listeriosis in Ghana, it was of interest to investigate whether consumption of traditionally processed fish poses a health risk. Illness largely depends on the number of organisms ingested. In laboratory tests, one bacterium showed the potential to cause disease in humans.[5] However, this problem is still the subject of heated discussions among experts. Most at risk are children, the elderly, pregnant women and people with a feeble immune system (for instance, those infected with HIV). This vulnerable group makes up a significant number of people in Ghana. Therefore, it was necessary to know which fish products are commonly consumed and how much is normally eaten at a time.

The commonly consumed products were identified through a survey of 450 consumers in Jamestown and Madina (in Accra) and Tema New Town (in Tema, near Accra). They were later sampled from five informal markets and analysed microbiologically to determine the presence and concentration of *Listeria monocytogenes*.

The suspects were:

- sundried sardines (*Sardinella aurita*)
- hot-smoked marine fish
    - tuna (*Katsuwonus pelamis*)

  - herrings (*Sardinella eba*)
  - mackerel, locally referred to as salmon (*Scomber japonicus*)
- salted-dried
  - tilapia (*Oreochromis niloticus*) locally known as *koobi*, from domestic freshwater lakes
  - ray fish (*Dasyatis centroura)* locally known as *kako*
- salted and fermented fish locally called *momoni*, made from marine fish bought by processors at a lower price as the fish would have otherwise been discarded.

The hazard is present but risk to public health is low

Listeria was detected in 93% of smoked mackerel, 80% of smoked tuna and 67% of the smoked herrings. Even though the bacteria were found in smoked fish, concentrations were generally very low. Salted and sundried fish were less contaminated than smoked fish.

Risk assessors are detectives, but the 'crime' they investigate is food contamination. In this case, researchers wanted answers to the question: Where did the fish get contaminated? Was it in the sea, on the boat, in the port, at the market or in the kitchen? To answer this question, typical processing chains for smoking, salting and drying were examined. Fish samples were taken along these chains from raw to processed products to determine the possible presence and concentration of *Listeria*.

The organism was detected in at least one sample from each step in the processing chains, except in frozen fresh mackerel and herrings, and hot-smoked fish (tuna, mackerel and herrings) sampled immediately after the smoking. We found that the source of contamination was most likely improper handling of the products after processing. Observations at the processing sites showed that sanitary facilities such as toilets and potable water sources were not available. Moreover, water used for washing the fish proved to be contaminated. However, the organism was not found in smoked fish right after the smoking but was found in the product at the point of sale to the consumer. In the markets, the fish were handled with bare hands and wrapped in materials of questionable cleanliness. It is therefore most likely that the product that was rendered safe during smoking ended up being contaminated at the point of sale. In another study in Ghana (Chapter 16), it was found that fermented milk not only contained *Listeria* but that this represented a public health risk. Would the same be true for fish?

Listeria can be eliminated by thorough cooking. Therefore, the survival of the bacterium in domestic cooking was evaluated in the laboratory by deliberately introducing large amounts of a control organism into some traditionally processed fish and using the contaminated fish to prepare typical Ghanaian soups using local recipes identified through a focus group discussion (Chapter 5). The experiment simulated a worst-case scenario. Additionally, Ghanaian street food was purchased and analysed for the presence of *Listeria*.

While some of the control organisms survived the experimental cooking, street food samples were found to be uncontaminated. Ultimately, falling sick with human listeriosis largely depends on the number of the bacteria ingested and the susceptibility of the person who eats the fish. In the survey, most consumers reported eating more than 200g of smoked mackerel and tuna at a time. However, due to the low contamination levels, the risk of a healthy person ingesting enough bacteria to fall sick was generally low.

The participants in the survey also gave information on the consumption patterns among the elderly, children and pregnant women in their households. This helped to assess whether and to what extent this highly vulnerable group was at risk. For example, for smoked tuna, whereas the risk of illness for the low-risk group ranged from one in a million to one in a hundred million, the risk of illness for the highly vulnerable group ranged from one in ten to one in a hundred.

The findings of this study contrast with those of the study on *Listeria* in fermented milk in Ghana, which found the risk to consumers was relatively high. Of course, fish has been consumed on a large scale for a long time in Ghana, while a large market for fresh milk is only starting to develop. It makes sense that when foods have been eaten for a long time, people will develop practices that reduce the risk of getting infections from them.

How the problem is handled overseas

The United States of America and the United Kingdom follow a zero-tolerance policy for the presence of *Listeria* in food. They argue that a minimum infection dose is not known and laboratory tests have shown that one single bacterium is able to cause disease. On the other hand, most countries in the EU have set tolerance limits with zero tolerance for infant food and food products given to the elderly or in hospitals. In the EU, listeriosis occurs at about the same rates as in the United States of America and the United Kingdom, suggesting that a zero-tolerance policy does not necessarily offer more protection to consumers. European experts argue that tests are not yet 100% reliable and *Listeria* is a widespread bacterium and difficult to eliminate, thus zero-tolerance regulations hamper international trade.

Very high quality standards for food obviously have costs; these include more expensive production and the destruction of food which does not meet the standards. In Africa, these costs fall most heavily on poor people who cannot afford expensive production and who often do not get enough food. High standards also make it difficult for Africa to trade with other countries. According to the former secretary general of the United Nations, Kofi Annan, the EU regulation on fungal contamination of peanuts 'cost Africa US$750 million each year in exports. And what does it achieve? It may possibly save the life of one citizen of the EU every two years.'[6] There is a lot of debate on what are the most appropriate standards for African countries; risk assessment can shed light on the matter by estimating the health impacts of different standards.

Recommendations

The hygienic conditions of traditional fish processing and post-processing handling should be improved through impact-driven participatory studies. This study suggests how good communication between veterinary and medical doctors can allow early warning of possible public health threats when zoonotic diseases are detected in animals. The findings support the theory that when people have a long tradition of consuming food products, they are likely to have developed ways of reducing the risk of food-borne illness, but food products that are less familiar to consumers are likely to be more risky.

Kennedy Bomfeh holds a Master's degree in food science from the University of Ghana. During his undergraduate and graduate studies he worked as a teaching assistant and research assistant at the University of Ghana in Accra.

Title and authors of the study

Risk assessment for *Listeria monocytogenes* in traditionally processed fish from informal markets in Accra and Tema, Ghana.

Kennedy Bomfeh,[1] *Kwaku Tano-Debrah,*[1] *Firibu K. Saalia*[1] and *Betty Bediako-Amoa*[1]
[1]University of Ghana

Contact details

Kennedy Bomfeh
Department of Nutrition and Food Science, University of Ghana
P.O. Box LG 134, Legon, Accra, Ghana
Email: kbomfeh@gmail.com

Notes

1. WHO. 2011. www.who.int/topics/listeria_infections/en (accessed 9 July 2014).
2. FAO. 2004. *Fishery country profile: Ghana.* ftp://ftp.fao.org/FI/DOCUMENT/fcp/en/FI_CP_GH.pdf
3. Mensah P, Yeboah-Manu D, Owusu-Darko K and Ablordey A. 2002. Street foods in Accra, Ghana: how safe are they? *Bulletin of the World Health Organization* 80: 546–554.
4. www.fao.org/fi/oldsite/FCP/en/gha/profile.htm (accessed 9 July 2014).
5. WHO. 2004. www.who.int/foodsafety/publications/micro/en/mra4.pdf (accessed 9 July 2014).
6. www.apsnet.org/publications/apsnetfeatures/Pages/Mycotoxins.aspx (accessed 9 July 2014).

33

EUROPEAN UNION TRADE REGULATIONS INFLUENCING FOOD PRODUCTION IN CÔTE D'IVOIRE

Yolande Aké Assi Datté, Kristina Roesel, Axel Sess, Henry Biego Godi, Mathias Koffi, Patrice Kouamé, Bassirou Bonfoh and Delia Grace

Key messages

- Diaspora populations offer an emerging market for African traditional foods, such as smoked fish, but may also be vulnerable to health risks associated with them.
- The study team found that more than 71% of smoked fat fish in Côte d'Ivoire is contaminated with polycyclic aromatic hydrocarbons (PAHs).
- The contamination exceeds the limit set by the EU for fresh fish.
- Identifying high-risk practices is the first step in taking action to change them; the study successfully identified high-risk practices including using resinous wood for smoking of fish.
- Only 10% of the producers knew about the risks associated with PAHs; this low level of awareness is a major obstacle to improving practices.
- Food safety is not just for the consumer; people involved in processing can also be exposed to high levels of hazards.

Background

It is said that 'when Paris sniffs, Abidjan catches a cold'. In an increasingly global world, connected by social and trade networks, no country stands alone. Partly due to historical links, there is a large community of Ivorian expatriates in France and, like many expatriates, they are hungry for the foods of home. This study came about after an incident whereby French regulators detected PAHs in fish smoked in Côte d'Ivoire and exported to France.

PAHs are formed by the incomplete combustion of coal, oil, petrol, wood, tobacco, charbroiled meats, garbage or other organic materials. Most PAHs are pollutants and have no known use. A few are used in medicines and to make dyes, plastics, pesticides and wood preservatives. The primary sources of emission are petroleum refineries, fossil fuel (coal and oil) power plants, wood product manufacturers, asphalt roads, motor vehicle exhaust, volcanoes and fires of all types (bush, forest, agricultural, home heating and cooking). They recently came to attention as a potential hazard to people who eat barbecued meats. Smoked and barbecued meats and fish may contain high levels of PAHs as a result of the smoking process. Exposure to PAHs can irritate the eyes, nose, throat and bronchial tubes. Contact with the skin can cause irritation or allergic reaction. Very high levels may cause headaches and nausea, damage the red blood cells, liver and kidneys, and may even cause death. The International Agency for Research on Cancer cites a number of PAHs as 'probably carcinogenic to humans' and others as 'possibly carcinogenic to humans'.[1]

PAHs enter the body by inhaling contaminated air or consuming contaminated food or water. Skin contact with heavy oils or other products (creosote, roofing tar, other tars and oils) containing PAHs will result in uptake too. Hence, PAHs are not only food hazards but also occupational hazards, and those smoking food are at risk. These chemical pollutants are poisonous to aquatic life and birds in the short to medium term. They are moderately persistent in the environment and can accumulate in the body, especially in fat. The concentration of PAHs found in fish and shellfish is expected to be much higher than that in the environment from which it was taken.

More than 80% of the fish landing in Côte d'Ivoire is traditionally smoked for sale in the local market and for export. During the smoking process, benzo(a)pyrene (BaP) – the PAH of reference which is likely to cause cancer – can be released. In 2006, a European by-law[2] determined the maximum acceptable levels of specific contaminants in food produce (BaP in smoked fish) and thus required surveillance of all smoked products destined for export to the EU.

In 2007, BaP was discovered in smoked fish from Côte d'Ivoire destined for export to Europe. In Europe the main purchasers of these fish products are the West African diaspora. This incident proved that the application of these regulations is a severe setback for this profitable market in Côte d'Ivoire. Smoked fish accounts for 0.73% of the total export volume which corresponds to 2.3% of foreign exchange, and the sector employs approximately 70,000 people who feed another 400,000.

The present study aimed to assess formation of PAHs in smoked fish and understand the practices that increase risk of exposure to PAHs. The ultimate aim was to promote safe smoking of fish marketed in Côte d'Ivoire. Factors that might increase the formation of PAHs during traditional fish processing, storing and preserving were investigated in four main centres in Abidjan: Port-Bouët, Boulay Island, Yopougon and Adjamé. These areas are close to the Gulf of Guinea where fish is traditionally smoked and marketed informally. The study team visited the production sites and interviewed producers, sellers and consumers of smoked fish, facilitated by the local authorities and local non-governmental organizations, consumer associations and producers in the informal sector. Samples of fish were also collected and tested.

Processors and consumers are at risk

Fish at the smoking site is received either fresh or frozen. The frozen fish is defrosted, and, depending on the type of fish, scaled. After rinsing, the fish is prepared for smoking (folded whole or in pieces). After draining, the fish is smoked for 45 minutes to one hour until it is cooked but damp. Afterwards it is cooled and sold or smoked again for another hour on a weak fire, resulting in dry-smoked fish (this largely depends on consumer demand). The final product is wrapped in paper or plastic, stored and sold on the local market.

Almost 90% of the 423 survey respondents were women, 59% of whom did not have secondary education. Most of them considered the revenues from their businesses to be satisfactory. Fat fish was preferred for smoking because the fat content enhances the taste as flavouring substances are mostly soluble in fat. The fish is smoked on home-made metal ovens, and 85% of the respondents said they smoked both sides of the fish at hot temperatures for more than two hours. Branches of rubber trees (*Hevea* spp. from the spurge family) were used for fuel by two-thirds of the operators.

The results of the survey showed that only 10% of the people questioned knew about the risks related to PAHs released during traditional smoking of fish. Concern over PAHs is relatively recent, and information about emerging hazards, especially those with complicated names and causes, may take a long time to trickle down to the people who need the information most. Although they were not aware of PAH-related risks, many participants had experienced fatigue, headaches and eyestrain. This could be due to many causes, but given the high levels of PAHs in the smoked fish, it is very likely that it is due to high levels of occupational exposure. During the visits to the markets, high-risk practices were noticed such as the use of resinous wood (branches of rubber trees) and high smoking temperatures. These practices, together with information gained from face-to-face talks, led to the conclusion that there is a risk of PAHs being formed during traditional smoking of fish.

The EU uses BaP as a marker for the occurrence of carcinogenic PAHs and has set the maximum level in fresh fish at 2μg per kilogram and 5μg per kilogram for smoked fish.[3] These levels are said not to cause long-term adverse effects on the health of consumers. The fat content of 49 samples of fresh and smoked fish was determined by validated international standards and compared to the maximum levels for BaP set by the EU. Fish at the study sites exceeded these threshold values by far; four-fold in fresh fish (8.53μg/kg) and more than five-fold (28.64μg/kg) in smoked fish. Over 71% of smoked fat fish tested was contaminated with BaP, with higher BaP levels in higher fat content fish.

The survey also determined the average consumption per person of fresh and smoked fish. Using these findings and estimates by the National Institute for Public Health and the Environment in the Netherlands, it was calculated that the consumers of smoked fish in Côte d'Ivoire are exposed to an almost two-fold higher risk of falling ill with cancer. Thus, apart from trade restrictions, Ivorians are likely to face increased risk of cancer if traditional methods of smoking and processing fish continue.

Recommendations

Quality control measures and risk mitigation techniques should be developed and strategies to reduce the risks of exposure to PAHs in smoked fish for human consumption promoted, for example education of fish processors on the types of wood suitable for smoking fish. Awareness of PAHs amongst the processors and consumers must be increased and operators at smoking sites should receive medical checks enforced by health officers.

Yolande Aké Assi Datté is a state veterinarian in Côte d'Ivoire and is the director of the Central Laboratory for Food Hygiene and Agribusiness at the Ministry of Animal Production and Fishery Resources. This study was undertaken towards her PhD degree from the Université Félix Houphouët-Boigny.

Title and authors of the study

Formation of polycyclic aromatic hydrocarbons in traditionally smoked fish sold and consumed in Côte d'Ivoire.

Yolande Aké Assi Datté,[1,2] *Axel Sess*,[1,2] *Henry Biego Godi*,[3] *Mathias Koffi*,[1,3] *Patrice Kouamé*[2] and *Bassirou Bonfoh*[4]

[1]Laboratoire Central pour l'Hygiène Alimentaire et l'Agro-Industrie, Ministère de l'Agriculture, Côte d'Ivoire; [2]Université Félix Houphouët-Boigny, Côte d'Ivoire; [3]Université Nanguy Abrogoua, Côte d'Ivoire; [4]Centre de Recherches Scientifiques en Côte d'Ivoire

Contact details

Yolande Aké Assi Datté
Laboratoire Central pour l'Hygiène Alimentaire et l'Agro-Industrie
Ministère de l'Agriculture, 04 B.P. 612 Abidjan 04, Côte d'Ivoire
Email: aaay02@yahoo.fr

Notes

1. National Pollutant Inventory, Department of Sustainability, Environment, Water, Population and Communities, Canberra, Australia. www.npi.gov.au/substances/polycyclic-aromatic/index.html (accessed 9 July 2014).
2. Commission regulation (EC) No. 1881/2006 of 19 December 2006 setting maximum levels for certain contaminants in foodstuffs http://eur-lex.europa.eu/LexUriServ/LexUriServ.do?uri=OJ:L:2006:364:0005:0024:EN:PDF
3. Commission regulation (EC) No. 1881/2006. http://eur-lex.europa.eu/LexUriServ/LexUriServ.do?uri=OJ:L:2006:364:0005:0024:EN:PDF, page 18.

34

SHELLFISH ON THE TABLE NOT TO BLAME FOR CHRONIC COUGH IN CÔTE D'IVOIRE

Sylvain Gnamien Traoré, Kristina Roesel, Régina Krabi, Koffi D. Adoubryn, Aka Assoumou, Solenne Costard, Kohei Makita, Delia Grace, Marina Koussémon and Bassirou Bonfoh

Key messages

- *Vibrio* and lung flukes were present in shellfish but there was little evidence to link them to human infection.
- Food preparation practices (for example, thorough cooking of shellfish) may reduce risk among consumers.

Background

Zoonotic diseases are often under-diagnosed. One reason is that the symptoms are often similar to those of more common diseases and laboratory tests that would allow differential diagnosis are often not available or too expensive. Brucellosis is a good example; it is so often wrongly diagnosed as malaria that suspected cases of brucellosis are identified by medical history of 'malaria that does not respond to anti-malarial treatment'. Twenty-one million people live in Côte d'Ivoire, 31,000 of whom are said to be infected with active tuberculosis.[1] Chronic cough is one of the symptoms of tuberculosis, although it may be caused by other types of infection, for instance lung fluke infection. What if the chronic cough of these patients is due not to the bacterium that causes tuberculosis but to something else? The present study investigated the presence of lung flukes in shellfish sold in markets in and around Abidjan and the possible link between shellfish consumption and chronic cough in patients at tuberculosis centres.

Lung flukes are one of the many types of worms that infect people. Humans can become infected with worms in numerous ways: schistosomiasis (bilharzia) is transmitted through contact with contaminated water, soil-transmitted helminthiasis (liver flukes) through infective soil and lymphatic filariasis (elephantiasis) through mosquito bites. Transmission via food is yet another route which currently affects more than 40 million people worldwide, specifically, via food related to water such as fish, shellfish and water plants. More than 70 species of the class of worms called trematodes (flukes) are known to infect humans through food but they are widely unknown, partly due to their complex life cycles and geographic distributions. Lung fluke infection (paragonimiasis) is among the four most important of these neglected tropical diseases.[2]

Humans are the definitive host of lung flukes, that is, the host where the adult stage of the worm lives. The eggs are coughed up by people and may also be found in human faeces if secretions from coughing are swallowed. Once shed, the eggs develop into larvae and invade snails in fresh water where they transform into cercariae (a stage of the complex life cycle) and are shed into the water again. They seek a crustacean, such as a crab, crayfish or shrimp, where they develop into another form that is infectious to the definitive host (humans). A person who eats infected freshwater crabs or shrimps can become infected and the worms invade the lungs. Other definitive hosts such as pigs, dogs and cats that eat shellfish can also shed eggs in their faeces and thus perpetuate the cycle of infection. The symptoms of lung fluke infection in humans are tuberculosis-like and include blood-stained sputum, chronic cough and chest pain.[3]

Lung fluke infections can be easily avoided by ensuring that fish, crabs and shellfish are well cooked. Treatment is easily administered with deworming medicine. Unfortunately, if symptoms of lung fluke infections are mistaken for those of tuberculosis, the patient will be treated with very expensive antibiotics that are not effective against worm infections. Differential diagnosis is therefore crucial. Raw shellfish from brackish saltwater is host to another agent likely to cause disease in humans: the *Vibrio* bacteria, including *Vibrio cholerae* that causes cholera.[4] Because shellfish are an important source of food in Abidjan and are associated with two major diseases – lung fluke infection and cholera – the study team investigated the possible risks of shellfish consumption to human health.

Hundreds of samples of shellfish were taken from markets in and around Abidjan and around 12% were found to contain lung fluke stages. In addition to testing of shellfish, several hundred patients at tuberculosis centres and children at schools were tested for worm infections by sampling stool and sputum. Worm eggs were found regularly but none were from lung flukes. This finding excluded lung flukes as the cause of chronic cough in the sampled patients. The study then sought to investigate at what point these parasites were eliminated.

Some 120 households in Abidjan were interviewed on shellfish preparation and eating habits. Almost everyone in Abidjan eats shellfish either occasionally or regularly. Over 80% of respondents said they cooked their shrimps and crabs thoroughly for more than 45 minutes. This is the most effective means of mitigating the risk of transmitting disease and can explain why – despite a high prevalence of lung fluke parasites in shellfish in the markets – the risk to human health is low. A key finding from our food safety research is that high levels of pathogens in food do not necessarily correspond to a high level of risk to human health, and therefore careful risk assessment is essential.

However, one observation from our study was left unexplained: more than three-quarters of the coughing patients who tested negative for lung flukes also tested negative for tuberculosis. This calls for further investigation to reveal other possible reasons for chronic cough among inhabitants of Abidjan.

Shellfish may not be to blame for cholera either

Every year an estimated 3–5 million people worldwide fall sick from cholera and 20% develop acute watery diarrhoea which causes several hundred thousand deaths. Cholera outbreaks are closely linked to inadequate environmental management. Peri-urban areas are particularly at risk where people are crowded and basic sanitary infrastructure is not available. The short incubation period of *Vibrio cholerae* of two hours to five days enhances the potentially explosive pattern of cholera outbreaks.[4]

Nearly 10% of the shellfish sampled contained *Vibrio* spp. but our study found that *Vibrio cholerae*, the causative agent of cholera, was absent in the shellfish. Nevertheless, the practice of prolonged cooking also helps to reduce the load of other disease-causing bacteria that may be present in the shellfish, thereby rendering it safe for human consumption.

Recommendations

Although the traditional practice of prolonged cooking of shellfish is effective at reducing the risk of bacterial infection, cross-contamination of other foods should be avoided, for example by separating raw shellfish and foods such as vegetables during purchase, transport, storage and preparation. Utensils used for preparing shellfish should be thoroughly cleaned before using them for other food. As earlier mentioned, the possible reasons for chronic cough in tuberculosis-negative patients should be investigated further.

Sylvain Gnamien Traoré holds a Master's degree in microbiology from the University Nanguy Abrogoua in Côte d'Ivoire and works at the Centre Suisse de Recherches Scientifiques en Côte d'Ivoire. The research work towards his PhD from the Université Nanguy Abrogoua was carried out at the Swiss Tropical and Public Health Institute in Basel, Switzerland.

Title and authors of the study

Risk for *Vibrio* and *Paragonimus* infections linked to shellfish consumption in Côte d'Ivoire.

Sylvain Gnamien Traoré,[1,2] *Régina Krabi,*[1,2] *Koffi D. Adoubryn,*[3] *Aka Assoumou,*[3] *Solenne Costard,*[4,5,6] *Kohei Makita,*[7] *Delia Grace,*[6] *Marina Koussémon*[1] and *Bassirou Bonfoh*[2]

[1]Université Nanguy Abrogoua, Côte d'Ivoire; [2]Centre Suisse de Recherches Scientifiques en Côte d'Ivoire; [3]Laboratoire de Parasitologie-Mycologie, Université Félix Houphouët-Boigny, Côte d'Ivoire; [4]Royal Veterinary College London, United Kingdom; [5]EpiX Analytics, USA; [6]International Livestock Research Institute, Kenya; [7]Rakuno Gakuen University, Japan.

Contact details

Sylvain Gnamien Traoré
Centre Suisse de Recherches Scientifiques en Côte d'Ivoire
Microbiology, Food Risk Analysis
01 B.P. 1303 Abidjan 01, Côte d'Ivoire
Email: sylvain.traore@csrs.ci

Notes

1. WHO. 2011. https://extranet.who.int/sree/Reports?op=Replet&name=%2FWHO_HQ_Reports%2FG2%2FPROD%2FEXT%2FTBCountryProfile&ISO2=CI&outtype=html (accessed 9 July 2014).
2. WHO. 2007. *Action against worms*. www.who.int/neglected_diseases/preventive_chemotherapy/Newsletter10.pdf (accessed 9 July 2014).
3. WHO. 2011. www.who.int/zoonoses/diseases/trematodosis/en/index.html (accessed 9 July 2014).
4. WHO. 2011. www.who.int/mediacentre/factsheets/fs107/en/index.html (accessed 9 July 2014).

PART 3

Annexes

ANNEX 1

PROJECT PARTNERS FROM 2008 TO 2011

National partners

Bassirou Bonfoh: Centre Suisse de Recherche Scientifique, Côte d'Ivoire
Cheryl McCrindle: University of Pretoria, South Africa
Erastus Kang'ethe: University of Nairobi, Kenya
Girma Zewde: Addis Ababa University, Ethiopia
Helena Matusse: Agricultural Research Institute of Mozambique
Kwaku Tano-Debrah: University of Ghana
Lusato Kurwijila: Sokoine University of Agriculture, Tanzania

German partners

Anne Valle Zárate: Universität Hohenheim
Marianna Siegmund-Schultze: Universität Hohenheim
André Markemann: Universität Hohenheim
Juliane Braeunig: Bundesinstitut für Risikobewertung
Max Baumann: Freie Universität Berlin

ILRI partners

Amos Omore
Bryony Jones
Delia Grace
Derek Baker
Kohei Makita (coordinator)
Kristina Roesel
Saskia Hendrickx
Siboniso Moyo
Solenne Costard

ANNEX 2

LIST OF PUBLICATIONS FROM THE SAFE FOOD, FAIR FOOD PROJECT

Theses

Amenu K. 2013. Assessment of water sources and quality for livestock and farmers in the Rift Valley area of Ethiopia: Implications for health and food safety. PhD thesis, University of Hohenheim, Stuttgart, Germany.

Appiah J. 2012. Assessment of the risk of consuming milk/milk products contaminated with *Listeria monocytogenes* from the informal markets. MPhil thesis, University of Ghana, Legon, Accra, Ghana.

Bomfeh K. 2011. Risk assessment for *Listeria monocytogenes* in traditionally processed fish from informal markets in Accra and Tema. MPhil thesis, University of Ghana, Legon, Accra, Ghana.

Desissa F. 2010. Quantitative risk assessment of consuming milk contaminated with *Staphylococcus aureus* in Debre-Zeit. MSc thesis, Addis Ababa University, Addis Ababa, Ethiopia.

Heeb AW. 2009. Participatory risk assessment of game products marketed through formal and informal chains: Hazard identification and risk assessment. MSc thesis, University of Hohenheim, Stuttgart, Germany.

Kabui KK. 2012. Assessment of milk quality and the potential of a quality-based payment system in smallholder farms in Limuru and Eldoret, Kenya. MSc thesis, University of Nairobi, Nairobi, Kenya.

Kilango K. 2011. Food safety in milk markets of smallholder farmers in Tanzania: A case of peri-urban wards in Temeke Municipality. MSc thesis, Sokoine University of Agriculture, Morogoro, Tanzania.

Koné VB. 2010. Représentation sociale de la qualité des aliments au Sahel: Perception et motivation des acteurs dans la sécurité sanitaire des denrées d'origine animale à Cinzana au Mali. MSc thesis, Université de Cocody, Abidjan, Côte d'Ivoire.

Mahundi E. 2010. Food safety risk analysis and marketing access of beef in Arusha Municipality, Tanzania. MSc thesis, Sokoine University of Agriculture, Morogoro, Tanzania.

Muchangos AB. 2012. Prerequisites for HACCP in small-scale poultry production and processing in Maputo, Mozambique. MSc thesis, University of Pretoria, Pretoria, South Africa.

Mwai C. 2011. Risk of contamination of beef carcasses with *Escherichia coli* O157:H7 from slaughterhouses in Nairobi, Kenya. MSc thesis, University of Nairobi, Nairobi, Kenya.

Ndongo FK. 2009. Choice of breeds and husbandry practices influencing the safety of milk and milk products from smallholder dairy cattle farms around Nairobi, focusing on brucellosis. MSc thesis, University of Hohenheim, Stuttgart, Germany.

Qekwana N. 2012. Occupational health and food safety risks associated with traditional slaughter practices of goats in Gauteng, South Africa. MMedVet thesis, University of Pretoria, Pretoria, South Africa.

Ramrajh S. 2012. Participatory risk assessment for harvesting of impala (*Aepyceros melampus*) and the distribution of byproducts. MMedVet thesis, University of Pretoria, Pretoria, South Africa.

Sow I. 2011. Evaluation du risque de brucellose lié à la consommation du lait frais dans la commune rurale de Cinzana, Mali. MSc thesis, Université de Bamako, Bamako, Mali.

Spengler M. 2011. Assessment of water and milk quality in rural mixed crop-livestock farming systems: A case study of Lume and Siraro districts, Ethiopia. BSc thesis, University of Hohenheim, Stuttgart, Germany.

Toyomaki H. 2012. An estimation of thermophilic *Campylobacter* population in ready-to-eat roast beef and chicken and the hygiene practices of sellers in beer bars in Arusha, Tanzania. BVSc thesis, Rakuno Gakuen University, Japan.

Traoré SG. 2013. Risques de contraction des affections à *Vibrio* spp. et à *Paragonimus* spp. liés à la consommation des crabes et des crevettes vendus sur les marchés d'Abidjan et de Dabou. PhD thesis, Université Nanguy Abrogoua, Côte d'Ivoire.

Peer-reviewed book chapters

Atwill ER, Li X, Grace D and Gannon V. 2012. Zoonotic waterborne pathogen loads in livestock. In Dufour A, Bartram J, Bos R and Gannon V (eds), *Animal waste, water quality and human health*. IWA Publishing, London, pp. 73–114.

Gannon V, Grace D and Atwill ER. 2012. Zoonotic waterborne pathogens in livestock and their excreta – Interventions. In Dufour A, Bartram J, Bos R and Gannon V (eds), *Animal waste, water quality and human health*. IWA Publishing, London, UK, pp. 115–156.

McDermott J and Grace D. 2012. Agriculture-associated diseases: Adapting agriculture to improve human health. In Fan S and Pandya-Lorch R (eds), *Reshaping agriculture for nutrition and health*. IFPRI (International Food Policy Research Institute), Washington, DC, pp. 103–111.

Journal articles

*Although they do not report findings from the project, these papers by scientists on the project team include concepts and thinking on participatory risk analysis, the development of which was supported by funding from the Safe Food, Fair Food project.

Aké-Assi Y, Biego GHM, Koffi KM, Kouamé P, Achi L and Bonfoh B. 2010. Validation de la méthode de détermination du benzo(a)pyrene dans des poissons frais et fumés vendus et consommés en Côte d'Ivoire. *Revue Africaine de Santé et de Productions Animales* 8(S): 53–58.

Amenu K, Markemann A and Zárate AV. 2013. Water for human and livestock consumption in rural settings of Ethiopia: Assessments of quality and health aspects. *Environmental Monitoring and Assessment*. doi 10.1007/s10661-013-3275-3.

Amenu K, Markemann A, Roessler R, Siegmund-Schultze M, Abebe G and Zárate AV. 2013. Constraints and challenges of meeting the water requirements of livestock in Ethiopia: Cases of Lume and Siraro districts. *Tropical Animal Health and Production*. doi 10.1007/s11250-013-0397-0.

Bonfoh B. 2010. Valeur ajoutée de la participation dans l'analyse de risques des aliments à l'intersection des secteurs formel et informel. *Revue Africaine de Santé et de Productions Animales* 8(S): 1–2.

Desissa F, Makita K, Teklu A and Grace D. 2012. Contamination of informally marketed bovine milk with *Staphylococcus aureus* in urban and peri urban areas of Debre-Zeit, Ethiopia. *African Journal of Microbiology Research* 6(29): 5852–5856.

Fokou G, Koné VB and Bonfoh B. 2010. 'Mon lait est pur et ne peut pas rendre malade': Motivations des acteurs du secteur informel et qualité du lait local au Mali. *Revue Africaine de Santé et de Productions Animales* 8(S): 75–86.

Grace D. 2012. The deadly gifts of livestock. *Agriculture for Development* 17: 14–16.

Grace D, Kang'ethe E and Waltner-Toews D. 2012. Participatory and integrative approaches to food safety in developing country cities. *Tropical Animal Health and Production* 44(Suppl 1): S1–S2.

Grace D, Makita K, Kang'ethe EK and Bonfoh B. 2010. Safe Food, Fair Food: Participatory risk analysis for improving the safety of informally produced and marketed food in sub-Saharan Africa. *Revue Africaine de Santé et de Productions Animales* 8(S): 3–11.

Herrero M, Grace D, Njuki J, Johnson N, Enahoro D, Silvestri S and Rufino MC. 2013. The roles of livestock in developing countries. *Animal* 7(Supplement s1): 3–18.

Kouamé-Sina SM, Makita K, Costard S, Grace D, Dadié A, Djè M and Bonfoh B. 2012. Hazard identification and exposure assessment for bacterial risk assessment of informally-marketed milk in Abidjan, Côte d'Ivoire. *Food and Nutrition Bulletin* 33(4): 223–234.

Kouamé-Sina SM, Makita K, Grace D, Dadié A, Djè M and Bonfoh B. 2010. Analyse des risques microbiens du lait cru local à Abidjan (Côte d'Ivoire). *Revue Africaine de Santé et de Productions Animales* 8(S): 35–42.

Kouamé-Sina SM, Dadié A, Makita K, Grace D, Djè M, Taminiau B, Daube G and Bonfoh B. 2011. Diversity, phylogenetic relationship and antibacterial potential of *Bifidobacterium* species isolated from raw milk production chain in Abidjan (Côte d'Ivoire). *African Journal of Microbiology Research* 5(21): 3394–3403.

Makita K, Desissa F, Teklu A, Zewde G and Grace D. 2012. Risk assessment of staphylococcal poisoning due to consumption of informally-marketed milk and home-made yoghurt in Debre Zeit, Ethiopia. *International Journal of Food Microbiology* 153(1-2): 135–141.

Makita K, Fèvre EM, Waiswa C, Eisler MC and Welburn SC. 2010. How human brucellosis incidence in urban Kampala can be reduced most efficiently? A stochastic risk assessment of informally-marketed milk. *PLoS ONE* 5(12): e14188. doi:10.1371/journal.pone.0014188.

Makita K, Grace D, Randolph TF, Baker D and Staal S. 2010. ILRI/BMZ Safe Food Fair Food: Building capacity to improve the safety of animal-source foods and ensure continued market access for poor farmers in sub-Saharan Africa. *Journal of Veterinary Epidemiology* 14(1):19–20.

Makita K, Fèvre EM, Waiswa C, Bronsvoort MDC, Eisler MC and Welburn SC. 2010. Population-dynamics focussed rapid rural mapping and characterization of the peri-urban interface of Kampala, Uganda. *Land Use Policy* 27(3): 888–897.

Makita K, Fèvre EM, Waiswa C, Kaboyo W, Eisler MC and Welburn SC. 2011. Evidence-based identification of the most important livestock related zoonotic diseases in Kampala, Uganda. *Journal of Veterinary Medical Science* 73(8): 991–1000.

*Omore A, Kurwijila L and Grace D. 2009. Improving livelihoods in East Africa through livestock research and extension: reflections on changes from the 1950s to the early twenty-first century. *Tropical Animal Production and Health* 41(7): 1051–1059.

Perry B and Grace D. 2009. The impacts of livestock diseases and their control on growth and development processes that are pro-poor. *Philosophical Transactions of the Royal Society B* 364(1530): 2643–2655.

Traoré SG, Koussémon M, Odermatt P, Aka ND, Adoubryn KD, Assoumou A, Dreyfuss G and Bonfoh B. 2010. Risque de contraction de trématodoses alimentaires avec la consommation des crustacés vendus sur les marchés d'Abidjan. *Revue Africaine de Santé et de Productions Animales* 8(S): 45–52.

Traoré SG, Odermatt P, Bonfoh B, Utzinger J, Aka ND, Adoubryn KD, Assoumou A, Dreyfuss G and Koussémon M. 2011. No *Paragonimus* in high-risk groups in Côte d'Ivoire, but considerable prevalence of helminths and intestinal protozoon infections. *Parasites & Vectors* 4: 96.

Traoré SG, Bonfoh B, Krabi R, Odermatt P, Utzinger J, Koffi-Nevry R, Tanner M, Frey J, Quilici ML and Koussémon M. 2012. Risk of *Vibrio* transmission linked to the consumption of crustaceans in coastal towns of Côte d'Ivoire. *Journal of Food Protection* 75(6): 1004–1011.

Yobouet BA, Dadié A, Bonfoh B, Makita K, Grace D, Djè KM and Meile L. 2013. Virulence factors and antibiotics resistance of *Bacillus cereus* group species isolated in traditionally marketed raw milk in Abidjan, Côte d'Ivoire. *Letters in Applied Microbiology* (submitted).

Yobouet BA, Kouamé-Sina SM, Dadié A, Makita K, Grace D, Djè KM and Bonfoh B. 2014. Contamination of raw milk with *Bacillus cereus* from farm to retail in Abidjan, Côte d'Ivoire and possible health implications. *Dairy Science & Technology*. 10.1007/s13594-013-0140-7.

Conference papers and posters

*Bin Qutub A, Deka R, Sarma D, Baker D, Thorpe W and Grace D. 2009. *Capacity building based on local risk mitigation strategies and value chain analysis may lead to better management of food-borne disease*. Symposium paper presented at Innovation Asia-Pacific held at Kathmandu, Nepal, 4–7 May 2009.

Bomfeh K, Tano-Debrah K, Saalia FK and Bediako-Amoa B. 2012. *Risk assessment for* Listeria monocytogenes *in hot-smoked fish in informal markets in Madina, Accra*. Paper presented at the 17th Faculty of Science Colloquium, University of Ghana, Accra, Ghana, 21 March 2012.

Fahrion A, Toan NN, Thuy DN, Lapar L and Grace D. 2010. *Risk assessment in the pork meat chain in 2 districts of Vietnam. A residency training project in collaboration with the International Livestock Research Institute*. Poster presented at the European College of Veterinary Public Health AGM and Annual Scientific Conference, Nottwil, Lucerne, Switzerland, 7–8 October 2010.

Fahrion AS, Grace D, Toan NN, Thuy DN, Staal S and Lapar L. 2010. *Risk assessment in the pork meat chain in two districts of Viet Nam*. Paper presented at Tropentag 2010, Zurich Switzerland, 14–16 September 2010.

Fahrion A, Richa K, Jamir L, Begum S, Rutsa V, Ao S, Padmakumar V and Grace D. 2010. *Risk assessment in the pork meat chain in Nagaland, India*. Poster presented at the annual conference of the Society for Veterinary Epidemiology and Preventive Medicine, Nantes, France, 24–26 March 2010.

Gervelmeyer A. 2009. *Food safety and food sovereignty: A possible linkage for rural development?* Paper presented at the VSF Europa symposium on food sovereignty, Pineto, Italy, 8–9 October 2009.

Grace D. 2010. *Risk-based approaches to food safety in developing countries.* Paper presented at the annual conference of the Australian Agricultural and Resource Economics Society, Adelaide, Australia, 9–12 February 2010.

*Grace D and Randolph T. 2009. *Exploded logit: More information from ranked data.* Poster presented at the annual conference of the Society for Veterinary Epidemiology and Preventive Medicine, London, UK, 1–3 April 2009.

*Grace D and Randolph T.F. 2009. *Development of a participatory methodology to prioritise milk borne disease in data-scarce environments.* Paper presented at the annual conference of the Society for Veterinary Epidemiology and Preventive Medicine, London, UK, 1–3 April 2009.

Grace D, Makita K, Baumann M, Bräunig J and Unger F. 2011. *ILRI/BMZ Safe Food Fair Food: Enhanced capacity to improve the safety of animal-source foods and ensure continued market access for poor farmers in sub-Saharan Africa.* Paper presented at the second international food safety and zoonoses symposium, Chiang Mai, Thailand, 21–22 July 2011.

Grace D, Thuy DN, Kang'ethe E, Fahrion A, Monda J and Lapar ML. 2010. *Don't eat your greens (or your mom may be wrong).* Paper presented at the 2010 EcoHealth Conference, London, UK, 18–20 August 2010.

Makita K, Grace D, Randolph TF, Baker D and Staal S. 2010. *Safe food, fair food: building capacity to improve the safety of animal-source foods and ensure continued market access for poor farmers in sub-Saharan Africa.* Poster presented at the 2010 ILRI Annual Program Meeting, Addis Ababa, Ethiopia, 14–17 April 2010.

Makita K, Grace D, Baumann M, Bräunig J, Randolph T, Baker D and Unger F. 2010. *ILRI/BMZ Safe Food Fair Food: Building capacity to improve the safety of animal-source foods and ensure continued market access for poor farmers in sub-Saharan Africa.* Poster presented at Tropentag 2010, Zurich, Switzerland, 14–16 September 2010.

Tano-Debrah K, Saalia FK, Bediako-Amoa B, Appiah J, Dogbe E and Bomfeh K. 2011. Listeria monocytogenes*: An emerging food-borne pathogen in Ghana?* Paper presented at the annual scientific conference of the University of Ghana's College of Health Sciences on 'The increasing burden of non-communicable diseases in Ghana', Accra, Ghana, 21–23 September 2011.

Tano-Debrah K, Bediako-Amoa B, Saalia FK and Bomfeh K. 2011. *Occurrence of* Listeria monocytogenes *in traditionally processed fish in informal markets in Accra, Ghana.* Paper presented at the 27th biennial conference of the Ghana Science Association on 'Promoting the development of agro-processing industries to enhance value addition for local and export markets: The role of science and technology', Kumasi, Ghana, 10–15 July 2011.

Tano-Debrah K, Appiah J, Makita K, Grace D and Bomfeh K. 2010. *Application of participatory methods in assessing the risk of consuming raw milk from informal markets in Ghana contaminated with* Listeria monocytogenes. Paper presented at the 15th World Congress on Food Science and Technology, Cape Town, South Africa, 22–26 August 2010.

Presentations at the first International Congress on Pathogens at the Human-Animal Interface

Aké Assi Datte Y, Sess A, Biego GH, Koffi M, Kouamé P and Bonfoh B. 2011. *Formation of polycyclic aromatic hydrocarbons in traditionally smoked fish released for consumption in Abidjan, Côte d'Ivoire.* Presentation at the first International Congress on Pathogens at the Human-Animal Interface (ICOPHAI 2011), Addis Ababa, Ethiopia, 15–17 September 2011.

Amenu K, Markemann A, Roessler R, Siegmund-Schultze M and Zárate AV. 2011. *Inadequate access to safe water for livestock and people in Ethiopian rural settings: Implications for health.* Poster presented at the first International Congress on Pathogens at the Human-Animal Interface (ICOPHAI 2011), Addis Ababa, Ethiopia, 15–17 September 2011.

Appiah J, Tano-Debrah K, Annor GA, Alpha MM, Makita K and Grace D. 2011. *Quantitative probabilistic assessment of the risk of listeriosis from the consumption of milk from informal markets in Ghana.* Paper presented at the first International Congress on Pathogens at the Human-Animal Interface (ICOPHAI 2011), Addis Ababa, Ethiopia, 15–17 September 2011.

Bomfeh K, Tano-Debrah K and Saalia FK. 2011. *Exposure assessment for* Listeria monocytogenes *in hot-smoked fish in Ghana.* Poster presented at the first International Congress on Pathogens at the Human-Animal Interface (ICOPHAI 2011), Addis Ababa, Ethiopia, 15–17 September 2011.

Desissa F, Makita K, Teklu A, Zewde G and Grace D. 2011. *Isolation and identification of* Staphylococcus aureus *from informally marketed bovine milk in urban and peri urban areas of Debre Zeit.* Poster presented at the first International Congress on Pathogens at the Human-Animal Interface (ICOPHAI 2011), Addis Ababa, Ethiopia, 15–17 September 2011.

Desissa F, Makita K, Teklu A, Zewde G and Grace D. 2011. *Raw milk consumption and its implication for public health.* Poster presented at the first International Congress on Pathogens at the Human-Animal Interface (ICOPHAI 2011), Addis Ababa, Ethiopia, 15–17 September 2011.

Heeb A, McCrindle CME, Zárate AV, Ramrajh S, Grace D and Siegmund-Schultze M. 2011. *The potential for game meat edible by-products to contribute to food security in South Africa and risk assessment.* Paper presented at the first International Congress on Pathogens at the Human-Animal Interface (ICOPHAI 2011), Addis Ababa, Ethiopia, 15–17 September 2011.

Heeb A, McCrindle CME, Zárate AV, Ramrajh S, Siegmund-Schultze M, Makita K and Grace D. 2011. *Informally marketed meat in South Africa: A qualitative risk assessment.* Paper presented at the first International Congress on Pathogens at the Human-Animal Interface (ICOPHAI 2011), Addis Ababa, Ethiopia, 15–17 September 2011.

Kasse FN, Makita K, Siegmund-Schultze M, Piepho HP, Grace D, Kang'ethe E and Zárate AV. 2011. *Choice of breeds and husbandry practices influencing the safety of milk and milk products in smallholder dairy farms in peri-urban Nairobi, focusing on brucellosis.* Presentation at the first International Congress on Pathogens at the Human–Animal Interface (ICOPHAI 2011), Addis Ababa, Ethiopia, 15–17 September 2011.

Kilango K, Makita K, Kurwijila L and Grace D. 2011. *Food safety in milk markets of smallholder farmers in Tanzania: A case study of peri-urban wards in Temeke.* Paper presented at the first International Congress on Pathogens at the Human-Animal Interface (ICOPHAI 2011), Addis Ababa, Ethiopia, 15–17 September 2011.

Koné VB, Fokou G, Makita K, Grace D and Gnabeli YR. 2011. *Social representation and perception of the quality of animal-source foods in Cinzana, Mali.* Presentation at the first International Congress on Pathogens at the Human-Animal Interface (ICOPHAI 2011), Addis Ababa, Ethiopia, 15–17 September 2011.

Kouamé-Sina SM, Yobouet BA, Dadié A, Makita K, Grace D, Djè KM and Bonfoh B. 2011. *Bacterial risk assessment in informally produced milk consumption in Côte d'Ivoire.* Presentation at the first International Congress on Pathogens at the Human-Animal Interface (ICOPHAI 2011), Addis Ababa, Ethiopia, 15–17 September 2011.

Mahundi E, Kurwijila LR, Karimuribo ED, Makita K, Ngowi HE and Grace D. 2011. *Food safety risk assessment in beef in Arusha municipality, Tanzania.* Presentation at the first

International Congress on Pathogens at the Human-Animal Interface (ICOPHAI 2011), Addis Ababa, Ethiopia, 15–17 September 2011.

Makita K, Kang'ethe E, Zewde G, Kurwijila L, Matusse H, McCrindle C, Tano-Debrah K, Bonfoh B, Costard S, Baker D and Grace D. 2011. *Participatory methods for risk analysis of informally marketed livestock products in sub-Saharan Africa: Advantages and challenges.* Presentation at the first International Congress on Pathogens at the Human-Animal Interface (ICOPHAI 2011), Addis Ababa, Ethiopia, 15–17 September 2011.

Molefe SM, McCrindle CME, Botha CJ, Makita K and Grace D. 2011. *A critical review of food safety legislation and policy applicable to products of animal origin in South Africa.* Presentation at the first International Congress on Pathogens at the Human-Animal Interface (ICOPHAI 2011), Addis Ababa, Ethiopia, 15–17 September 2011.

Molefe SM, McCrindle CME, Botha CJ, Makita K and Grace D. 2011. *Situation analysis on South African animal medicines, animal health and animal residues in foodstuffs.* Paper presented at the first International Congress on Pathogens at the Human-Animal Interface (ICOPHAI 2011), Addis Ababa, Ethiopia, 15–17 September 2011.

Muchangos AC, McCrindle C, Matusse H, Makita K and Grace D. 2011. *Prerequisites for HACCP in small-scale poultry production in Maputo, Mozambique.* Paper presented at the first International Congress on Pathogens at the Human-Animal Interface (ICOPHAI 2011), Addis Ababa, Ethiopia, 15–17 September 2011.

Mwai CW, Makita K, Arimi SM, Kang'ethe EK and Grace D. 2011. Escherichia coli (E. coli) *O157 in beef carcasses in slaughterhouses in Nairobi, Kenya.* Poster presented at the first International Congress on Pathogens at the Human-Animal Interface (ICOPHAI 2011), Addis Ababa, Ethiopia, 15–17 September 2011.

Ramrajh S, McCrindle CME, Heeb AW, Makita K and Grace D. 2011. *Participatory risk analysis to ensure food safety of edible offal from game meat.* Paper presented at the first International Congress on Pathogens at the Human-Animal Interface (ICOPHAI 2011), Addis Ababa, Ethiopia, 15–17 September 2011.

Sow I, Fanè A, Niang M, Makita K, Costard S, Grace D and Bonfoh B. 2011. *Investigation on the risk of brucellosis linked to the production and consumption of milk in rural Cinzana, Mali.* Presentation at the first International Congress on Pathogens at the Human-Animal Interface (ICOPHAI 2011), Addis Ababa, Ethiopia, 15–17 September 2011.

Tano-Debrah K, Appiah J, Annor GA, Alpha MM, Makita K and Grace D. 2011. *Qualitative assessment of* Listeria monocytogenes *exposure among consumers of milk in informal markets in Ghana.* Presentation at the first International Congress on Pathogens at the Human-Animal Interface (ICOPHAI 2011), Addis Ababa, Ethiopia, 15–17 September 2011.

Toyomaki H, Ishihara K, Sanka P, Kurwijila LR, Grace D and Makita K. 2011. *An estimation of thermophilic* Campylobacter *population in ready-to-eat roast beef and chicken sold and hygiene practices of sellers in beer bars in Arusha, Tanzania.* Paper presented at the first International Congress on Pathogens at the Human-Animal Interface (ICOPHAI 2011), Addis Ababa, Ethiopia, 15–17 September 2011.

Traoré SG, Krabi R, Odermatt P, Utzinger J, Costard S, Makita K, Grace D, Koussémon M and Bonfoh B. 2011. *Risk for* Vibrio *and* Paragonimus *infections linked to shellfish consumption in Côte d'Ivoire.* Presentation at the first International Congress on Pathogens at the Human-Animal Interface (ICOPHAI 2011), Addis Ababa, Ethiopia, 15–17 September 2011.

van Zyl E, McCrindle CME, Makita K and Grace D. 2011. *Hazard identification and characterization for quality control of biltong through application of appropriate microbiology and biotechnology methods.* Paper presented at the first International Congress on Pathogens at the Human-Animal Interface (ICOPHAI 2011), Addis Ababa, Ethiopia, 15–17 September 2011.

Yobouet BA, Kouamé-Sina SM, Dadié A, Makita K, Grace D, Meile L, Djè KM and Bonfoh B. 2011. Bacillus cereus *risk assessment in raw milk consumed in the informal dairy sector in Côte d'Ivoire.* Presentation at the first International Congress on Pathogens at the Human-Animal Interface (ICOPHAI 2011), Addis Ababa, Ethiopia, 15–17 September 2011.

Presentations at the 13th biennial conference of the International Society for Veterinary Epidemiology and Economics

Mahundi E, Makita K, Toyomaki H, Grace D and Kurwijila LR. 2012. *Quantitative assessment of the risk of acquiring campylobacteriosis from consumption of ready-to-eat beef in Arusha Municipality, Tanzania.* Poster presented at the 13th biennial conference of the International Society for Veterinary Epidemiology and Economics (ISVEE 13) held at Maastricht, the Netherlands, 20–24 August 2012.

Makita K, Kang'ethe E, Zewde G, Kurwijila L, Matusse H, McCrindle C, Tano-Debrah K, Bonfoh B, Costard S and Grace D. 2012. *Key messages from Safe Food Fair Food project: Food safety in informally marketed livestock products in sub-Saharan Africa.* Poster presented at the 13th biennial conference of the International Society for Veterinary Epidemiology and Economics (ISVEE 13) held at Maastricht, the Netherlands, 20–24 August 2012.

Muchangos AC, McCrindle CME, Matusse H and Makita K. 2012. *Prerequisites for HACCP in poultry processing in Maputo, Mozambique.* Poster presented at the 13th biennial conference of the International Society for Veterinary Epidemiology and Economics (ISVEE 13) held at Maastricht, the Netherlands, 20–24 August 2012.

Traoré SG, Costard S, Krabi R, Odermatt P, Utzinger J, Makita K, Grace D, Koussémon M and Bonfoh B. 2012. *Assessment of exposure to* Vibrio *in shellfish consumed in Abidjan, Côte d'Ivoire.* Poster presented at the 13th biennial conference of the International Society for Veterinary Epidemiology and Economics (ISVEE 13) held at Maastricht, the Netherlands, 20–24 August 2012.

Other presentations

Desissa F and Grace D. 2012. *Raw milk consumption behaviour and assessment of its risk factors among dairy producers in urban and peri-urban areas of Debre Zeit, Ethiopia: Implication for public health.* Presentation at Tropentag 2012, Göttingen, Germany, 19–21 September 2012.

Grace D. 2011. *Risk-based approaches to food safety in developing countries.* Presentation at a workshop on 'Safety of animal-source foods with an emphasis on the informal sectors', New Delhi, India, 8 February 2011.

Grace D. 2011. *Safe foods in informal markets: Agriculture-associated disease work at ILRI.* Presentation at the ILRI Livestock Exchange, Addis Ababa, Ethiopia, 9–10 November 2011.

Grace D and McDermott J. 2012. *Agriculture for nutrition and health.* Presented at the 2012 Ecohealth conference, Kunming, China, 15-18 October 2012.

Grace D and McDermott J. 2012. *International agricultural research and agricultural associated diseases.* Presentation at the International One Health Summit, Davos, Switzerland, 19–22 February 2012.

Grace D and Randolph T. 2012. *CGIAR Research Program on Livestock and Fish and its synergies with the CGIAR Research Program on Agriculture for Nutrition and Health.* Presentation at the third annual conference on Agricultural Research for Development: Innovations and incentives, Uppsala, Sweden, 26–27 September 2012.

Grace D and Randolph T. 2012. *Innovations and incentives in agricultural research for poor countries.* Presentation at the third annual conference on Agricultural Research for Development: Innovations and incentives, Uppsala, Sweden, 26–27 September 2012.

Kilango K, Makita K, Kurwijila LR and Grace D. 2012. *Boiled milk, food safety and the risk of exposure to milk borne pathogens in informal dairy markets in Tanzania.* Oral presentation at the 2012 IDF World Dairy Summit, Cape Town, South Africa, 4–8 November 2012.

Kouamé-Sina SM, Makita K, Grace D, Dadié A, Djè M and Bonfoh B. 2013. *Bacterial risk assessment of milk produced locally in Abidjan, Côte d'Ivoire.* Poster presented at the 5th Congress of European Microbiologists (FEMS 2013), Leipzig, Germany, 21–25 July 2013.

Kouamé-Sina SM, Dadié A, Makita K, Grace D, Djè M, Taminiau B, Daube G and Bonfoh B. 2010. *Biodiversity, phylogenetic relationship and antibacterial potential of* Bifidobacterium *species isolated from raw milk production chain in Abidjan (Côte d'Ivoire).* Presentation at the CSRS Scientific Seminar No. 11, Abidjan, Côte d'Ivoire, 4 November 2010.

Kurwijila LR and Mdegela RH. 2012. *Management to prevent* S. aureus *mastitis in small-scale dairy farms in Tanzania.* Oral presentation at the 2012 IDF World Dairy Summit, Cape Town, South Africa, 4–8 November 2012.

Muchangos AC, Matusse H, Hendrickx SCJ and McCrindle CME. 2013. *Food safety in Mozambique: From research to implementation.* Presentation at the 14th international conference of the Association of Institutions for Tropical Veterinary Medicine (AITVM), Johannesburg, South Africa, 25–29 August 2013.

Roesel K, Holmes K, Kung'u J, Grace D, Pezo DQ, Ouma EA, Baumann M, Fries R, Ejobi F and Clausen PH. 2013. *Fit for human consumption? A qualitative survey at a Ugandan pig abattoir.* Presented at the 14th International Conference of the Association of Institutions for Tropical Veterinary Medicine (AITVM), Johannesburg, South Africa, 25–29 August 2013.

Shija F, Misinzo G, Nonga H, Kurwijila LR, Roesel K and Grace D. 2013. *The use of polymerase chain reaction (PCR) to confirm the presence of selected pathogenic bacteria along the milk value chain in Tanga region.* Presented at the 14th International Conference of the Association of Institutions for Tropical Veterinary Medicine (AITVM), Johannesburg, South Africa, 25–29 August 2013.

Toyomaki H, Mahundi E, Ishihara K, Kurwijila L, Grace D and Makita K. 2012. *Quantitative risk assessment of acquiring campylobacteriosis from consumption of ready-to-eat beef in Arusha Municipality, Tanzania.* Presented at the annual conference of the Japan Society of Veterinary Epidemiology, Saitama, Japan, 29 March 2012.

Project factsheets and brochures

GTZ Advisory Service on Agriculture Research for Development (BEAF). 2009. *Safe Food Fair Food.* GTZ project factsheet.

ILRI. 2012. *Aliments sains, aliments équitables.* Profil du Projet ILRI. ILRI, Nairobi, Kenya.

ILRI. 2012. *Alimentos seguros, alimentos equitáveis.* ILRI, Nairobi, Kenya.

ILRI. 2012. *Safe Food, Fair Food.* ILRI Project Profile. ILRI, Nairobi, Kenya.

INDEX